When Worlds Collide

When Worlds Collide

Exploring the Ideological and
Political Foundations of the
Clash of Civilizations

Gene W. Heck

ROWMAN & LITTLEFIELD PUBLISHERS, INC.
Lanham • Boulder • New York • Toronto • Plymouth, UK

ROWMAN & LITTLEFIELD PUBLISHERS, INC.

Published in the United States of America
by Rowman & Littlefield Publishers, Inc.
A wholly owned subsidary of The Rowman & Littlefield Publishing Group, Inc.
4501 Forbes Boulevard, Suite 200, Lanham, Maryland 20706
www.rowmanlittlefield.com

Estover Road
Plymouth PL6 7PY
United Kingdom

British Library Cataloguing in Publication Information Available

Library of Congress Cataloging-in-Publication Data

Heck, Gene W.
  When worlds collide : exploring the ideological and political foundations of the
clash of civilizations / Gene W. Heck.
     p. cm.
  Includes bibliographical references and index.
  ISBN-13: 978-0-7425-5856-4 (cloth : alk. paper)
  ISBN-10: 0-7425-5856-8 (cloth : alk. paper)
  1. Jihad. 2. War—Religious aspects—Islam. 3. Terrorism—Religious aspects—
Islam. 4. Islamic fundamentalism. 5. Islam and politics. 6. Qaida (Organization)
I. Title.
  BP182.H43 2007
  303.48'2176701821—dc22   2007020799

Printed in the United States of America

∞™ The paper used in this publication meets the minimum requirements of
American National Standard for Information Sciences—Permanence of Paper
for Printed Library Materials, ANSI/NISO Z39.48-1992.

To rebuilding trust between
the East and the West through
mutual understanding

On the Eternal Universality of Reasoned Law

There is, in fact, a true law, namely right reason, which is in accordance with nature, which applies to all men and is interchangeable and eternal. . . . It will not lay down one rule at Rome and another at Athens, nor will it be one rule today and another tomorrow. But there will be one rule eternal and interchangeable binding at all times and upon all peoples.

—Cicero, Roman Senator-Philosopher

Contents

Competing Doctrines of War

WHAT ISLAMIC DOCTRINE PRESCRIBES

The Qur'anic Prescription for War

Fight in the name of Allah against those who would fight against you, but begin not hostilities. Lo, Allah loveth not transgressors. Slay them wherever you find them, and drive them from whence they drove you out, for such persecution is worse than slaughter.

—Surat al-Baqarah 2:190–191

WHAT CHRISTIAN DOCTRINE PRESCRIBES

The Biblical Prescription for War

And when the Lord thy God shall deliver thine enemies before thee, thou shalt smite them and utterly destroy them; thou shalt make no covenant with them nor show mercy unto them . . . and thou shalt destroy all the peoples that the Lord thy God giveth over to thee, and thy eye shall not pity them. . . . In the cities that the Lord thy God giveth you for an inheritance, ye shall save alive nothing that breatheth, but ye shall utterly destroy them.

—Deuteronomy 20:13–16

Acknowledgments

The author acknowledges his debt and gratitude to many for making publication of this book possible. Foremost among them is the publisher Rowman & Littlefield and to its superb editors, Chris Anzalone and Karen Ackermann, for making publication not only possible but enjoyable; to Tiffani Adams and Doug Baldwin, as always, for their ongoing comment, wit, and wisdom; and finally, but certainly not least, to my wife, Adrienne, whose counsel and support have been a source of strength for many years. Thank you all!

Introduction

Fight against those who believe not in Allah nor in the Last Day, nor forbid that which has been forbidden by Allah and His Messenger, and those who acknowledge not the religion of truth until they pay the poll tax (*jizyah*) willingly and feel themselves subdued.

—Surat al-Tawbah 9:29[1]

PRINCIPAL FOCI OF THIS INQUIRY

The tragic events of September 11, 2001 have transformed the historic East-West relationship, with the media's coverage of the "war on terrorism" forever changing world perception. Indeed, its pervasive global outreach has created its own counterculture—causing geopolitics to correspondingly irrevocably change. For too often today, civilized society is confronted, via television's ubiquitous cameras, with barbarous acts of terrorism committed by Middle Eastern–looking men ranging in age from fifteen to forty-five—often followed by Web site claims that these were "sacred acts of violence" perpetrated in Islam's name.[2]

Too often, the planet's intellectual elite—scholars, politicians, and the media alike—succumb to the resulting false perceptions as well. Exposed to orientalist exegesis of passages such as the Qur'an's famed "sword verse" cited above, the world at large concludes that Islam is the "Dark Age" religion of a barbaric netherworld that not only espouses

1

and embraces terror but also considers it a "badge of honor." Accordingly, when analysts and casual viewers alike span the bloody panorama of atrocities today being perpetrated in God's name, the question too often ceases to be "What can Islam do for humanity?" and becomes instead "What has humankind done to Islam?"

The ramifications of this reality are equally critical for humanity and for security. Stereotyping is invariably inherently unfair, and as such has rightly been decried as a tool of prejudice and hate. The moral dilemma develops, however, precisely at that juncture where impression and reality intersect—a dilemma whose operational ramifications are significant both for humankind and human safety. For while members of the U.S. Transportation Safety Administration (TSA) are devoutly engaged in random airport shakedowns of eighty-year-old wheelchair-ridden Republican grandmothers seeking to avoid stereotyping allegations, real time terrorists with box cutters may well be walking blithely by.

As at the realpolitik bottom line, profiling is no more than a common sense starting point in sound detective work based upon plausible suspicion—for Mormons did not blow up the World Trade Centers and political correctness doesn't win wars on terror. Better ways, therefore, are needed to avert potential threats through enhanced ability to distinguish actual friend from foe on a "real time" basis. This work strives for improved understanding to that end.

The search for answers merits careful contemplation. For the issue of stereotyping being inherently unfair invokes more basic questions, among them: "Does terrorism have a particular religion?" "If so, who exactly is a terrorist?" And, "Does the term apply exclusively to Muslim males in the modern age?"

The doctrinal issue thus is a starting point. To wit: Are the so-called Qur'anic sword verses more chilling in their perceived intent than biblical Jeremiah 48:10 which would become the favored battle cry of Crusaders:[3]

Cursed is the one who is slack in doing the work of the Lord; and accursed is the one who keeps back the sword from bloodshed.

And do they substantially differ in their projection and intent from such well-known biblical descriptions of an avenging "Christian God":

If I whet my glittering sword, and my hand take hold on judgment, I will render vengeance onto my enemies and reward them that hate me. I will make my arrows drunk with blood and my sword shall devour flesh; and that with the blood of the slain and the captives, from the beginning of revenge upon the enemy. (Deuteronomy 32:41–43)

The Lord thy God is a man of war, and the Lord is His Name. (Exodus 15:3)

The book of Joshua is similarly knee-deep in blood, as are other Old Testament books, as perception again becomes one of perspective—reflecting the twin realities that truth is not just about facts, it is equally about how facts are perceived—and also the ubiquitous conviction that "the terrorists" are invariable never "us" but "them." Or as eighteenth-century British philosopher Edmund Burke famously observed: "Scratch any ideology and beneath it you will find a terrorist!"[4]

This may well be an inordinately pessimistic view. But if not, the crucial issue then becomes: "Is any society defined by the proclamations of a few or instead by the tenor of millennia-old literature that is intrinsic to its heritage?" Islam—no less than Judaism or Christianity, Buddhism, or Hinduism—is shaped by its global historic context. The corollary to this near universal truth is that religious constitutions—be they the Qur'an, Torah, or Bible—were undeniably addressed to the challenges of their particular age. Lawgivers in ancient time were predisposed to draconian means.

The Qur'an was revealed to an early seventh-century Near East civilization. The Torah and the Bible's Old Testament, in turn, were the spiritual beacons of Bronze Age tribes then resident in the same region two millennia before. They too appear onerous in their prescriptions. Indeed, the penalties that they impose project as barbarous in a modern age—overkill, perhaps, within the context of what contemporary society may deem to be banal infractions.

Yet in a more modern context, consider the somber admonition of Burke's French contemporary Maximilien Robespierre who would author the capstone to the much heralded democratic revolution that issued from his nation's vaunted Age of Enlightenment by serving as progenitor of its attendant Reign of Terror:

If *virtue* is indeed a mainstay of a democratic government in time of peace, then in time of revolution, a democratic government must rely upon both virtue and *terror*. . . . For terror is no more than justice swift, severe and inflexible; it is an emanation of virtue . . . It has been said that terror is a mainstay of despotic governance. The government of the revolution is the despotism of liberty against the forces of tyranny![5]

Robespierre's claims thus lend substance to the time-proven maxim:

One man's terrorist is another man's freedom fighter![6]

Indeed, sometimes today's freedom fighters can mutate into tomorrow's nihilists, as is the case of Afghanistan's erstwhile mujahidin, as analysis will show.

To lend perspective to this perplexing paradox of time and place, it is illuminating to consider parallels between Biblical prescriptions for war and those of the Qur'an:

BIBLE: King James Version*

When thou come nigh unto a city to fight against it, then proclaim peace unto it. And it shall be, if it make the answer of peace, and open unto thee, then it shall be that all people found therein shall be tributaries unto thee, and shall serve thee. And if it will make no peace with thee, but will make war against thee, then thou shalt besiege it. And when the Lord thy God hath delivered it into thy hands, thou shall smite every male thereof with the sword.—Deuteronomy 20:10–147.

---

*Counterpart Jewish Torah equivalents of cited biblical Old Testament passages are, of course, identical save for idiosyncratic translation variants, as follows:

> When you approach a town to attack it, then you shall offer it terms of peace. If it responds reasonably and lets you in, all persons present therein shall serve you at forced labor. If it does not surrender to you but would join battle with you, you shall lay siege to it; and when the Lord your God delivers it into your hand, you shall put all its males to the sword. Torah, New JPS Version, 20:10–11.

Qur'an: Al-Madinah Version

And when We decide to destroy a town (population), We send an order (to obey Allah and be righteous) to those among them who lead a life of luxury. If then, they transgress therein, thus the word is justified, and we destroy it with complete destruction.—Surat al-Isra' 17:16

Unfortunately, notwithstanding the proximity in modus operandi, too often, those with preconceived notions concurrently fall victim to the trap of selective extraction. While some, for instance, are wont to quote the stentorian stipulation in Surat al-Anfal—

> Let not the Unbelievers think that they can get the better (of the Godly) . . .
> Against them make ready your strength to the utmost of your power, including steeds of war, to strike terror into the hearts of the enemies of Allah and your enemies. (8:59–60)

—they neglect to note that this austere exhortation is immediately followed by the admonition:

> But if the enemy incline toward peace, do thou (also) incline toward peace, and trust in Allah. (Surat al-Anfal 8:61)

In like manner, they are fond of quoting God's instruction to Prophet Muhammad regarding polytheists delivered in Surat al-Tawbah:

> Then, when the "sacred months" have passed, slay the polytheists wherever you may find them, and take them captive and besiege them, and prepare to ambush them. (9:5)

But they forget that this stern passage is immediately followed by:

> But if they repent and establish worship and pay the poor due, then leave their way free. Lo! Allah is Forgiving and Merciful. And if any of the polytheists seeks your protection, then protect them so that they may hear the Word of God; and afterward convey them to their place of safety. For that is because they are a folk who know not. (9:5–6)

They likewise overlook the fact that this particular passage was aimed primarily at the Quraysh—Islam's polytheistic prime archenemy of the day—as well as at their partisans at the oasis of Yathrib, a city targeted to be the seat of governance for the nascent Islamic state once occupied and rechristened al-Madinah.[7]

They neglect, too, to recall that the Bible portrays in equally doomsday terms visions of anti-Christs and beasts from the bowels of hell and fiery furnaces and avenging Angels of the Apocalypse leading forces of light in cosmic mortal combat against forces of darkness arrayed on the battlefield of Armageddon—as Surat al-Tawbah is matched, in intensity, blow-for-blow, by the Book of Revelation.

This reality makes blaming terrorism on select passages from the Qur'an no more than, and indeed is tantamount to, blaming the Crusades on passages from the Bible. For in this instance, neither are the cause. They merely provided the rally slogans.

As the concurrent requisite quest for peaceful coexistence is equally enjoined by the Qur'an—wherein Muslims are constantly counseled that their fellow monotheists, the Jews and the Christians, "Peoples of the Book," are coreligionists worthy of respect and deference:

> And argue not with Peoples of the Scripture unless it be (in a way) that is better, except with such of them as do wrong; and say: "We believe in that which was revealed to us and revealed to you; our God is your God; and to Him we surrender (as Muslims)." (Surat al-'Ankabut 29:46)

Say (O Muhammad): We believe in Allah and that which is revealed to us and that which was revealed to Abraham and Ishmael and Isaac and Jacob and the Tribes, and that which was given to Moses and Jesus and the Prophets by their Lord. We make no distinction between any of them, and to Him (alone) have we surrendered (in Islam). (Surat Al-i 'Imran 3:84)

Lo! Those who believe, and who are Jews and Sabians, and Christians— whosoever believes in Allah and the Last Day and does right—no fear shall come upon them neither shall they grieve. (Surat al-Ma'idah 5:69)

Thus, the Qur'an traces a lineage issuing not only from the good news Gospels but also from a Judeo-Christian Old Testament more draconian in its prescriptions as a divine "Constitution for Believers" revealed in Bronze Age times than that of the Muslims revealed at the onset of the Middle Ages. The contrast is compelling.

THE IMPERATIVE OF THIS INQUIRY

Any religion, of course, can be demonized by a failure to perceive its prescriptions within their proper context. Certainly biblical prescriptions for the pursuit of a pious life, as shown, are demonstrably no less austere, exacting, and frightening in their approach than their Qur'anic counterparts. Yet it is Islam that bears the baggage of such unfortunate stereotypes. Examples, even at the hands of perceived "experts," are legion.

Eminent orientalist Bernard Lewis, for instance, has determined Islam to be "a military religion—fanatic warriors engaged in forcibly spreading their faith and their law through armed might"—a theme echoed by the famed German sociologist Max Weber. Samuel Huntington, in turn, calls Islam a faith "deeply steeped in bloody borders."[8]

These perceptions or misperceptions, then, have led to a mounting moral sense that there is something terribly wrong within Islam and, hence, it is that Bernard Lewis is found speaking of the "Crisis of Islam" and asking: "What Went Wrong?" Whereas Samuel Huntington has issued deterministic explanations positing an apocalyptic "Clash of Civilizations," and Irshad Manji has lamented "The Trouble with Islam."[9]

Such contentions build, of course, upon mass accretions of nearly a millennium of negative advertising that set its roots in Pope Urban II's proclamation of the first Crusade at Clermont, France, on November 26, 1095— a "reverse jihad" that depicted Islamic warriors as barbaric apostates of the anti-Christ blasphemously occupying Sacred Jerusalem—the very "navel of the universe" from whence Christianity was born—while calling for its liberation and redemption.[10]

When Pope Urban II had finished this homily, the medieval Church doctors advise, the assembled multitudes cried out in affirmative unison: *Deus hoc volt!* ("God wills it!"), and upon hearing this stirring invocation, more than 150,000 of God's finest warriors, mostly Franks and Normans, took up the "call of the Cross"—so named because of a replica of the cross that each participant wore as a symbolic badge of honor. Thus, the epic of the Crusades was born.[11]

The Crusaders, of course, were improbable "liberators" or "illuminators"—as this was, at the least, a curiously culturally unbalanced "clash of civilizations"—with the peoples targeted for liberation clearly the socially superior of the two combatants. Indeed, even as medieval Muslims were preserving Graeco-Roman knowledge and forging mathematics and science—practically inventing algebra and astronomy and other sciences—a belligerent Holy Roman Empire persisted in portraying Islam as "the religion of the sword."

A critical question that issues from these realities thus becomes: Was this a genuine religious conflict, a cultural one, or instead merely one of overt prejudice bred of ignorance and misperception that has been perpetuated to the present day?

Certainly, fundamentalist evangelists—Muslim and Christian alike, ranging from the most virulent and vocal of jihadi clerics to the Reverends Franklin Graham, Jerry Falwell, Pat Robertson, and Jerry Vines—have conveyed it as a cosmic clash of "theisms." As for every Muslim cleric calling for the "demise of the infidel West," there have been literally dozens of Western clerics, intellectuals, and members of government who have addressed Islam and Arabs in equally regrettable terms.[12]

Conjured up within their pronouncements are stark images of a time-warped twenty-first century transfer back into the heartland of the early Middle Ages—finding bearded mullahs surging rabidly from their mosques to attack modern-day Babylon while seeking to re-create a bygone reactionary, irrational, and violent world.

It is within this convoluted context, then, that such terms as "Wahhabi," "Islamic fundamentalism," "political Islam," "radical Islam," "Islamic extremism," "Islamo-fascism" "militant jihadism," and "Islamic terrorism" have too often come to be confounded as synonymous in Western media portrayals, notwithstanding that all with the exception of the first are all terms that speak to *political power*, not spiritual salvation—to sedition, and not religion.[13]

Yet, though religions should not be demonized because every disciple is not a saint, the conspiratorial debate nonetheless today still unwinds in Armageddon-like fashion as one of imperialist "Crusaders" and "Zionists" arrayed in mortal combat against "barbaric apostates from the netherworld"—with civilization no richer for the dialogue.

Is there a basis for such charges? Is there validity to the debate: Does Islam prescribe a wanton killing of civilians through suicide bombings? Is there a defining difference between so-called Wahhabi Qur'anic translation and exegesis and that of more traditional Islamic schools of thought that produces violence and vitriol within its ranks? This inquiry produces findings that are at once illuminating in its mission to ascertain if, at a doctrinal level, Islam is indeed a religion misunderstood. To wit, consistent with popular perception, does the Qu'ran:

- Direct its followers to initiate hostilities against unbelievers?
- Require them to reject peace overtures from would-be adversaries?
- Permit them to seek peace prior to armed engagement?
- Ban formal treaties with potential enemies?
- Promote the employment of independent clandestine terror cells?
- Permit them to engage in torture and attack of civilian populations?
- Condone suicide in quest of martyrdom?
- Deny the status of Jews and Christians as monotheistic coreligionists or prohibit peaceful coexistence with them? And,
- In addressing such doctrines, are there substantive differences between so-called Wahhabi Qur'anic translations and interpretations and those of more traditional Islamic schools of thought?

More succinctly put: Is Islam an inherently and irreconcilably intolerant religion? Does it oblige its adherents to wage unending jihad against those who do not share its beliefs? If not, cognizant that most holy books contain passages that can be literally misinterpreted by uncritical minds, why are there many Muslim suicide bombers but relatively few Christian, Jewish, Buddhist, or Hindu ones?

And equally germane: if not, is it fair to blame 1.4 billion Muslims and more than 200 million Arabs for the malevolent handiwork of an ideologically deviant few? And just who are these so-called infidels that some of its adherents forever rail against anyway?

In the quest for answers, the challenge thus becomes one of peeling back fiction to perceive fact—of removing the barnacles upon barnacles of misperception that have accreted upon popular perception until often even the original intent—the very tenets of Islam's Founding Fathers—have been lost, buried beneath a murky veneer of errant exegesis.

As a consequence, too often what is perceived as Islam today is instead an evil incarnate that is its antithesis. The reason goes to the very structures of the terrorist organizations themselves, for all civilizations have historically organized themselves into essentially the same socioeconomic units—first into families, then into clans, then into tribes, then ultimately into the greater formalities of nation-states.

Extremist groups such as Hezbollah and Hamas, to the contrary, are not so structured—but rather are founded on toxi-centric resentments— reactions bred of perceived suppression, envy of the success of others, the politics of "victimization," and hatred of "the enemy," expressed in poisonous platitudes and virulent vendettas that render them instruments of unbridled violence rather than as subscribers to normative codes of conduct for war. In countenancing, indeed encouraging, attacks on civilians executed through suicide bombings by their youth, some have come to hate the enemy even more than they love their own children.

How is the evolution of this animus best explained? To fathom the flowering of a faith, inquiry must trace it back to its historic roots. Unfortunately, too often would-be revivalist movements never get back that far—in the case of Islam, often not beyond the eighteenth century of Muhammad b. 'Abd al-Wahhab back to the seventh-century Age of Muhammad; and in that of Christianity, not beyond the seventeenth-century era of King James back to the first-century Age of Christ.[14]

Yet such a course is critical for fuller understanding, for the Crusades have now been over for eight centuries. The time is overdue for those on both sides of the cultural divide to acknowledge that classic Islam, as defined by its doctrine, has been a historic civilizing force whose societal contributions have, over time, greatly leavened the global socioeconomy and culture. This inquiry is dedicated to developing evidence demonstrating that reality.

In so doing, analysis concurrently explores the sources of misperception—discerning how, for instance, dissonant elements of the Wahhabi movement, with Egypt's Muslim Brotherhood acting as a catalyst, have over time transformed a small portion of an essentially benign religious cause into a politically lethal one. Or, as one Egyptian commentator has aptly put it:[15]

Allah conceived Islam as a religion.
Men have transformed it into politics.

A religion is defined by its doctrine; its doctrine by its sacred writings. This inquiry endeavors to divine Islam's precise prescriptions for war and peace by digging to their doctrinal roots—the Qur'an and its attendant juridic body of Muslim common law, Prophetic Tradition. In this process—seeking definitive answers—an Islam emerges quite different from that often seen on CNN when viewed through a prism that dramatically transforms the global framework of analytic reference— one that, in seeking to rectify misconception, concludes with new perception.

This, then, is an investigation overdue. For to date there has been no genuine quest to doctrinally discern a formal Islamic Code of Conduct for War and Peace—no serious longitudinal study of the concept or practice of jihad based upon its treatment within the Qur'an and associated Prophetic Tradition that offers the intensity of illumination needed to reach the level of human understanding required for cognizant and effective policy making.

This inquiry is concurrently intended as a critical first step toward the goal of East-West reconciliation in a longstanding interface tragically torn apart by the terrible events of 9/11. Only enhanced bilateral understanding can restore the amity of the historic relationship—and must, if comity is to prevail.[16]

The case for greater intercultural understanding could not be more compelling, as it is not tautologous to say that the facts of life are, in large part, demographic—and those facts are not on the side of the West. The gravity of a prospective "clash of civilization" is more than ample to preclude needless alienation, because while America's demographic challenges are unique, she is not unique in having demographic challenges. Indeed, they are endemic to Western civilization.

For with the West in population decline—with a 2.1 child birthrate required to sustain the status quo, and the populations of the native-born in the United States now growing at less than 2.0 percent—and with fertility rates registering at 1.17 percent in Russia, 1.20 percent in Italy, 1.33 percent in Germany, 1.41 percent in Japan, 1.60 percent in Canada, 1.66 percent in Britain, and 1.73 percent in France, yet that of the 1.4 billion citizens of the Islamic world achieving 3.5 percent and often higher—if present trends continue Christian Europe within this century will instead become "Eurabia." Time thus is clearly not supporting those who fail to discern between a tiny minority of terrorists and the vast majority of Muslims who share common values of humanity and decency and aspire to a common vision of a world wherein amity is valued.

Today, as the West is demographically dying, the Islamic world retains values that it has lost—a desire to procreate and the will to perpetrate families, faith, values, culture, and civilization. Within that world, so-called "Islamic terrorists" indeed constitute a minuscule share, albeit a potent one. But let there be no doubt that they are an enemy more invidious than America has ever faced before—one that genuinely believes that the prevalence of its political views takes precedence *uber allis*—and that the killing of innocent civilians is justified in that quest.

Such people do not belong in power—they belong in cells and cemeteries, not in seats of governance wherein amity is an aspired goal. It becomes imperative, therefore, for the peoples of the West to identify that vast majority of Muslims who are their allies in the war on terror and enlist them in the victory drive that will ensure ultimate success.

SIGNIFICANT FINDINGS OF THIS INQUIRY

In the last analysis, then, this inquiry seeks a focused study of the ideological and political bases for modern Middle East terrorism. What are its incipient sources? Who and what abetted them? What is their ultimate remedy? Its initiative is dedicated to seeking answers to these questions. Characterized by a revisit of primary sources in its quest to discern the root causes of ongoing terror, it produces a sequence of incontrovertible interrelated, on-the-ground realities that directly challenge a multitude of conventional wisdoms as to its underlying causes—for its dozen principal findings are at once contra-intuitive and revisionist, as the analyses that follow reveal.

Yet the revelations, though revisionist, are not entirely earth breaking. Fragments of the story already have been told. Graphic events have been documented. But the fully integrated spectrum of political developments has until now not been developed. As a consequence, in filling in the missing pieces of an intricate, evolutionary puzzle, then filling in the blanks of the picture so produced, the evidence is compelling that it is the fingerprints of Egypt's radical Muslim Brotherhood—and neither classic Islamic doctrine nor Saudi Arabia's highly introspective Wahhabi movement—that indelibly appear as the proverbial smoking gun of the current reign of terror being perpetuated in Islam's name within the region. The investigation's principal findings thus address:

What are the Sources of Modern Middle East Terror?

1. That they cannot be directly traced to a classic religious doctrinal cause. As at their most basic, the modus vivendi dicta of the Qur'an, the living constitution of a seventh-century Near East tribe, are no more draconian in their prescriptions than those of the biblical Old Testament, the living constitution of an early Bronze Age Near East tribe.
2. That the Muslim Codes of Conduct for War and Peace, as defined by the Qur'an and its affiliate body of Prophetic Tradition—the corpus juris of the traditional seventh century medieval Islamic state—if actually applied as doctrinally delineated, are fully consonant with the dictates of the modern Hague and Geneva Conventions.

3. That as such, though classic Islamic doctrinal literature is now often cited as a source, the verses of the Qur'an can no more be identified as an incitement to modern terror than can those of the Old Testament be blamed for the Crusades. Indeed, such a foray into the fantasy of logic is tantamount to an ipso facto indiscriminate labeling of those today who adhere to fundamental religious beliefs on each side of the ideological divide as "active terrorists."

4. To the contrary, the facts of life being largely economic, there *is* instead a direct linkage between Middle East levels of per capita income and the evolution of political incubators capable of spawning metastasizing cells of terror. Sudan, Algeria, Egypt, the Yemen, Afghanistan, Pakistan, Kashmir, and less affluent districts of Saudi Arabia serve as prime examples.

This reality does not mean that the demagogic leaders of modern Middle East terrorist movements necessarily come from modest means—as people such as Osama bin Laden and his spiritual guru, Dr. Ayman al-Zawahiri, both university graduates born of affluent families, most certainly do not—but only that the overwhelming masses of their deputies and devotees were born in lower income strata wherein perceptions of relative economic deprivation lend religion resounding political reverberation.

It is such human-reduced conditions, then, that terrorist organizations such as Hezbollah and Hamas deftly exploit by serving as self-appointed quasi-nongovernmental organizations providing welfare, shelter, education, medical, and other social services to the proximate region's destitute and disillusioned.

What Are the Causes of Modern Middle East Terror?

5. That the so-called Wahhabi movement is often unjustly maligned for alleged doctrines and precepts that do not comport with the actual teachings of the movement's eighteenth-century founder, Muhammad ibn 'Abd al-Wahhab, who advocated jihad by peaceful, not militant, means.

6. That much of the basic infrastructure for, and inducements to, modern Mid-East terrorism, on the other hand, were actually forged by regional operatives of Western intelligence agencies seeking to engage radical elements of "Political Islam" as a counterbalance to perceived enemies of their own political and economic interests and designs.

7. That the Egyptian Muslim Brotherhood, founded in the second quarter of the twentieth century, was created with both the encouragement and funding of an affiliate of the British foreign intelligence agency,

MI6, to counter the spread initially of the rise of Wafdist Party nationalism, then of Nazism, and subsequently of communism—all, in their time, viewed as threats to London's diplomatic and financial ambitions in the environs of the Suez Canal.

8. That when Egyptian intelligence drove the Muslim Brotherhood underground after its attempted assassination of Jamal Abdul Nasser in 1954, it took refuge in the western half of the Arabian Peninsula wherein it proceeded to convert dissonant elements within the traditionally benign *religiously fundamentalist* Wahhabi movement into a virulent, covert, *politically activist* one—thereby establishing an ideological milieu propitious for modern jihadism to be spawned.

9. That it was the equally diligent efforts of MI6's U.S. counterpart, the CIA, to spark jihad as a "homegrown" counterinsurgency to repel the Soviet invasion of Afghanistan throughout the late 1970s and early 1980s that served as the delivery room for the birth of many modern Mid-East terrorist movements—for which today, Iraq serves as a prime nurturing incubator.

Coming on the heels of hindsight afforded by MI6 attempts to co-opt Islam's religious right a quarter of a century before, this experiment thus became instead a colossal failure of foresight, providing the requisite operating milieu, infrastructure, equipment, and training that would, a decade later, give birth to al-Qaeda—affirming the sage admonition of John Kennedy that "those who would ride the back of the tiger too often instead wind up inside."

10. That the flowering of al-Qaeda, the latest offspring of what some call radical Islam, today continues to be sustained by deep Egyptian Muslim Brotherhood roots in that:[17]
    - Osama bin Laden was raised in a part of what is modern day Saudi Arabia that the Brotherhood had deeply penetrated;
    - He reads and quotes the works of its chief theorist Sayyid Qutb;
    - Some of the organization's most prominent members, including Sayyid Qutb's brother Muhammad and Abdullah 'Azzam, who was key in establishing the Muslim Brotherhood's Palestinian Hamas spin-off, were amongst his foremost college mentors;
    - Egypt's "blind sheikh," 'Umar 'Abd al-Rahman, later implicated in the 1993 World Trade Center bombings, and his two sons, served with bin Laden in Afghanistan;
    - Ayman al-Zawahiri—a disciple of Sayyid Qutb and the head of his own Egyptian Jihad group—is concurrently al-Qaeda's doctrinal leader and chief spokesman;

- Muhammad 'Atif, al-Qaeda 's chief military commander until his death in a U.S. air strike in the Afghan War in November, 2001, was Egyptian;
- Abu Muhammad al-Misri, former general manager of al-Qaeda's former training camps in Afghanistan, likewise is Egyptian;
- Muhammad 'Atta, al-Qaeda's lead 9/11 hijacker who died in the World Trade Center disaster, also was Egyptian; and
- The linkages go on ad infinitum, as much of the infrastructure of al-Qaeda has been built upon the foundations of Egyptian jihadist groups.

In short, it can be convincingly demonstrated that some of the West's foremost geopolitical challenges today result from aborted intelligence efforts to co-opt Political Islam as a countervailing force against other emerging global ideologies deemed more politically dangerous. As there is compelling evidence documenting that it was Britain's vaunted foreign intelligence unit, MI6, that early in the twentieth century knowingly, yet without great forethought, jump-started Egypt's Muslim Brotherhood—an organization whose interests with which it was frequently in conflict—and which, commencing at mid-century, proceeded to corrupt a small, economically marginalized element of Saudi Arabia's indigenous Wahhabi movement, who, in the mid-1980s, joined volunteers trained by the CIA in its jihad to repel the Soviet invasion of Afghanistan.

And then, at that war's successful close, its unemployed veterans, like those of Vietnam, feeling largely unappreciated—and absent what they perceived to be a meaningful follow-on mission—developed the vision that led to the creation of al-Qaeda as a logical extension of their training and conviction. In this sense, therefore, it may be concluded that the Muslim Brotherhood and al-Qaeda are each unfortunate end-products of creative, albeit, naive Western intelligence efforts to engage the Islamic politico-religious establishment—as the symmetry of their efforts to co-opt esoteric allies—in a manner analogous to Israel's encouragement of Hamas as a counterbalance to Yasser Arafat's Palestinian Liberation Organization—is mirrored in their common failure to succeed. These realities, in themselves, make the compelling case for a better understanding of the motives and methods of Political Islam.

What, Then, Are the *Cures* for Modern Middle East Terror?

Reflecting these grim on-the-ground realities, then, effective remedy must be pursued by seeking to critically evaluate equally what does and doesn't work. To these ends, realizations are imperative that:

11. The propagation of the notion of Anglo-American democracy as a counterterrorism tool—the overarching leitmotif ostensibly guiding Western intelligence agencies in their machinations in the Islamic Middle East for the past seven decades—really doesn't work, and indeed is a precept fatally flawed within a region doctrinally committed to the establishment of an Islamic theocratic state while concurrently conspiring to create an overarching caliphal one. Thus, though today, many Mid-East states have crafted practical accommodations to reconcile democratic aspirations to the dictates of modern governance, the underlying classic impelling religious ideology nonetheless remains intact, finding traction on the current Islamic "political street." And, finally, that

12. At the economic bottom line, if there is a Western solution to the many problems and challenges confronted within the Middle East, that answer must include reducing both actual economic disparities and the perceptions of relative economic deprivation that today lend religion within the region its evangelic back-to-basics resonance. To these ends, the promulgation of constructive economic development programs that ensure greater distributions of wealth to economically disenfranchised citizens across the Islamic world may prove to be a more effective remedy for ongoing insurgency and political unrest than the construction of multitudes of Anti-Terrorism Centers in the quest for an ultimate cure.

In the development of these themes, then, this inquiry is organized into four sections. The first, covered in chapters 1 and 2, explores the Islamic doctrine of war and its permutations in modern insurgent activities. The second, presented in chapters 3 and 4, describes the historical evolution of modern Middle East terrorism. The third, detailed in chapters 5 and 6, examines the origins and development of contemporary terrorist infrastructures, with particular focus on the underground organization known as al-Qaeda. Finally, chapters 7 and 8 seek political and economic solutions to the vexing problems of violence presently afflicting the Islamic world. More detailed analyses of these phenomena are presented in the appendices.

METHODOLOGICAL NOTE

Throughout the text, a modified version of the Library of Congress transliteration of Arabic is employed wherein—due to limitations of the word processing system employed—no distinction is made between long and short vowels, nor is differentiation made between two Arabic consonants that invoke the same English consonant (e.g., "d" is used for each, not "d" for one and "d" with a dot subscript for the other). The exception is that conventional spellings of words in common usage are employed. Hence, Osama bin Laden's (not Usamah bin Ladin's) underground organization is depicted as "al-Qaeda" and not "al-Qa'idah" and the pro-Iranian Lebanese political faction as "Hezbollah" and not the more proper "Hizb Allah." Unless otherwise explicitly indicated, the M. Pickthall translation is employed throughout the analysis.

1

The Concept of "Jihad" in Historic Context

Finally, my brethren, be strong in the Lord and His might. Put on the whole armor of God that you may be able to stand against the wiles of the devil. For we do not wrestle against flesh and blood but against principalities, against powers, against the rulers of darkness of this age, against the spiritual hosts of wickedness in the heavenly places.

—St. Paul in the Bible, Ephesians 6:10–12

REFLECTIONS ON THE NATURE
OF THE ISLAMIC CODE FOR WAR

To discern what constitutes deviant behavior in the conduct of what some purport to be modern militant Muslim foreign policy, it is, at the onset, crucial to establish what constitutes a doctrinal norm.[1] This is a critical undertaking. For a definitive work on the phenomenon of terror must not only document its manifestations, it must contribute to fuller understanding of its sources. To these ends, inquiry explores at some length why a preponderance of acts of terrorism today is seemingly committed by Muslim male extremists between the ages of fifteen and forty-five and who then revel in their accomplishments in affiliated Web sites.

As with fifteen of the nineteen terrorists who perpetrated the heinous acts of September 11, 2001, in New York and Washington, D.C., bearing Saudi Arabian passports, analysis quite naturally focuses in particular upon the educational systems and social mores of that country and its so-called Wahhabi movement that is often accused of fostering a draconian, fanatically puritanical interpretation of Islamic doctrine that creates a socioeconomic milieu propitious for spawning militant extremism. In this quest, employing original source documents, two phenomena are exegetically explored:[2]

1. Is the doctrinal interpretation of the Qur'an by the founder and adherents of the Wahhabi movement more strident in interpretation than other doctrinal exegeses of the Qur'an? To this end, particular scrutiny is focused upon the writings of the movement's founder, the eighteenth-century Saudi-Najdi Islamic reformer Muhammad Ibn 'Abd al-Wahhab.
2. If not, are there external factors impacting on the operating environment of the Wahhabi movement that have corrupted the original intent of its Islamic creed and transformed it, for a minor component of its adherents, from an essentially fundamentalist religious movement into an incendiary political one?

These are critical questions that must be comprehensively answered in the quest to cope with the very real threats that they pose—as understanding the origins and sponsors of global terror is a crucial first step in separating friend from foe in a murky world wherein polemic does not invariably signal actual intent and is critical in distinguishing dangerous radicals from natural allies who follow traditional Islam.[3] As those who today indulge in doomsday jeremiads notwithstanding, this campaign is not directed just against the West but indeed against all of humanity—not a clash of civilizations but instead a battle for civilization itself.

For with al-Qaeda claiming to have defeated one great global superpower, the Soviet Union, in the mountains of Afghanistan, if they now, operating in league with disparate other groups, are enabled to take credit for driving the remaining one, the United States, from the Iraqi desert, not because of military superiority or strategic guile but because of partisan discord in Washington, they will have developed a religious validation replete with political resonance throughout the entire Islamic world—increasing their motivation to pursue radical jihadism as well as assaulting traditional moderate Islamic values through violent means—while concurrently igniting an eclectic variety of retrograde Middle East dissidents engaged in a rearguard action taking as its form a direct frontal assault upon modern civilized progress as it is now conceived.

Such is no idle conjecture. In early 2003, Osama bin Laden publicly sought to ratchet up Middle East public opinion by charging:

The preparations for an attack upon Iraq are but one link in a chain of attacks. . . . With the start of the (1991) Gulf War, the Americans established important and dangerous military bases which have spread throughout the "Land of the Two Holy Places" (Saudi Arabia). One of the most important objectives of the new Crusader attack (in 2003) is to pave the way and prepare the region, after its fragmentation, for what will be known as the Greater State of Israel, whose borders will include extensive areas of Iraq, Egypt, Syria, Lebanon, all of Palestine, and large parts of the Land of the Two Holy Places.[4]

To deter this posited adverse outcome, bin Laden stipulated his military objectives, as articulated by his principal doctrinal advisor Dr. Ayman al-Zawahiri:[5]

The masters in Washington are using the local regimes to protect their interests and to fight the battle against the Muslims on their behalf. But if shrapnel from the battle reaches their homes and their bodies, they will face one of two bitter choices:

Either they will wage war against the Muslims, which means the battle will turn into jihad against the infidels; or they will reconsider after acknowledging the failure of their brutal and violent confrontation against the Muslims. Hence, we must move the battle *to the enemy's grounds* to burn the hands of those who ignite fire in our countries.

As the tragic events of 9/11 make vivid, these are not idle threats. Those who view Iraq as another Vietnam, therefore, must be made intently aware that in this case, there is a defining difference—that while the Vietnamese wanted nothing more than national reunification, al-Qaeda seeks to destroy all of democratic free society in the name of their vengeful God—and they particularly want to achieve their victory not in Fallujah, Najaf, or Ramadi but in the Western world and Washington itself.[6]

It comes as no surprise, then, that in a videotape broadcast on January 6, 2006, al-Zawahiri was already prematurely proclaiming victory in Iraq—as the reality is that, at the bottom line, these are fanatic ideologues committed not only to bringing down the more moderate Muslim regimes throughout the Middle East, but equally to attacking the decadent West and establishing a global theocratic caliphate molded in the image of their deviant world view.

To this end, they stop at nothing. For if they succeed, word will again be out that the American will to win is fragile—that it can be outlasted—with those who today advocate precipitous withdrawal for sheer partisan advantage aimed at defeat at any cost creating a world wherein victory will be pyrrhic at best and in no way conducive to the enduring peace to which they may aspire. As amidst somber echoes of Neville Chamberlain's cane on the cobblestones of Munich, the same pacific, equivocating, ideologically liberal

Washington political crowd that snatched American defeat from the jaws of success in Vietnam will again cut and run—and will have handed this toxic terrorist cabal its most noteworthy global victory. In such a context, then, prevailing can be the *only* exit strategy.

An April 6, 2006, National Security Council National Intelligence Estimate precisely makes this point:[7]

> We assess that the Iraq jihad is shaping a new generation of terrorist leaders and operatives; perceived jihadist success there would inspire more fighters to continue the struggle elsewhere. . . . (But) should jihadists leaving Iraq perceive themselves, and be perceived to have failed, we judge that fewer fighters will be inspired to carry on the fight.[8]

In other words, if terrorists are today permitted to prevail in Iraq, their activity will fuel the global jihadist movement everywhere, and conversely. This reality, in turn, is underscored in a January, 2007 National Intelligence Estimate:

> If Coalition forces were withdrawn rapidly . . . we judge that this almost certainly would lead to a significant increase in the scale and scope of sectarian conflict in Iraq, intensify Sunni resistance to the Iraqi Government, and have adverse consequences for national reconciliation.
>
> If such a rapid withdrawal were to take place, we judge that the [Iraqi Security Forces] would be unlikely to survive as a nonsectarian national institution; neighboring countries . . . might intervene openly in the conflict; massive civilian casualties and forced population displacement would be probable; [al-Qaeda in Iraq] would attempt to use parts of the country—particularly al-Anbar province—to plan increased attacks in and outside of Iraq.[9]

Indeed, Osama bin Laden has already explicitly heralded this course. Asserting that "America has divided the entire world into two spheres—one of faith wherein there is no hypocrisy, and one of infidelity from which Allah must save us," he continues:

> If Americans do not respond, then they will face the same fate as the Soviets who ran away from Afghanistan to face military defeat, political fragmentation, economic bankruptcy, and ideological collapse. This is our message to the Americans in response to theirs. Have they not realized why we resist, and why, with Allah's permission, we will win?[10]

Whither, then, the course? Political genius, it is said, is the art of lasting five minutes longer than one's enemy—a timeless maxim that must again be tested now. Its corollary in its pursuit in forging prudent approaches for effectively combating terrorism is "expect the unexpected." Hence, from a policy formulation standpoint, developing the fullest possible understanding of the self-proclaimed enemy that civilized society today confronts is quintessential to avoiding those misdirected remedies that derive from inadvertent misperception.

Accordingly, in exploring the multifaceted dimensions to the metastasizing mutant of Political Islam now emerging, establishing doctrinal bases for that devolution, based upon critical evaluation of original sources of the participants themselves, becomes of the highest priority. To wit, developing:

1. A fuller, more complete comprehension of the historic Islamic Code of Conduct for War and Peace as articulated in the Qur'an and Prophetic Tradition; and then determining
2. A sound methodological approach, founded upon classic Islamic sources, for conducting empirical evaluation.

Subsequent analysis thereby develops findings respecting terrorism's modern evolution quite revolutionary in impact, surprising even to many who have spent decades living within the Middle East while experiencing its unfolding course and its key contributing developments. In this process, the analyses of chapters 2 through 9 proceed methodologically in their pursuit of classic ideological pretexts for the modern practice of invoking terror in Allah's name. Before accurate biopsy of possible doctrinal bases for the evolution of current cells of terror under Islam's umbrella can be completed, however, certain historical foundations must be established to fix proper contextual matrices for evaluation.

To this end, the possibility of substantive differences between western and moderate Arabic translations of the Qur'an with the so-called Wahhabi version, produced at al-Madinah, are first explored without meaningful variances being established between the iterations. Analysis then moves to exploring whether there are instead substantive differences in modern doctrinal interpretation of the Qur'an and the vast corpus of Prophetic Tradition that provide justification for invoking terror as an instrument of foreign policy—with particular scrutiny centered upon the writings of the progenitor of the Wahhabi movement, Muhammad Ibn 'Abd al-Wahhab.

Again finding no identifiable correlation, focus turns to examining possible exogenous politico-religious influences in a quest to identify causes that have today metastasized certain segments of the traditionally fundamentalist *religious* Wahhabi movement into a virulent *political* one—with particular attention devoted to the gradual infiltration of Egypt's Muslim Brotherhood into Western Arabia commencing in the mid-twentieth century, and the affiliated impacts of the writings of its doctrinal apostle Sayyid Qutb and his disciples openly aimed at igniting lethality through violence.

As a precursor to these examinations, however, inquiry commences by turning to historical evaluation of the evolution of the international character of early medieval Muslim civilization itself in an age wherein the faith was characterized both by dynamism in its global outreach and tolerance in its application.

For to fathom why a civilization is where it is, it is first important to understand where it historically has been—as the xenophobia that today pervades significant elements of Islamic society is a relatively new phenomenon—an unfortunate by-product of retrenchment that has evolved in recent centuries for socioeconomic and political reasons explored at greater depth in chapter 9 to this inquiry.

Historically, the intellectual realm of Islam was strikingly different—aggressive in its quest for learning and conspicuously open to new ideas. Indeed, because of its vast absorptive capacity for knowledge in early medieval times, it rapidly became the uncontested military and commercial superpower of its age—both the global fount of learning and ever-zealous in its quest for more. Yet in the Western renaissance and early modern era, the sun surprisingly set upon the radiance of medieval Islamic civilization at high noon—at a point that should have been its zenith—and it has not recovered since. This inquiry seeks the reasons why. Accordingly, it is to extensive examination of the doctrinal bases for Islam's meteoric intellectual rise and fall that inquiry now turns.

In this quest, however, understanding how, and why, a faith behaves as it does also requires an a priori understanding of its self-image—how it views itself. Global perceptions of Islam, or of any religion or movement for that matter, are thus undeniably important—as internal and international reactions are often mutually reinforcing.

Certainly central to the relationship between the Islamic world and its counterpart in the West is a legacy of entwined and complex history, of course. But from an overarching public-policy perspective, it bears repeating that understanding the Islamic world must commence not with how the religion relates to other cultures but rather with knowledge of how it relates to itself.

Critical to a fuller understanding of Islam, then, is the realization that just as there is no single America or Europe today, there also is no monolithic entity or common uniform culture called "Islam." The Muslim world is instead at least as pluralistic as the West—spanning all of Asia and Africa and much of Europe, extending well beyond the confines of the Arabian Peninsula, which is the tunnel vision currently conjured up by many who contemplate the linear extent of projection of the faith.

For the Arabian Peninsula is, at best, no more than Islam in microcosm—the place where the faith began—with Saudi Arabia's 23.7 million plus populace no more than 1.7 percent of the estimated more than 1.4 billion Muslims today spread across the world. Indeed, the more basic reality is that while Muslims total more than a quarter of the world's population, Arab Muslims account for no more than one-eighth of that total. The rest are spread across East Asia, Africa, and the remainder of the planet.

Given this diverse mosaic, then, the would-be political analyst cannot rely upon stereotypes but must instead proceed with consummate caution in advancing any generalizations about "what really is Islam" and who "really are Muslims"—reflecting the reality that only about 13 percent of all Muslims are Arabs; the same percentage of all Arabs are Saudis; and less than 0.001 percent of all Saudis—and less than 0.00001 percent of all Muslims—are militant terrorists.[11]

These realizations become the more relevant when probing dimensions to what are frequently advanced as stereotyped representations of Islamic behavior. For the great majority of Muslims today share values typical of global society at large. Prominent among them is a strong commitment to family values, social justice, and the merits of free trade. They are not radicals; they are not revolutionaries. Indeed, as analysis will show, those who now spread terror in Islam's name, may, in reality, not be Muslims at all, but instead deadly carriers of an ever-metastasizing mutant ideology.

In pursuit of objective analysis, therefore, discretion must be invoked in approaching ultimate conclusions. Cognizant of the unfortunate media-generated perceptions of Islam cited in the introduction, this inquiry focuses upon the strategies and tactics of terror, and the beliefs that underlie them—as both historically and currently practiced within the Near East—recognizing that, while like everyone else, Muslim peoples are shaped by their history, unlike most, they are also intimately aware of it.

For Islam's rich history, for those privileged to engage in forging it, enjoys not only a unique religious significance but a profound legal consequence, as it reflects the workings of God's purpose for His Community of Believers—for those who not only accept the teachings of the faith but are likewise subject to its law. To ultimately understand its essence—and the unique theocracy that it has engendered—then, one must first probe its depths of origins.[12]

Hence, while in contemporary Western vernacular, the phrase—"that's history"—may dismiss a given matter of as little consequence; for the Muslim East, it is the embodiment of being and thus, must be carefully consulted by those who would pulse the quintessence of its civilization.

Before such a course can be effectively traversed, however, establishing certain historic perspectives and analytic methodologies is in order.

THE NATURE AND DIMENSIONS OF
THE EARLY ISLAMIC CONQUESTS

In this context, therefore, the early Islamic conquests must be perceived within the historical milieux wherein they unfolded—not as savage acts of illegal seizure but instead as the workings of a natural order that then obtained throughout the known universe—with jihad an instrument of *juhd*, (effort), serving at the pleasure of both God and State. For early medieval states generally did not possess frontiers or precise borders in the most modern sense. For them, on land, as with the concept of time, there was no precise line of demarcation but rather a border zone or "band," or "interval."

These were delineations sufficient for most pragmatic purposes, to be sure—as such laws as did exist regulated people, not places. A ruler ruled as far as he could collect taxes and maintain order—ruling a domain that was not static in its geography but determined to be ever expanding—bounded only by intraversable deserts and distant seas. Where there were no taxes to collect, therefore, exact borders didn't matter—as at specifically that point, the desire for imperial conquest usually ended, with further war no more than an extension of ongoing routine existence at the perimeter.[13]

In this sense, war was, in reality, an extension of life; that is, a state of war was presumed to exist between one's own tribe and all others unless a particular treaty or agreement had been reached with another tribe or tribal confederation that established amicable relations—thus rendering it to be at once a dual political and religious function at its inception. In this context, then, today's jihad, to some, is seen as little more than yet another tenuous step in a procession along a prolonged fourteenth-century continuum—building upon the still more millennia that preceded it—of a longstanding, now modern, tradition that commenced with the Arabs' first irruption from their peninsula in 634.

Scoped from this vantage point, therefore, while most Westerners have historically viewed their ruling polities as nations containing various religions, many fundamentalist Muslims have traditionally viewed theirs as a single religious polity, a Community of Believers artificially divided into tribes and nations—perceiving Islam to be creed *and* empire—bearing the baggage of rendering jihadist ideology diametrically opposed to the modern concepts of nationalism, secular sovereignty, democracy, freedom of speech and religion, and the Geneva Convention—all of which they deem to be the handiwork of infidels.

Thus, their vision, antistatist at its roots, does not commit Islam's Community of Believers to a secular democratic course founded in the future but instead consigns them to an autocratic, theocratic one firmly rooted in an oriental past. Indeed, given the diplomatic mores of that past that then prevailed on both sides of the East-West ideological divide, for medieval Muslims, the jihad was no more than foreign policy waged against infidels—a normal path to territorial expansion—a religious obligation as intrinsic to the faith as the sacrament of communion was to medieval Christendom.[14]

It is in this context that Arab militaries have traditionally been referred to as "the armies of Islam" and their leaders as "the rulers of Islam"—that the success of the early Islamic conquests became a watershed in human history—and thus must be viewed as such in retrospect. For at their apogee, the Muslims acquired a landmass that was the most expansive to that age—an empire larger than that of imperial Rome, which they succeeded as the foremost superpower on the planet.

In this era, in fact, Islam represented not only the greatest military power but also the greatest economic power in the world, trading in multitudes of commodities through a far-flung network of commerce connecting Asia, Africa, and Europe—exchanging wide varieties of foodstuffs and manufactured goods with the civilized countries of Asia; importing slaves, gold, gems, and base metals from Africa; and procuring slaves, wool, and timber from Europe.

At the same time, in a classic case of "the flag following trade," the Muslims were invading many of the very same countries with whom they were pacifically engaged in amicable, productive commerce—again in a manner consistent with the medieval notion of borderless domains.[15]

Yet this was no accident—no happenstance of fate—as the early Arab conquests were accomplished decisively and with uncommon swiftness. Indeed, within just a century of their seventh century eruption from the Arabian Peninsula, the Muslims came to rule a vast political and commercial hegemony that stretched from the Indian Ocean in the East, across the Near East and North Africa, to the Atlantic in the West.

By the time of Prophet Muhammad's death in 632, not only the Arabian Peninsula, but also most of the lower Levant, had been subjected to their direct control. In autumn 633, Muslim military operations commenced in southern Syria as well.[16] Simultaneously, the famed Arab general Khalid b. al-Walid undertook the pacification of Iraq.[17] Damascus surrendered to the Arabs in the autumn of 635.[18]

In late summer 637, the Muslim army achieved a major victory over its Byzantine counterpart at Yarmuk in the Jordan Valley, thereby paving the way for the conquest of the rest of Syria. On this occasion, the ninth century Arab historian/geographer al-Baladhuri conveys what he purports to be the prophetic lamentation of Byzantine Emperor Heraclius:

> May peace be with you now, O Syria, and what an excellent country you shall make for our enemy![19]

Shortly thereafter, in 638, Jerusalem surrendered, followed by Caesarea in 640; and with these conquests, the subjugation of Syria, except for its northern province of Qinnasrin, was complete.[20]

Meanwhile, the decisive battle for Persia took place at al-Qadisiyah on 1 June 637, with a sizable Muslim army commanded by Sa'd b. Abi Waqqas utterly destroying a massive Sasanid military force. Pushing forward, he seized Ctesiphon, the Persian capital, in that same month—and with the subsequent capture of Mukran in 644, the Arabs had reached the borders of India.[21]

In the West, the Islamic imperial quest was pursued with equally spectacular success. Most of Egypt, except for Alexandria, was captured in April 637.[22] The latter city, which boasted a garrison of 50,000 troops, held out until 6 December 641. Moving westward across North Africa, the noted Arab conqueror of Egypt, 'Amr b. al-'As, proceeded to take Barqah, Tripoli, and Carthage in rapid succession. Consolidation of the remaining Maghrib then continued thereafter at a casual, albeit steady, pace over the course of the next half century.[23]

In July 710, Muslim military units first set foot in Spain.[24] In the following year, the Battle for Europe commenced in earnest. On 19 July 712, a 12,000 man Muslim military contingent, commanded by Tariq b. Ziyad, routed a larger Visigothic army of King Roderick at the mouth of the Barbate River near Gibraltar. Soon thereafter, all of Spain fell with minor opposition.[25]

In 720, the Muslim military was at the southern borders of France. Narbonne was captured in that year.[26] By 732, they had crossed the Pyrenees Mountains and were threatening Tours and Poitiers. There, though, they were finally defeated by Charles Martel, mayor of Paris, in October 732, in the Battle of Tours, famously celebrated in the West as the decisive engagement that saved European Christendom from Muslim subjugation.[27]

At last, the Muslims' relentless drive westward had been stopped. But within the century following the death of Prophet Muhammad in 632, they had conquered, and now ruled, an empire that stretched from the southern borders of France in the West to those of India in the East. From a geopolitical standpoint, Pax Islamica had reached its most expansive form.

Yet even now, the Muslims' dramatic Age of Engagement was not yet over—as for a full millennium from their first irruption from the Arabian Peninsula in 634, armies bearing the banner of Islam continued to invade Christian territories. From 668–718, they made several attempts to take Constantinople.[28]

Indeed, in 846, a Muslim navy entered the River Tiber, and Arab forces sacked Ostia and Rome—*de Civitate Dei*—the City of God itself. In a terrified Europe, thereafter for many centuries, Christian Sunday services throughout the continent would end with the supplication: "From the fury of the Mahomedan, spare us, Lord!" And in 1453, the Muslims at last captured Constantinople—the city wherein Constantine had first embraced Christ—the secular Capital of Christendom, the "Second Rome," converting it into the capital city of the Ottoman Islamic state.[29]

In 1389, Ottoman armies also seized Kosovo. In 1430, they prevailed at Salonika. In 1470, they won at Negroponte. As late as 1521, Turkish Sultan Suleiman the Magnificent sacked Belgrade and conducted raids throughout the Balkans. In 1529, he lay siege to Vienna, and in 1683, Ottoman armies were again at Vienna's gates only there to be stopped by the army of Polish king John Sobieski—continuing a campaign against Christendom that had commenced in Andalusia in 732, nearly a millennium before.[30]

Similar campaigns were being carried out on the Eastern Front as well. From 1162 to 1192, Persian Muslim armies were intensely engaged in India. Concurrently, between 1237 and 1240, the Tatars of the Golden Horde conquered Russia and the hitherto Christian land of Anatolia. Indeed, as late as 1562, Mogul Muslim sultans deployed south of Bombay—all geopolitical realities that render devout Muslims' lingering angst even today over the Crusades is a somewhat double standard.[31]

ISLAM'S AVARICIOUS QUEST FOR KNOWLEDGE

Though fervent in its pursuit of just war—as will be delineated in the formulae of chapter 2—the early Islamic state was equally imbued with a religion characterized equally by its tolerance for, and appreciation of, other cultures and expansive in its global outreach in the quest to learn from them. Indeed, a Qur'anic verse exhorted Muslims to seek out learning:

> Proclaim that your Lord is most Benevolent, who taught human beings through the pen that which they did not know. (Surat al-A'laq 96:3–5)

In their pursuit of this objective, the Qur'an explicitly encouraged them to seek out learning wherever it could be acquired. Indeed, a tradition attributed to the Prophet Muhammad beseeched them to even go as far as China, if need be, to acquire knowledge. And pursue learning, they did—attaining the highest levels then achieved in human history in the arts and sciences of civilization.

For inheriting the knowledge, arts, and skills of the ancient Middle East—including the resplendent intellectual legacies of Greece and Persia—it imported and appended to them new and important external innovations such as the use and manufacture of paper from China and Arab numerals and decimal positioning from India.

To this rich inheritance, diligent scholars throughout the Islamic world added vital contributions through their own ideas and experiments. In most of the arts and sciences of civilization that they nurtured, Christian Europe clearly was the pupil, not the teacher—an intellectual dependent of the Islamic world relying upon Arabic versions for even many otherwise lost ancient Greek and Roman works.[32]

Almost from the beginning, Muslim intellectuals had developed an interest in the arts and sciences. This profound religious mandate—deeply interwoven into the highly international character of Islamic society that evolved over time—would soon become a prime factor leading the Islamic realm (*Dar al-Islam*) to acquire a wide and in-depth knowledge of bygone civilizations and to employ that knowledge to develop their contemporary one.

For it was Muslim scholars who at this time preserved Graeco-Roman science and philosophy throughout medieval Europe's prolonged Dark Ages—an era when, in the words of historian Phillip Hitti, Arab rulers were delving into Greek and Persian technologies "while Charlemagne and his lords were dabbling in the art of writing their own names."[33]

Khalid b. Yazid, son of the second Umayyad caliph Yazid I, for instance, oversaw the translation of numerous Greek works on astronomy and chemistry into Arabic. The fourth Umayyad caliph, Marwan I, ordered the translation, with addenda and commentaries, of the famous medical treatise of Aaron of Alexandria. The translation of medical literature was, in fact, a principal aspect of the scientific progress that distinguished the rule of the Umayyads.

When the 'Abbasids established their new capital in Baghdad in 762, moreover, al-Mansur, that dynasty's second caliph, further encouraged the translation of works of medicine and astronomy from Greek and Syriac. To facilitate this effort, he sent a special envoy to Constantinople to procure scientific books. The Byzantine emperor reciprocated by providing him with the geometries of Euclid and several books on the natural sciences.

During the reign of the great 'Abbasid caliph Harun al-Rashid, many works on philosophy and logic were also translated into Arabic, as books continued to be brought to Baghdad from the conquered cities of Byzantium. Indeed, the very first Arabic treatise on geometry, a translation of Euclid, appeared in his time. This famed caliph likewise founded an academy of science in Baghdad that his son and eventual successor, al-Ma'mun, developed into a major center of learning. This academy, the House of Wisdom, engaged in original research into many branches of science and letters, as well as in the translation and dissemination of a wide variety of foreign scientific, literary, and philosophical works.

From the Greek, Muslim scholars at this great research center learned, translated, and published the philosophies of Plato, the logic of Aristotle, the medical works of Hippocrates and Galen, and the mathematics and astronomies of Euclid, Archimedes, and Ptolemy. Most of the translations from Persian, in turn, dealt with historic and literary subjects; from Sanskrit, mathematics, medicine, astronomy, and literature; from Syriac and Nabatean, agriculture and engineering; and from Latin and Hebrew, major scientific and literary compositions.

Caliph al-Ma'mun likewise reportedly dispatched a special envoy to Sicily requesting that its ruler send to Baghdad the Library of Syracuse, which was one of the most famous of that era. He also acquired numerous Greek texts from other parts of Byzantium and the Western world, including the works of Plato, Aristotle, Hippocrates, Galen, Ptolemy, and other intellectual luminaries of classic antiquity. His reign, in fact, has been called the Golden Age of Arabic Translation, as numerous scientific works were reproduced in Arabic from Greek, Roman, Syriac, Aramaic, Nabatean, Persian, and Sanskrit primary sources.

Soon, with the onset of the Dark Ages in Europe, many of these priceless works of Graeco-Roman scholarship would be lost to the West. Indeed, it was only because of their careful preservation at the hands of the Muslims that they were initially saved and later retransmitted to Christian West Europe in the twelfth to thirteenth centuries when the Dark Ages were over.

The town of Toledo, in Umayyad Spain, was an especially important knowledge transfer center. There, the works of Aristotle and Plato were again converted into Western tongues. One Gerard of Cremona, before his death in 1187, translated seventy-one works from Arabic into Latin—including Ptolemy's *Al-Majest*, Euclid's *Elements*, and various treatises of Galen, Hippocrates, and Aristotle—as well as al-Farabi's famed Aristotelian commentary.[34]

Not only were previous Western works retransmitted, but original Arabic scientific and literary contributions were converted into Western languages as well. It was in Muslim Toledo, for instance, that the renowned scholar Adelard of Bath translated the astronomic tables of al-Khwarizmi and other Arabic mathematic and astronomic tables into Latin.[35]

It was there that Michael the Scot translated al-Bitruji's astronomy, *Al-Hayah*, and Ibn Sina's version of Aristotelian zoology. It was in Umayyad Spain that John of Seville, midway through the twelfth century, translated into Western vernacular a variety of other works on arithmetic, astronomy, medicine, and philosophy written by such Muslim savants as al-Farghani, al-Kindi, and al-Ghazali.[36]

This milieu of tolerance and thirst for knowledge was evident internally as well. For the medieval Muslim scholars were far more than just great translators, many were extremely accomplished scientists in their own rights. Beginning about 771, they developed a particular interest in astronomy. Early in the ninth century, in fact, the 'Abbasid caliph al-Ma'mun commissioned the building of a new observatory at Baghdad. There, astronomers not only made highly systematic observances of the celestial movements, they also verified with astounding accuracy the obliquity of the ecliptic, the precession of the equinoxes, the length of a solar year, and that of a terrestrial degree.[37]

Indeed, the astronomers at this pioneering facility—as well as at others soon to be developed at Cairo, Cordova, and Toledo—developed the theoretical foundations for the astronomic sciences, and introduced new formulae, calculations, procedures, and tables that were, for centuries, taught at the great universities of Europe. Their works would, in fact, later become the principal references for such great Western astronomers as Tycho Brahe, Kepler, Copernicus, and Galileo.

The contributions of one giant of medieval Muslim science, Muhammad b. Musa al-Khwarizmi, were particularly monumental. In addition to compiling the oldest astronomical tables still in existence, he likewise composed the oldest known Middle Eastern works on both mathematics and algebra—the latter discipline generally considered to be a Muslim invention. The name "algebra" itself, in fact, derives from the Arabic term *al-jabr*—which means "bone-setting" and al-Khwarizmi likened to the "factoring of quadratic equations" in his renowned treatise *Calculation of Integration and Equation*.[38]

'Umar al-Khayyam, who was famed for his collection of poems, was also a master of the mathematical sciences and wrote a definitive work on algebra. Another ninth-century mathematician, Thabit b. Qura, wrote the pioneering scholarly work produced on spherical geometry, and al-Battani's contributions to the same topic continue to be respected by scientists to this day. The modern system of numbers, as noted, likewise was transmitted to the West from the Indians via the Arabs, who also introduced the concept of zero and provided the English equivalent for it, cipher, as well.[39]

Yet this dynamic process of intellectual transfer was not limited to applied sciences, as the treatises of Islamic academics contributed greatly to global commerce as well. For much Western business vocabulary, mercantile ideology, concepts of profit motivation, contracts of corporate association, and its commercial tools of trade likewise now were all profoundly revolutionized by the ongoing, firsthand exposure of European merchants to the superior economic methods at work in the Islamic East—with the commercial renaissance of the Christian West evolving in late medieval times a product of this transformation.

THE USE OF QUR'ANIC MOTIVATION FOR MILITANT PROPAGANDA PURPOSES

Given medieval Muslims' concurrent commitment to just war and equitable peace, the key analytic question in defining their foreign policy motivations inevitably becomes one of determining a precise, exacting methodology for engaging in Qur'anic exegesis, for in Islamic affairs both political and diplomatic, the Qur'an is the quintessential guide—the "final revelation" of the "final prophet" Muhammad.

Not only is it integral to all Muslims' daily lives, it is the living constitution of the Islamic state. Reflecting this reality, eminent orientalist Bernard Lewis asserts that in contrast to the other major world religions:

> Islam from the lifetime of its founder was the state, and the identity of religion and the government is indelibly stamped on the awareness and memories of the faithful from their sacred writings, history, and experience.[40]

It is not at all surprising, therefore, to find that most of the significant political and movements in modern Muslim history have drawn heavily upon classic Islam as a unifying and motivating force. For the employment of religious iconography, and in particular, Qur'anic verses, as both political slogans and battle cries, has been richly documented in Islamic history almost from its inception—making careful study of their employment as political communication not only useful from a current strategic analytic standpoint but also of historic consequence.

This is a crucial stepping-stone in framing analysis. For in a contemporary context, Near East political scientist Peter Marsden, supported by T. P. Schwartz Barcott, among others, assert that much usage of Qur'anic references by modern Muslim political leaders originated with the underground insurgent movement known as the Muslim Brotherhood that coalesced in Egypt in 1928. Deeming Islam's doctrinal legacy to have derived from two primary sources—the Qur'an and Prophetic Tradition—it is said to have adopted as its slogan from that of the seventh century *khawarij* insurgent movements waged against the formal Islamic establishment, which proclaimed:

> The Qur'an is our constitution; the Prophet is our guide. Death for the glory of Allah is our supreme ambition.[41]

But Marsden's claim is true only to the extent that he applies it to a *modern* context. For a classic use of Qur'anic verses in battlefield motivation was intrinsic to the entire history of Islam from its inception. Yet recognition of their longstanding use in militant symbolism should come as no surprise. For the Qur'an—Islam's principal holy work, comprised of some 80,000 words organized into 6,219 verses subdivided into 114 chapters—is, as Bernard Lewis has asserted, the "living constitution" for all Muslims.[42]

Of its 6,219 verses, in fact, more than 500 contain legal applications and more than 80 are explicit in their legal construction and prescription. Indeed, the entire body of Islamic sacred literature—the Qur'an and Prophetic Tradition—plus fourteen centuries of subsequent analytic commentary—not only constitutes the religious constitution for the creed, but in so doing, concomitantly directly refutes the vitriolic polemic of modern jihadist ideology, as subsequent discourse will reveal.[43]

Accordingly, based upon careful exegesis of such Qur'anic verses, it is possible to retrospectively construct both a doctrinally prescribed medieval Islamic operational military model—in a modern sense, a "classic formula for war"—and a clearly delineated Muslim "code of conduct" for pursuing peace—as detailed throughout this work. In the process, analysis concurrently explores the course whereby, and the milieu wherein, the current Middle East "culture of terror" has evolved.

2

On the Islamic Doctrine of War

Warfare is ordained for you though it is hateful unto you; but it may happen that you hate a thing that is good for you; and it may happen that you may love a thing that is bad for you. Allah knows. You know not.

—Surat al-Baqarah 2:216

THE GEOPOLITICAL CONTEXT

With the traditional Muslim terms of military engagement having been defined in chapter 1, it is now critical to detail and evaluate the doctrine that drove it. To that end, it is first crucial to bear in mind that civilizations, and their motivating ideologies, must be judged not only by their time and place, but also by the tone and temperament wherein they evolved.

Islam was born within a harsh and violent operating environment and received a correspondingly harsh and aggressive reception from surrounding tribes. Indeed, the first Muslims had to fight tenaciously for sheer survival from the initial proclamation of their faith until Arabia had at last been subjugated by Islam at the death of Prophet Muhammad in 632—a volatile age wherein preexisting norms of intertribal behavior were directly dependent upon the threat or actual use of force by the claimant of any right, including the right to survive.[1]

The threat or use of force was also the norm among the various surrounding major polities of the region, including the superpowers to the north and northeast: the Byzantines and Sasanids, respectively. When Islam's empire was established in seventh-century Arabia, therefore, it was the accepted method of conducting what is today commonly known as international diplomacy.

Thus, it was normative, indeed inevitable, that Islam should doctrinally endorse the use of military means in its relations with non-Muslims. Yet in so doing, it concurrently introduced new, more civil standards for rationalizing and controlling its actual practice, as this inquiry, in subsequent chapters, demonstrates.[2]

Among them, whereas previous proximate warfare had been motivated by such material considerations as territorial sovereignty, economic greed, and intertribal rivalry, the Qur'an restricted the use of force in the pursuit of geopolitical relations to self-defense and expansion of the propagation of God's Word—with a stipulation that the latter type of jihad need not be militant perforce and could as readily be pursued by missionary means as well as by good example. In this context, then, jihad became institutionalized as an obligation beside the Five Pillars of the Faith as a prime vehicle to protect the Community of Believers as well as to expand it.

These, then, became the only sanctioned reasons for going to war. Moreover, as subsequent analysis reveals, Muslims were likewise closely constrained by certain rules concerning the actual conduct of war. Prior to engagement, for instance, they were required to offer their opponents an opportunity to accept the faith without combat—and if it then became necessary to fight, hostilities must perforce be restricted to combatant soldiers and only on the battlefield.[3]

Islam is thus unequivocal in its militant prescriptions. Not only does the Qur'an delineate fixed guidelines for conventional war, it also sets strict restrictions on unconventional (asymmetric) warfare practices conducted by irregulars (soldiers without portfolios), which it carefully constrains.

Within this battlefield context, as analysis will also demonstrate, the polyvalence of the concept of jihad is painstakingly defined. For, as noted, the concept does not invariably mean holy war or often even conventional war. Indeed, it frequently doesn't even mean war at all but instead the unending struggle of the devout to be good Muslims—deriving its meaning from a saying attributed to Prophet Muhammad that:

It is the duty of every Muslim to command good and forbid evil with sincerity of heart (devotion), tongue (outreach), and hand (sword).[4]

Islam's preconditions for war, therefore, are founded on four precepts:

1. It must be essentially defensive in nature (*difa'i*) and be sanctioned by competent authority, a duly enfranchised Islamic leader capable of both engaging war and assessing its mandating virtue and potential for success.
2. There must be just cause (justice in war = *jus in bello*)—to ward off forces of evil and corruption and thereby expand the domain of Islam.
3. It must be preceded by a declaration of intent, inviting unbelievers to either embrace Islam or alternately to pay tribute in recognition of its sovereignty.
4. It must be conducted in accordance with Islamic values—not for personal glory, but to glorify God—for a cause and a path that leads to lasting peace.[5]

In this context, therefore, the parallels between Islam's rules for war and traditional Christian prescriptions for just war are strikingly similar. Competent authority, just cause, right intent, reasonable expectations for success, and a desire and quest for peace—all of the criteria for the pursuit of the Western concept of justifiable recourse to war (*jus ad bellum*) are equally present in Islam's rules for war——not just at its inception, at the commencement of hostilities, but equally throughout its conduct, and at its close—observing the limits to war in the quest for lasting peace.

In both, as defined in East and West alike, then, *jus ad bellum* contains three main requirements—just cause, legal competence to declare and wage war, and right reason—together with the stipulations that (1) recourse to the use of force be a last resort; and (2) that its overarching goal be to reestablish the peace. *Jus in bello*, in turn, levies two further conditions:

1. The means used must be proportionate to the remedies sought.
2. Noncombatants must be immunized or indemnified against harm to the maximum extent possible.[6]

Taken in concert, then, the coalescing of the precepts of *jus ad bellum* and *jus in bello* have led to a near universal consensus, in both medieval and modern times, and for East and West alike, that for a war to be fought justly, it must be:[7]

- publicly declared;
- proclaimed by recognized authority;
- engaged with the right intention;
- waged for just cause;
- pursued with proportionate reason;

- undertaken as a last resort; and
- only sought in the ongoing quest for a just peace.

THE DOCTRINAL CONTEXT

These precepts, then, form the doctrinal foundations for an integrated Islamic Code of Conduct for War that, from its inception, was concurrently a formula for peace that deployed with consummate success. Indeed, early on, medieval Muslim exegetes explicitly focused upon the role of war as an important transport vehicle on the path to peace.

Among them, the late University of Michigan orientalist George Scanlon cites more than forty classic Arabic doctrinal texts on the equity of warfare written between the eighth and fifteenth centuries in prefacing his edition of the fourteenth century 'Umar al-Ansari's "Dispelling of Fears in the Management of Wars." Muhammad al-Shaybani's eighth century "Book of the Law of Nations" also provides details on the legalities, types, rules of engagement, and justifications for just war set within the context of the early Islamic conquests.[8]

The composite of these classics makes clear that the Islamic rules for war are neither unfathomable nor arcane. Indeed, their prescriptions for (1) an overarching quest for peace; (2) legitimate pretexts for war; (3) types of permissible combat; and (4) personal conduct in war's pursuit are strikingly similar to St. Thomas Aquinas's precepts of just war (*bellum justum*). They also closely parallel the four basic principles of the Law of War as codified by The Hague Conventions at the onset of the twentieth century and the Geneva Convention in 1949. To wit:[9]

Table 2.1.

Modern Law of War	as reflected in the	Islamic Code for War
Legitimacy	as reflected in	righteous intent
Proportionality	as reflected in	measured response
Distinction	as reflected in	discrimination
Humanity	as reflected in	aggression avoidance

Precisely defining each of these precepts is illuminating in perceiving their intent. As for devout Muslims, "legitimacy" means actions bred of operational necessity executed pursuant to a lawful order issued by a duly constituted authority and carried with righteous goals. As such, it is an obligation of both daily life and war.

Indeed, "operational necessity," as manifest in "religious intent," is replete throughout the Qur'an and needs no elaboration here. In war, however, its pursuit is circumscribed. It must be carried out "in the way of God" to serve His purpose—to wit, a religious *casus belli*—conducted as only He would want it conducted. It must never be pursued for self-aggrandizement or personal gain.

The Islamic Code of Conduct for War, as Qur'anically prescribed, thus is explicit. Its tenets—founded on precepts of (1) legitimacy, (2) proportionality, (3) distinction, and (4) humanity today deemed modern—are detailed in the following fifteen integrated, sequential precepts.

Legitimacy

Precept 1: *War against unrepentant idolaters is legitimate.*
Polytheists, it is clear, were the prime battlefield enemy targeted by Islam. Yet even as such, a mandate for war against them must be preconditioned by a démarche for peace. Once commissioned, however, it becomes irrevocably unconditional.
Verse:
When the sacred months are passed, kill the polytheists wherever you find them; and take them captive and besiege them and prepare to ambush them. But if they repent, establish worship, and pay the zakat, *then leave them their way free.* (Surat al-Tawbah 9:5)
Comment:
Hence, while the mandate to wage jihad against polytheists is unequivocal, it is concurrently tempered by an obligation to be merciful to the would-be compliant in the quest to expand the jurisdiction of the faith.

Precept 2: *A call to war must be preceded by a call for peace.*
Indeed, predicated upon a Qur'anic injunction calling for war against the polytheists of Makkah, Muslim jurists held that any call for war must first be preceded by a call for peace and conversion to Islam pursuant to the precept that: "We never punish until We have first sent an Apostle," thereby invoking a trucial waiting period for response that, juridical concurrence generally held, was to be three days in duration.[10]
Verse:
And when We would destroy a township, We send a commandment to its folks who live at ease, and if afterward they commit abomination therein, so the Word (of punishment) has effect for it, and We annihilate it with complete annihilation. (Surat al-Isra' 17:16)
Comment:
This order, then, was deemed to fulfill the precondition of the requisite call for amicable submission.

Precept 3: *If the call is rejected, then armed conflict may proceed.*
If, however, the call was not requited, military engagement became fully sanctioned.
Verse:
If they repent and establish worship and pay the poor due, then they are your brothers in religion. We detail Our revelations for people who have knowledge. And if they break their pledges after their treaty (has been made), then fight the heads of disbelief. Lo! They have no binding oaths in order that they may desist. Will you not fight a folk who broke their solemn pledge, proposed to drive out the Messenger, and attacked you first? (Surat al-Tawbah 9:11–13)
Comment:
After exhausting the possibility of peace, therefore, the Qur'an does sanction war against those who are perceived to have blasphemed the faith.

Precept 4: *On the imperative of then fighting in the cause of God.*
This reality is best evidenced in Surat al-Nisa', wherein "fighting to preserve the faith" is made a Divine Mandate.
Verse:
Let those who fight in the way of Allah, those who would sell the life of this world for the other, those who fight in the way of Allah, be he slain or be he victorious, for him, We shall bestow a vast reward. (Surat al-Nisa' 4:74)
Comment:
The verse thus makes evident that (1) the sole justification for war is in pursuit of Divine will and mandate; but (2), in that quest, zealous activism will be justly rewarded.

Proportionality

Precept 5: *Warfare must be measured in response.*
Proportionality, that is, measured response, is the second precondition for the honorable conduct of modern warfare, and is equally manifest within Islamic tradition.
Verse:
And one who attacketh you, attack him in like manner as he attacked you. (Surat al-Baqarah 2:194)
Comment:
The Qur'an thus prescribes that the response to any perceived hostility must be discriminate and measured. In the words of noted Islamic scholar Muhammad Haleem: "Only combatants are to be fought, and no more harm should be caused to them then they have caused. Thus, weapons of destruction that destroy civilians and their towns are ruled out by the

Qur'an and the word and deed of the Prophet, these being the only binding authority in Islamic law."[11]

Precept 6: *Proportionality must be meted out with temperance.*
Response must not be measured in proportionate reaction only, it is best served when delivered with compassion.[12]
Verse:
And we prescribed there for them therein: a life for a life, an eye for an eye, a nose for a nose, an ear for an ear, a tooth for a tooth, and for wounds, retaliation. But whoso foregoeth it (in the way of charity), it shall be expiation for him. (Surat al-Ma'idah 5:4)
Comment:
Islam's doctrine of defensive, proportionately measured response thus dictates that any retaliation may not exceed, but must instead be equal or less than, the original transgression, thereby establishing a full spectrum of flexible operational parameters that include full forgiveness.

Distinction

Precept 7: *Discrimination must be applied in war's pursuit.*
Distinction in the form of discrimination—refraining from attacking for personal gain "targets of opportunity," that is, those not actively seeking to be adversaries—is the third precondition for the honorable conduct of modern warfare.
Verse:
O ye who believe! When ye go forth (to fight) in the way of Allah, be careful to discriminate and say not unto one who offereth you peace: "Thou are not a believer," seeking chance profits of this like (so that ye may despoil him). With Allah are plenteous spoils. Even thus (as he is now) were ye before; but Allah has since been gracious unto you. Therefore, take care to discriminate. Allah is informed of what you do. (Surat al-Nisa' 4:94)
Comment:
The verse thus clarifies that attack upon those who would seek peace is not sanctioned within Islam.

Humanity

Precept 8: *The Qur'an emphasizes the criticality of humanity.*
Finally, humanity, in the form of aggression avoidance, the fourth and final for the honorable conduct of modern warfare, is equally clearly manifest within the Qur'an.

Verses:
*The faithful of the Beneficent are those who walk upon the earth modestly,
and when the foolish ones address them answer: "Peace!"* (Surat al-Furqan
25:63)
*And make not Allah, by your oaths, a hindrance to being righteous and observ-
ing your duty unto Him and making peace among mankind.* (Surat al-Baqarah
2:224)
Comment:
The quest for peace, then, is a quintessential precondition for commencing war. Set within the context of Islam's more general principles of war,
these four preconditions for the honorable conduct of war are thus fully
consonant with those that obtain today.

On the General Principles of War

Precept 9: *The primacy of peace is paramount.*
The Islamic rules for war, therefore, are not radically removed from the
most modern prescriptions for its civilized pursuit. Indeed, at least a
dozen Qur'anic verses clearly emphasize the theme that striving for peace
must be a paramount first option for Muslims. For example:
Verse:
If they incline to peace, incline thou to it and trust in Allah. (Surat al-Anfal
8:61)
Comment:
Accordingly, the context of the verse makes clear that a devout Muslim
should, first and foremost, strive to make peace with his enemies—rendering war, therefore, no more than a recourse of last resort in the conduct
of diplomatic affairs.

Precept 10: *Equity is critical to war's pursuit.*
Indeed, the pursuit of peace must not only be the overarching first recourse of all Muslims, it must unequivocally be intended to ensure equity
among mankind.
Verse:
*And if two parties of Believers fall to fighting, then make peace among them. And
if one party of them doeth wrong to the other, fight ye that which doeth wrong until it return unto the ordinance of Allah; then, if it return, make peace between them
justly and act equitably. Lo, Allah loveth the equitable.* (Surat al-Hujurat 49:9)
Comment:
The Qur'an is thus uncompromising in prescribing equitable justice in
militant pursuits.

Precept 11: *The initiation of aggression is strictly prohibited.*
The Qur'an further makes clear that initiating unprovoked aggression
likewise is prohibited.
Verse:
*Except those who seek refuge with a people between whom and you there is a
covenant, or come unto you because their hearts forbid them war on you or to
make war on their own folk. Had Allah willed, he could have given them power
over you so that assuredly they would have fought you. So if they hold aloof from
you, and wage not war against you, and offer you peace, Allah alloweth you no
way against them.* (Surat al-Nisa' 4:90)
Comment:
Here again, war against nonaggressors with whom there are binding
treaties or who offer peace is expressly prohibited.

Precept 12: *Enemy abstention from aggression mandates a cease fire.*
Indeed, the Qur'an establishes that if the enemy desists from further re-
sistance, then hostilities must cease.
Verse:
*And fight them until persecution is no more and religion is for Allah (alone). But
if they desist, then let there be no hostility except against wrongdoers.* (Surat al-
Baqarah 2:193)
Comment:
It must again be recalled that this verse was targeted primarily against the
aristocratic polytheists of Makkah who posed an ever-present physical
threat to the nascent forces of Islam. It also safeguards the well-being of
noncombatants.

Precept 13: *Just war is mandated only when attacked.*
While condemning unprovoked aggression, however, the Qur'an
nonetheless makes it clear that if unjustifiably incited, war can be a legitimate option for a Muslim.
Verse:
*Fight in the way of Allah against those who fight against you, but begin not hos-
tilities. Lo! Allah loveth not aggressors.* (Surat al-Baqarah 2:190)
Comment:
The words *aggressor* and *transgressor* appear interchangeable in this
context—constituting an absolute prohibition of the initiation of aggression but nonetheless admonishing Muslims to fight in the way of
Allah those who would fight them in pursuit of a war defensive in its
nature, and in a manner that is honorable and just—with this verse
being followed by Surah 2:194: *"But if they give over, surely Allah is All-
forgiving, All-compassionate."*

Precept 14: *The prescription for just war is thus Qur'anically prescribed.*
This precept is fully consonant, then, with the Prophetic Tradition: "Do
not desire an encounter with the enemy, but when you encounter them,
be firm."[13] The conditions that allow for such just war are prescribed in
Surat al-Nisa':
Verse:
*How should you not fight for the cause of Allah and of the feeble among men and
of the women and the children who are crying: "O Lord! Bring us forth from out
of this town of which the people are oppressors! Oh, give us from You some protection! Oh send us from You some defender!"* (Surat al-Nisa' 4:75)
Comment:
The Qur'an thereby makes clear that the prime justifications for war must
be to advance the faith, redress wrongdoing, and to protect the weak and
helpless.

Precept 15: *The objectives of just war are likewise Qur'anically pre-
scribed.*
The prime objectives of just war are to ensure equitable treatment for all
and to rid the world of corruption, unbelief, and wrong-doing.
Verse:
*If Allah had not repelled some people by others, the earth would have been cor-
rupted. But Allah is the Lord of Kindness to (His) creatures.* (Surat al-Baqarah
2:251)
Comment:
This admonition is further buttressed by the scriptural verse:

> *Allah forbids you not, as regards those who have not fought you in religion's cause,
> nor expelled you from your habitations, that you should be kindly to them and act
> justly to them; surely Allah loves the just.* (Surat al-Mumtahinah 60:8)

As such, the scriptures concur in a compelling way that the prime purpose of just war is to eradicate wrongdoing so that the less fortunate may
be protected and that justice is preserved for all mankind.

Jihad—just war—is thus not war for national or personal gain but instead both an *internal* struggle to follow God and all that He commands
and an *external* struggle to bring His truth to mankind. In this context,
then, the fifteenth-century Arab historian Ibn Khaldun distinguishes between wars of jihad and justice and wars of sedition and anarchy—making clear that a war's ultimate objective must be to establish a communal
good and purpose—while concurrently revealing that Islam's precise prescriptions for cause in declaring war, though written fourteen centuries
before, comport fully with the modern standards codified in The Hague
Convention on the Opening of Hostilities of 1907.[14]

In war's pursuit, moreover, as appendices which follow clarify, only the religious leader of the Islamic community, the *imam*, may declare war, whereupon, once proclaimed, it may be waged against four types of enemies:[15]

1. infidels,
2. apostates,
3. bandits, and
4. rebels.

But though warfare against all four enemy types is legitimate, only the first two are jihad, which, as noted, differs significantly from conventional secular war—as they are to be pursued in direct fulfillment of a religious obligation. As such, there is often considerable scholarly debate over whether jihad can possess offensive as well as defensive dimensions.

To this end, the distinction frequently is made that jihad—is a "communal obligation" (*fard kifayah*) when offensive and an "individual obligation" (*fard 'ayn*) when defensive. The case for defensive war is founded on the Qur'anic verse:[16]

If they incline to peace, incline thee also to peace; and put thy trust in Allah. (Surat al-Anfal 8:61)

This injunction—which, as suggested earlier, must be preceded by a call for peace when initiating conflict—is reinforced by the Prophetic Tradition related in the ninth-century compiler Muslim's *Sahih*:

Whenever the Prophet appointed a commander to an army or an expedition, he would say
When you meet your pagan enemies, summon them to three things. Accept whatever they agree to and refrain from fighting them. Summon them to become Muslims. If they agree, accept their conversion. . . .
In that case, summon them to dwell in the "Abode of the Emigrants." If they refuse, let them know that they are like the Bedouin who share only in the booty proceeds when they fight together with other Muslims.
If they refuse conversion, then ask them to pay the poll tax. If they agree, accept their submission. But if they refuse, then ask Allah for assistance and fight them.[17]

If a war is to be *offensive*, on the one hand, some maintain, it is considered to be a communal obligation. If deemed *defensive*, on the other—in response to an attack on the Islamic state, for example—then some hold that it must, or may, also be pursued individually, in which case it becomes incumbent upon the individual to do what he can for the cause of the faith.[18]

Either way, it is a somewhat paradoxical "optional obligation"—for unlike the Judeo-Christian ethic, Islam does not compel its devout to either "turn the other cheek" or "turn their swords into plowshares," as Isaiah 2:4 prescribes.[19]

It is this "individual option to take up the sword" that remains in scholarly debate and that Osama bin Laden has repeatedly invoked in proclaiming his jihad against America and the West at large, as well as, without discrimination, against perceived backsliding Islamic theocracies.[20]

3

Getting From "There"
to "Here"

Nationalism is our belief, the homeland is the Dar al-Islam, the ruler is
Allah, and the constitution is the Qur'an.

—Sayyid Qutb, Doctrinal Leader, Muslim Brotherhood

THE DOCTRINAL EVOLUTION

Preceding analysis presents compelling arguments for exonerating classic Islamic doctrine and its follow-on exegesis from complicity in the
rise of modern Islamic terrorism. This chapter, in turn, seeks to identify
the prime external catalysts that gradually transformed a segment, albeit
minor, of Saudi Arabia's fundamentalist Wahhabi *religious* movement into
a strident, lethal *militant* one; to wit: the ideological influence of a gradual
infiltration of the kingdom's western region, the Hijaz, over the course of
the second half of the twentieth century by disciples of Egypt's politically
virulent Muslim Brotherhood.

This seminal development—immediately following that organization's
suppression into underground operations by Egyptian intelligence after
its attempt to assassinate that nation's president, Jamal Abdul Nasser, in
1954—was a watershed in the gradual evolution of modern global terror
now being perpetrated in Islam's name. Accordingly, it becomes critical to
explore the political and socioeconomic milieux wherein the kingdom's
present mutant cells of terror that metastasized from that ideological infiltration were spawned.

The gradual evolution of the so-called Wahhabi movement within Saudi Arabia, as noted, is quite complex, with its lineage traced to sundry tangled roots. Accurate understanding of their interweaving is perhaps thus best approached commencing with a perfunctory review of the theological evolution of Islam itself. For religions become institutions only when the rituals that once shaped their sacred histories later become politically transformed into authoritative models of orthodox law.

Within Islam, that tipping point came in the ninth century, midway through the rule of the 'Abbasids, in the form of intense public inquisition as to the eternal nature of the Qur'an—a two-century-long proxy clash for power between the caliphs and the clergy that commenced with the reign of al-Ma'mun, reached its apex in that of al-Mutawakkil, and was gradually completed by that of al-Qadir two centuries later.[1]

This was, in reality, an intellectual confrontation wherein al-Ma'mun unsuccessfully set out to impose the rule of state upon religion—to select a particular doctrine and enforce it, thereby attempting to create a quasi-Erastian regime. Eventually, though, he and his successors were compelled to concede primary exclusivity of doctrinal power to Islam's traditionalist religious establishment, the 'ulama'—the "learned men," the "doctors of law," the closest that Islam has come to a developing vested clergy.[2]

The issues in debate focused directly upon how God's realm, the Dar al-Islam, and His ummah, the fundamental transtribal Community of Believers, should be governed—and centered around whether the secular ruler:

- is knowledgeable in, and capable of, making judgments on the bases of the Qur'an and Prophetic Tradition (*ahadith*: = *sunnah* = custom = common law); or
- though primarily a political figure, should nonetheless consult with the clergy—the 'ulama'—in reaching decisions on matters of policy; or instead merely
- provide nominal lip service to Islamic values, yet not order anything directly opposed to the consensus of the juridic scholars.

At the apex of the contentious constitutional debate, then, was the ruler's religious affiliation as head of state—and thus, by implication, the relationship of the caliph vis-à-vis the clergy—with the latter's position clearly articulated by famed thirteenth/fourteenth–century Hanbali jurist Ibn Qayyim al-Jawziyah as:

Properly speaking, these rulers are obeyed only to the extent that their commands are consistent with the articulations of religious science. Hence, a ruler's duty to obey derives from his obligation to obey the jurists. This is because such obedience is due only in what is known to be virtuous and what is required by religious science.[3]

Thus, Ibn Qayyim clearly subordinated the ideological desires and dictates of the caliphs to the doctrinal determinations and demands of the clergy.

This evolutionary intellectual confrontation was no mere happenstance—as almost from the onset, a classic traditionalist vs. rationalist debate had evolved within Islamic doctrine in several phases. Early on, it was recognized that hermeneutics focused upon the Qur'an and corpus of Prophetic Tradition alone could not explicitly address every possible challenge confronting mortal man, particularly as the burgeoning ummah rapidly expanded into the vast and complex empire that would soon come to be the Dar al-Islam.

Accordingly, a process of analogy (*qiyas*) over time concurrently developed that permitted religious scholars, when responding to unfamiliar legal dilemmas, to draw rational comparisons or parallels between their particular circumstance and similar ones that had been confronted by Prophet Muhammad.[4]

Large segments of the *'ulama'*, however, felt a distinct measure of discomfort over placing undue emphasis upon rationale and reason over revelation in formulating the Islamic corpus juris. Accordingly, they ultimately became more dependent in the development of the *shari'ah* upon a fourth generally recognized source of Islamic law—juridical consent (*ijma'*).

Predicated upon the proposition that a unanimous consensus amongst legal scholars on a particular issue could establish both a binding legal decision and a juridical precedent that could justifiably be passed along as fully obligatory upon succeeding generations of Muslim jurists, the *'ulama'* proceeded to consolidate their authority as sole arbiters of doctrinal belief.[5]

There was yet a fifth basis for the formulation of Islamic law that could be applied in those circumstances wherein the Qur'an and *ahadith* were silent and wherein analogy or consensus could not be reached. Called *ijtihad* (independent juridical rationalization), pursuant to it, a qualified legal scholar could engage his personal juristic reasoning to issue a decision (*fatwa* = the *shari'ah* equivalent of *responsa prudentium* in Roman law) that could be accepted or rejected by the ummah as appropriate.[6]

Ijtihad would prove to be an important source of Islamic law until the close of the tenth century when the traditionalist *'ulama'* ultimately effectively succeeded in outlawing it (*saddu bab al-ijtihad* = closed the door of deductive reasoning) as a legitimate tool of juridical exegesis—thereby signaling the beginning of the end for those who believed that, provided that it did not contradict Divine Revelation, religious truth could be derived through a process of reasoned logic.[7]

One dimension to this intensely divisive rationalist vs. traditionalist debate centered around the concept of whether the *Umm al-Kitab*—the heavenly Mother of Books from whence the Torah, Bible, and Qur'an all derived as described in appendix C—as directly handed down to man in the form of the sacred Qur'an with Prophet Muhammad as its conduit—were the actual words of God. If so, according to traditionalist rationale, the Qur'an not only reveals God's will, it reveals God's self—and if the doctrine of *tawhid* forbids a division or sharing of Divine Unity, then it is not just the Word of God, it is God Himself.[8]

It was precisely this position that the *'ulama'* effectively argued and was the one that, by midway through the eleventh century, prevailed and continued to ascend to an apogee of dominance by the end of the thirteenth century. Thereafter, the traditionalists were in total control within Sunni (though not Shi'i) Islam, with the rationalists branded as heretics—a condition that prevails until the present day in ideologically more conservative Islamic countries such as Saudi Arabia.[9]

The results were reverberating—as henceforth, with this doctrinal victory, the *'ulama'* moved to a position of unquestioned authority within the ummah—which they then used to both institutionalize their theological opinions into distinct schools of legal thought and to distill their rationales into that binding code of conduct now known as the *shari'ah* that effectively transformed Islam from a formalized religion into an all encompassing way of life—as well as a holistic lifestyle which the *'ulama'* claimed sole authority to define and sanction.[10]

THE POLITICAL EVOLUTION

This circumstance would come to be seriously challenged, however, commencing at the dawn of the eighteenth century with the birth of the aforesaid Muhammad ibn 'Abd al-Wahhab in the central Arabian Najdi village of 'Uyaynah, in al-'Arid, forty kilometers northwest of Riyadh. Clearly imbued with religious zeal and a passionate affinity for Qur'anic exegesis, his father sent him first to al-Madinah and then to al-Basrah in Iraq in the 1730s to pursue Islamic studies.[11]

There, he developed intense anger at what he believed to be a gradual adulteration of the religion that was soon to be transformed into an all-encompassing obsession to strip it of its "superstitious innovations" and restore it to its original precepts as defined by its pious Founding Fathers (*al-aslaf*) as he viewed them. Central to his thesis was the doctrine of *tawhid*—the "unity of God"—the concept that God alone has sovereignty, and that His laws alone—as delineated in the Qur'an and *ahadith* are normative.

Accordingly, returning to the Najd, Muhammad ibn 'Abd al-Wahhab embarked upon his puritanical crusade commonly known as Wahhabism—as an Islamic fundamentalist revival movement urging a return to ancestral (*salafiyah*) precepts movement now set root.[12] He abhorred many popular religious practices that had issued from what he deemed to be the pre-Islamic Age of Ignorance (*al-'Asr al-Jahili*) such as *sufism* and the veneration of saints and tombs, which he condemned both as superstitions and idolatry; unwarranted innovations, which he believed led to polytheism; and unbelief which he deemed to be amongst the worst of sins.

Fancying himself to be a revivalist (*mujaddid*) seeking to obliterate accretions to the religion that had been instituted by the *'ulama'*, he instigated in their stead strict implementation of *shari'ah* law free from external influence or interpretation. Central to his thesis was that the classic doctrine of *tawhid* must be devoutly respected.[13]

Muhammad ibn 'Abd al-Wahhab divined much of his religious inspiration from Ibn Taymiyah, a self-proclaimed thirteenth/fourteenth–century Damascene legal reformer trained in the Hanbali School of Islamic jurisprudence. Challenging the stasis and rigidity of the then prevailing exegetical practice of *taqlid* (adherence to tradition), he sought a reopening of the *bab al-ijtihad* that had been closed since the early eleventh century in a quest to restore the prevailing juridical doctrine to the faith and belief of its original Founding Fathers—the Righteous Ancestors of Islam.[14]

Concurrently, within the Najd, an ambitious, albeit minor, sheikh of a clan headquartered in a small oasis called al-Dar'iyah in Wadi Hanifah just below Riyadh, Muhammad ibn Sa'ud, controlled both the wells and the trade routes within the proximate region. In the process of expanding the coverage of his commercial influence when an itinerant preacher, Muhammad ibn 'Abd al-Wahhab, arrived in his oasis seeking protection, he did not hesitate to seize the opportunity to establish an allied secular-religious condominium of rule that would strengthen both his economic prosperity and his military prowess. The pact of loyalty committed between them in 1744, therefore, marked not only the formation of a genuine Saudi state but one solidly founded on conservative theocratic values.[15]

In the process, the House of Saud and the region's indigenous religious element, the Family of the Shaykh, concurrently proceeded to create a hybrid paramilitary religious unit consisting of Wahhabi warriors—who numbered around 11,000 by 1912 and totaled more than 50,000 in the 1920s—and who ultimately came to be known simply as the Brotherhood. Thus, the Saudi-Al-Shaykh ruling alliance that still stands was born.

Accordingly, inspired by the intense fervor of a resonant new creed, Wahhabism impregnated the nascent Saudi leadership with a powerful moral force that would prove crucial for the consolidation and expansion of their tribal rule. Contemptuous of the secular Bedouin, its attention was focused upon winning the loyalty of the region's more sedentary population.[16]

Integral to their success was the new ruling "bureaucratic condominium" that soon evolved. For the Najdi equivalent of the traditional Islamic 'ulama' religious establishment were then known as the mutawwa'in. Students of locally observed Hanbali jurisprudence, they consisted primarily of part-time religious ritual specialists—an avocation that they pursued in conjunction with their primary livelihoods in trade and agriculture.

Often quasi-literate and untrained in doctrinal matters, they were generally less concerned with overarching issues regarding the role of the "just ruler" within the Islamic theory of state than with more day-to-day parochial moral issues as they divined them from the Qur'an, as well as with ensuring strict obedience to the local Muslim community leader. Among their primary roles was enforcement of strict discipline of others in their observances of, and submission to, major imposed Islamic obligations such as prayer, fasting, the pilgrimage, and payment of the zakat tax.[17]

It was this primitive religious infrastructure that 'Abd al-'Aziz ibn Sa'ud inherited when he wrested control of Riyadh from the appointed proxies of the banu Rashid who ruled the region from their northwest capital, Ha'il, in 1902. Prudently seeking to co-opt it into his service, he proceeded to formally employ them as salaried oath-bound employees of the state—thereby effectively transforming them from mere itinerant preacher-farmers into full-time religious specialists loyal to him and fully dependent upon his resources. Thereby enfranchised, while operating under the aegis and pretext of "religious education," they piously ensured the submission and loyalty of the portion of Arabian populace that came under Ibn Sa'ud's jurisdiction between 1902 and 1932.[18]

The mutawwa'in likewise soon came to play a major role in the creation of that other half of the uniquely symbiotic bureaucratic ruling condominium that operated under Ibn Sa'ud's rule—the indigenous paramilitary fighting force known as the Ikhwan (Brotherhood)—as because of their educational outreach, he was able to draft from the region's tribal confederation a religio-tribal corps of semipermanent military cadres that, using al-Dar'i yah as a base, would eventually subjugate all of Arabia under his control.

Primarily Bedouin who devoutly accepted the fundamentals of puritanical orthodox Islam that issued from the rigid Hanbali religious doctrine that Muhammad ibn 'Abd al-Wahhab had taught, they thus came to constitute a standing military force that abandoned its nomadic heritage to live in formal urbanized military cantonments—mushrooming in total from 52 in 1920 to 120 by 1929—where they were subjected to the constant regenerative religious indoctrination of the *mutawwa'in*. Part and parcel of that austere indoctrination was an unqualified acceptance of Ibn Sa'ud as supreme *imam* of the Muslim community.[19]

Renouncing nomadism in favor of a more sedentary lifestyle of learning and land cultivation, therefore, Saudi Arabia's *Ikwan* was formed—and with his religio-secular tandem thereby effectively forged into a powerful theocratic-militaristic movement, Ibn Saud, together with his Al Sa'ud-Al Shaykh ruling condominium, was able to transform it into a jihad that, over the course of the next half century, would gradually defeat Wahhabi tribal foes both ideologically and militarily.[20]

MODERN ADAPTATIONS OF WAHHABI DOCTRINE

Meanwhile in Egypt, in the late nineteenth to early twentieth centuries, such religious reformers as Jamal al-Din al-Afghani (the ideological great-great-grandfather of Osama bin Laden), his pupil Muhammad 'Abduh, and 'Abduh's disciple Rashid Rida were similarly contending that Muslims did not need the guidance of the traditionalist *'ulama'* to interpret God's secret revelations—that the *bab al-ijtihad* should be reopened—and that every manmade source of law—*ahadith*, *qiyas*, and *ijma'*—should be reopened to rational discourse and reinterpretation in a quest to restore the religion to its original precepts. Thus, Islam's *salafiyah* movement set even deeper roots.[21]

It was into this disquieting setting of intellectual ferment, then, that Hassan al-Banna, a school teacher from Egypt's Nile Delta who would found his own version of a Muslim Brotherhood (not to be confused with that of Saudi Arabia), was born. Arriving in Cairo in 1923 to pursue a college degree in higher education, he was appalled by the depravity and rampant secularism that gripped the city. A devotee of Rashid Rida—whose magazine, *al-Manar* (*The Beacon*), he perpetuated, and upon whose precepts he founded his back-to-basics fundamentalist philosophy—maintaining that jihad was as incumbent upon Muslims as the "five pillars of Islam"—and on this foundation, committed to his campaign of Islamic reform.[22]

But though he appealed to local religious authorities, he found them to be irrelevant and ineffective. Also rejecting the contemporary popular nationalistic appeals of Pan-Arabism, as with al-Afghani, Rida, and 'Abduh before him, he concluded that "Islam is the only answer"—and proceeded to create his own radical *salafiyah* ideological movement. Preaching a program of jihad, he argued that:

> He who dies and has not fought, and has not resolved to fight, has died a *jahiliyah* ("ignorant") death. . . . Death is art![23]

Over time, and particularly after World War II, his Muslim Brotherhood flourished and evolved as a socialist-type organization driven by religious ambition—committed to a conviction that Islam was a universal ideology superior to all other systems of human organization. Following the earlier leads of Muhammad ibn 'Abd al-Wahhab, al-Afghani, 'Abduh, and Rida, it rejected the classic precept of *taqlid* and upheld the right of *ijtihad*.

Though the movement was avowedly apolitical and did not advocate the overthrow of Egypt's khedival government, it was nonetheless perceived by some to be a mounting political threat. Accordingly, on December 8, 1948, it was dissolved by governmental decree; and on February 12, 1949—in apparent reprisal for the assassination of Egyptian prime minister Mahmud al-Nuqrashi on the preceding December 28, ostensibly at the hands of a Brotherhood member—Hassan al-Banna was gunned down on a Cairo street by Egyptian political police. Undeterred, and now given his martyr status as a rally point, however, the Brotherhood would become even stronger in his wake.[24]

Thus, notwithstanding al-Banna's initial commitment to the precepts of Egypt's Free Officers movement and enjoying a modicum of comity with it, as Jamal Abdul Nasser set out to implement his 1952 postrevolution nationalistic agenda, his distinctly secular agenda, combined with his authoritarian rule, soon came to clash with the egalitarian nature of the Brotherhood. Accordingly, in October 1954, when eight shots were fired as Nasser delivered a speech in Alexandria, a propitious opportunity to seriously dismantle the fractious group presented itself to Egyptian authorities. Blaming the assassination attempt on its conspiracy, Nasser outlawed the Muslim Brotherhood and proceeded to torture, imprison, and execute its leaders.[25]

In so doing, however, he would unleash a leviathan. For al-Banna's soon-to-be-ideological successor, the American-educated, Egyptian-born ideological progenitor of Islamic radical reform, Sayyid Qutb—while languishing in his confinement cell in a Cairo prison as a result of the ongoing dissident crackdown—perceived a revelation.

Preaching in itself, he concluded, was not enough—more tangible political progress was required. Railing against the political, economic, and cultural domination of Egypt by the West, he contended that the most basic divisions within humanity were religious rather than racial or nationalist—a societal weakness issuing from "moral causation"— and that rectifying righteous war was the only form of killing that was legitimately sanctioned.[26]

For the manifest superiority of Islam to prevail, therefore, it must renew and reassert itself as a complete, fully integrated political, social, and economic system. God's Kingdom must be established on earth not with a centralized executive power such as a president or a king, but as an *ummah*—a divine society governed by Islamic values whose sole ruler would be God and whose sole sources of law would be the *shari'ah* and a return to the practice of *ijtihad*. In place of the Age of Ignorance that had engulfed the world, he wrote, there is a "true Islam" wherein nationalism is belief, homeland is the Dar al-Islam, the ruler is Allah, and the constitution is the Qur'an.[27]

To counter what he perceived to be pandemic "infidelity," he practiced the precept pioneered by thirteenth/fourteenth–century Damascene Hanbali reformer Ibn Taymiyah of accusing the so-called infidels of apostasy (*takfir*), both individually and systemically. To restore the religion, he thus called for a *salafiyah* movement—an immediate return to the founding tenets of the faith. Through the traditional process of religious renewal, therefore, political Islam was to be born—and though hanged on August 29, 1966, for his alleged involvement in plotting Nasser's assassination twelve years before, Sayyid Qutb's radical doctrine would continue to live after him with reverberating resonance.[28]

For in his aftermath, two catalytic—indeed catastrophic—courses of events would unfold and coalesce. First, it spawned a virulent offshoot, the Egyptian *Tanzim al-Jihad*, an organization over which today the al-Qaeda doctrinal leader Ayman al-Zawahiri—a disciple of Sayyid Qutb— continues to serves as military chief, and which in 1981, claimed responsibility for assassinating Egyptian president Anwar Sadat. This group has since amalgamated with al-Qaeda in a curious union that al-Zawahiri himself has confided is little more than a marriage of convenience to keep the institution of jihad alive."[29]

Second, concurrent with his acts of suppression, Nasser would create still another Frankenstein-like monster—driving the suppressed activist remnants of Egypt's erstwhile Muslim Brotherhood into exile in Southwest Arabia centered on that country's southwest 'Asir region. Indeed, their arrival in Saudi Arabia would come at a critically pivotal time—as the country remained unique within the Islamic world as one wherein the *'ulama'* had not largely lost their grip over society.

For unlike Egypt and the Levant, on the Arabian Peninsula, there was no widespread ongoing popular debate on the manifest virtues of modernism,

Pan-Arabism, Pan-Islamism, or Islamic socialism. Instead, the sole doctrine that enjoyed any significant social resonance within the Saudi kingdom was Wahhabi fundamentalist Islamic ideology.[30]

THE IMPACT OF REGIONAL POLITICAL EVENTS

At the same time, these events were not developing in a vacuum but rather as part of a cascading ideological process—making it critical to evaluate parallel political developments concurrently unfolding in the region. Among them, it becomes crucial to survey the contemporary international political landscape—called by some the "age of the Arab cold war"—many rooted in Saudi geostrategic needs as viewed through the prism of the Saudi global view. As then, within the learned political science departments of the West, it was conventional wisdom that Nasserite socialism was the Middle East wave of the future—and that it was just a matter of time before the rickety monarchies of the Arabian Peninsula would fall in its wake.

Indeed, already King Faruq of Egypt had been deposed by Nasser's Free Officer forces in 1952—and in 1955, a plot by Egyptian-trained Saudi army officers to overthrow King Sa'ud and Prince Faysal and establish a Nasserite-model socialistic government in their stead was uncovered just days before the coup was to take place, sending profound shockwaves through the Saudi royal family. To further compound royal concerns, the centuries-long-reigning imamate of the Yemen would be overthrown a decade later in a military coup d'état orchestrated by an Egyptian-backed officer, 'Abdallah al-Sallal, in September 1962.[31]

Not comfortable, of course, with the dangerous precedent of allowing a succession of regional monarchies to fall unchallenged, the stage was now set for Saudi military intervention in the Yemen supporting the religious Royalists then engaged in a proxy battle against a large Egyptian army supporting the more secular Republican Army in an ensuing highly divisive civil war. For with the newly proclaimed Yemen Arab Republic being the first nonmonarchic regime on the Arabian Peninsula, this ominous development would become a major Saudi security concern, mandating the removal of the occupying Egyptian military forces, estimated at over 20,000 troops in 1963, from the country as expeditiously as possible.[32]

Concurrently, to the north, Iraq had resurfaced as a source of worry to the Saudis with its Ba'thi Party takeover in 1968. For though the prospect of a wave of Nasserite socialism cresting through the region had dominated Arab politics in the 1950s and early 1960s, by the decade's close, "Ba'thi socialism," in both its Iraq and Syrian variants, had sprung up as a prime parallel concern, undermining Saudi claims to leadership amongst the region's ruling elites. The threat was not inconsequential.

For whereas in the early 1960s, Cairo had been the principal headquarters for anti-Saudi activity, by the onset of the 1970s, Baghdad had become a major alternate destination for Saudi Ba'thists and dissident Shi'is from the kingdom's Eastern Province where its oil industry was based—home to an anti-Saudi newspaper, *Sawt al-Tali'ah*, and opposition radio broadcasts sanctioned by Iraq's new leadership. Indeed, in June 1969, a coup organized by twenty-eight Saudi army officers, thirty-four air force pilots, numerous police, and sundry civilians against King Faisal—upon which Iraqi fingerprints were perceived—was discovered and suppressed.[33]

Meanwhile, as this external tension was ongoing, internally frustrated at the continuing unwillingness of King Sa'ud to sanction the creation of a partially elected "consultative council" and cede more power to the appointed cabinet as precursors to establishing a constitutional monarchy, certain senior Saudi Royals, among them Talal bin 'Abd al-'Aziz—who had led domestic reform movements from 1958 to 1962—and his full brothers 'Abd al-Muhsin, Badr, Nawaf, and Fawaz—together with a coterie of other Saudi intellectuals influenced by the lure of Nasserism, would flee to Cairo, there to set up an opposition group known as the Free Princes—a take-off on Nasser's Free Officers movement responsible for Egypt's 1952 coup—returning only in 1964 when finance minister Prince Faisal succeeded the profligate Sa'ud as king in a family-sanctioned coup de état.[34]

Thus perceiving a military coup in support of Nasserite and/or Syrian/Iraqi Ba'thi socialism to be its greatest internal threat, these developments coalesced into a firm determination by senior Saudi leadership that certain domestic security elements be front-end-loaded with tribal and religious leadership to the detriment of a more secular officer corps.

Responsibility for national defense and internal security were, in turn, reposed within three distinct and separate armed services: (1) the Ministry of Defense and Aviation, a modern tri-service military force; (2) the Saudi Arabian National Guard, which is, in reality, amalgamated remnants of the old tribal *Ikhwan*; and (3) the Ministry of the Interior, responsible for internal security. Each was headed by one of the most senior Saudi princes.

Consequently, desiring to upgrade his inventory of modern Western weaponry, primarily with U.S. defense/security systems, King Faisal—in seeking a genuine alternative to mounting Arab socialism—concurrently turned to the nurturing, and global export, of Islam, couching a Pan-Islamic policy within the rhetoric of calls for Muslim unity in a fervent quest to create an Islamic bloc to counter threatening nationalistic ideologies then emerging throughout the Arab world, some of which appealed to more liberal elements of his own constituency as well.[35]

Thereby hoping to curb growing secular political influence within the Muslim world, the arrival to southwest Arabia of Nasser's avowed enemies—remnant elements of the erstwhile and now exiled Egyptian Muslim Brotherhood—was, therefore, initially not viewed internally with particularly great alarm. To the contrary, they and their dissident counterparts from other secular Arab states such as Syria and Iraq were, from the onset, extended shelter and support consistent with traditional Arab hospitality. Indeed, some became academicians, journalists, bankers, and other business people. Only their participation in politics was banned.[36]

But while in southwest Arabia, Egypt's residual Muslim Brotherhood became beneficiaries of a surprise bonus far more utilitarian than shelter. They discovered Wahhabi Islam and then, surreptitiously co-opting a small segment of it, succeeded in converting a few impressionable young minds and at least a small portion of lesser affluent adherents to their cause, thereby radically transforming a tiny grouping of adherents to its indigenous, heretofore essentially fundamentalist religious character into a politically activist movement, fascist in nature to the extent that it aspired to global ambitions. It was in this highly charged socioeconomic setting, then, that Osama bin Laden was nurtured and where the Qahtanis, Ghamdis, and Shihris—names prominent in the September 11, 2001, World Trade Center attacks—lived.[37]

Following Sayyid Qutb's execution in August 1966 and the attendant suppression of the Muslim Brotherhood in Egypt, moreover, a number of the intelligentsia within its key leadership, including Muhammad Qutb, Sayyid Qutb's brother and later mentor of Osama bin Laden, and others also would flee to west Saudi Arabia. Arriving at a time when there was a shortage of professional educators in Saudi Arabia, they were welcomed with open arms and employed in major universities, including the "mother ship" University of al-Madinah, as well as King 'Abd al-'Aziz University in Jiddah attended by Osama bin Laden and other influential members of contemporary society.

Lent impetus by Nasser's regionwide loss of prestige following the disastrous 1967 Arab-Israeli war, while concurrently seeking to create a new "Islamic awakening," they then proceeded to ideologically grip many who attended Saudi academic institutions in the 1970s to 1980s in a new religious zeal.[38] As there, their thoughts and teachings would find fertile, fallow soil in the minds of young Saudi religious militants who advocated a more extremist brand of Wahhabi Islam than that being preached and taught in universities. Indeed, though focused on economics and engineering, bin Laden was also a keen pursuer of Islamic studies.

Consequently, he was exposed to the more radical theological interpretations of Islam then present among both Saudi and resident foreign Muslim professors—influences that would later come to intellectual fruition in his self-proclaimed jihad.[39] For among the various lectures whose sessions at King 'Abd al-'Aziz University bin Laden attended were those of the local chapter of the Muslim Brotherhood, which featured such luminaries as Muhammad Qutb and Dr. Abdullah 'Azzam—the latter an al-Azhar–educated member of the Palestinian Muslim Brotherhood, a reported founding member of its militant Hamas wing, and soon to become the architect of Islamic radical jihadism in Afghanistan—both of whom possessed strong academic and Islamic activist credentials and espoused the Qutbist ideology of politics through violent means.

The latter, an advocate of a militant global jihadist ideology and culture which he perceived as a duty incumbent upon all Muslims—causing him to become known as *amir al-jihad* ("prince" of jihad)—would, commencing in 1982, become prominent in exporting this volatile doctrine to Afghanistan. As assessed by Islamic scholar Reza Aslan:[40]

> Within Saudi Arabia, Dr. Abdullah Yusuf 'Azzam, professor of Islamic philosophy at King Abdulaziz University, used his great influence amongst the country's disaffected youth to promote a most uncompromising and belligerent interpretation of jihad that, he argued, was incumbent upon all Muslims. "Jihad and the rifle alone," Dr. 'Azzam proclaimed to his students. "No negotiations, no conferences, no dialogues. . . ."
>
> His teachings had an exceptional impact on one student in particular: Osama bin Laden, who would eventually put into practice his mentor's ideology by calling for a world-wide Muslim campaign of jihad against the West, a campaign that climaxed with the 9/11 terrorist attacks. It is no accident, then, that, first in Jiddah, then in Peshawar, Pakistan, and later in Afghanistan itself, 'Azzam would welcome young bin Laden—later to become the foremost proponent of radical jihadism—to the stridently violent doctrine and tactics of the Muslim Brothers—introducing him to a world view that transcended the Arabian desert and channeled him toward ardent devotion to the cause of Islamist reform.[41]

The arrival of the Egyptian exiles to Saudi Arabia, many of whom were from pious, educated, often multilingual families, thus was initially quite gradual and uneventful. Indeed, their antisocialist credentials afforded them access to positions of rank and influence within the kingdom on the condition that they did not engage directly in internal politics. In addition, the Muslim Brothers added a veneer of intellectual value to in-country Islamist thought at a time when unvarnished Wahhabism was not readily exportable.[42]

The first groups of Egyptians arrived in the 1950s, to be followed over the next decade by Syrians and Iraqis fleeing newly installed Ba'thi regimes in Damascus and Baghdad, then followed by yet another contingent of Egyptians fleeing further suppression of the Muslim Brotherhood subsequent to the execution of Sayyid Qutb in 1966—concurrently accompanied by intermittent waves of Palestinians both political and religious in their ideological orientations.

Among the Egyptians relocating to Jiddah at this time was the aforesaid physician from a longstanding family of physicians, Ayman al-Zawahiri, who found employment in a clinic there. Just an hour's drive from Makkah—the seat of two principal organizations linked to the Muslim Brotherhood, the Muslim World League created in 1962, and the World Assembly for Muslim Youth established in 1972—Jiddah likewise was the prime commercial bastion of the massive bin Laden business empire as well as later becoming a principal recruitment center, via Peshawar in Pakistan, for enlistees in the Afghani jihad. It was there that al-Zawahiri would meet the man who would provide him with the financial wherewithal to empower him to fulfill his radical, militant, religious ambitions: Osama bin Laden.[43]

Initially, Saudi Arabia did not appear to be seriously concerned with these political developments. To the contrary, putting émigré Egyptian fundamentalist intellectuals to work in Saudi Arabia—particularly throughout all levels of education—came off in the immediate Arab world as a convenient trump to the secular Nasserite socialistic propaganda that then pervasively floated throughout the Middle East region.[44]

THE COMPOUNDING OF INTERNAL POLITICAL EVENTS

Moreover, later, in the early 1980s, there appeared to be only a genuine propaganda upside to a guerilla engagement with Russia's Red Army, an insurgent war that not only enjoyed U.S. acquiescence and encouragement, but also one that America encouraged and financed. The reasons for this marriage of convenience were both numerous and complex. Regionally, a struggle in name of Islam against communistic atheism would provide a useful counterbalance to the resonance of Ayatollah Khomeini's incessant and impassioned calls to war against Russia's rival, the "Great Satan": America.

In addition, in 1979, the country's government had been shaken when a young group of local activists, together with foreign students educated at its universities, occupied the most sacred of all sites within Islam, the Grand Mosque in Makkah, with the expressed intent of carrying out internal jihad against its monarchic rule. The timing of the call to jihad in south central Asia therefore was most fortuitous. For by exporting the most zealous of the militant activists to the distant Afghan theater, their energies ceased to be internally directed and could more productively be spent abroad. Hence, the stage was set for the strange American-inspired, Saudi-financed, Pakistani-trained jihad against godless Russia that was soon to come.[45]

Indeed, the aforesaid violent seizure of Makkah's Grand Mosque on November 20, 1979, by Juhayman bin Muhammad al-'Utaybi—a self-proclaimed *salafi jihadi*—and his brother-in-law, Muhammad bin 'Abdallah al-Qahtani, together with over two hundred other Saudi and non-Saudi followers, coming as a mainstream internal threat, had been an especially sobering wake-up call for the Saudi senior leadership. As promptly declaring himself to be the *Mahdi*—the "messiah" or "promised one" of Islam—al-Qahtani decried what he perceived to be undue Western influence and royal family excess. His aim, therefore, was to purify Islam through a return to its well-established traditions of justice and equality.[46]

Crushing this insurrection would last two weeks with significant casualties on both sides—with the December 3, 1979, killing of the would-be Mahdi, al-Qahtani, and the attendant capture and subsequent execution of the rebellion's mastermind Juhayman, together with sixty-two of his followers.[47] This was a seminal event. Indeed, some see the Makkah incident as a tipping point in Saudi internal politics, contending that it—combined with concurrent calls by the Ayatollah Khomeini for the bloody overthrow of Saudi Arabia's satanic ally, the United States, Iraq's invasion of Iran, and the heating up of jihad in Afghanistan—compelled the Saudi government to seek much closer ties with the country's *'ulama'* in exchange for their support.[48]

In the decade following the dramatic events of 1979, therefore, the kingdom would enter into yet another of its recurring phases of "controlled Islamization"—with substantial sums of money invested in generous religious land grants and acts of piety and with a policy of evacuating its most militant activists to the Afghani war zone.[49]

Yet Saudi Arabia's annus horribilis—its "year of internal strife"—was not yet over. As immediately thereafter, the Shi'is of its Eastern Province, the home to its oil industry, took to the streets in open demonstration during their annual observance of *'ashurah*, commemorating the seventh-century martyrdoms of Caliph 'Ali's sons Hassan and Husayn—a practice forbidden by the state and confined to the Shi'is' private domains ever since their incorporation within the Saudi realm in 1913. Some 20,000 National Guard troops were required to put down this uprising of mourners.[50]

In early 1980, moreover, the Shi'is once again took to the streets to celebrate the first anniversary of the return of Ayatollah Khomeini to Iran—and to simultaneously protest what they perceived to be their second class citizenship status within the Saudi kingdom. Again, the National Guard was required to disperse this demonstration—today recalled in dissident lore as the "the uprising (*intifada*) of the Eastern Province"—again with numerous casualties.

Hence, intellectual ferment now ran rampant. Many followers of the Juhayman-al-Qahtani uprising had been educated at the Islamic University of al-Madinah, wherein, as noted, Muslim Brotherhood influence was particularly strong. Indeed, King Faisal, in the 1960s, had welcomed this development, even encouraging the movement to become more active in several newly established religious institutions as a counterbalance to the rising tide of Arab secular socialism.

Thus, the radical teachings of the group fell as seminal ideological seeds upon fallow intellectual soil and rapidly sprouted and took root—a process that continues to the present day. But each time, the Saudi senior leadership has sought to reach out to the country's more radical religious elements—as King Faisal had and King Khalid and King Fahd did subsequent to the 1979 Makkah mosque incident—those elements have inclined still further to the fringes of the ultraright.[51]

Indeed, it is precisely the perpetuation of such radical teachings that today has led in many Sunni pulpits to the invidious practice of *takfir* (or *takfir mu'ayyan*)—a concept lent credence by the thirteenth/fourteenth-century Hanbali Muslim jurist Ibn Taymiyah and reintroduced by his modern day disciple, Sayyid Qutb, of declaring those of a differing faith to be infidels.

This was, in effect, an institution of both incrimination and excommunication believed to have originated with the seventh-century Islamic secessionists, the *khawarij*, who, operating under the slogan, "There is no judgment but God's," and deeply obsessed with establishing who could and who could not be deemed a true Muslim, determined that anyone who disobeyed Qur'anic prescriptions or the Prophetic Traditions was an infidel to be expelled from the Community of Believers.[52]

In the second half of the twentieth century, the practice would be revived and given new life by such modern would-be reformers as Sayyid Qutb and the Pakistani Islamic theorist Abu al-A'la al-Mawdudi—ironically, the founder of the Pakistani *Jama'ati Islami* group that, in the 1980s, would work very closely with Pakistani and U.S. intelligence interests in recruiting the earliest precursors of al-Qaeda to resist the Soviet Union's invasion of Afghanistan.[53]

As a consequence, today the excommunication practice of labeling non-Muslims (or even other Muslims) as infidels, of perceiving the non-Islamic portion of the planet to be in an ignorant state, and of viewing jihad as the sole path to the eradication of injustice, not only factionalizes the Islamic world, but, as demonstrated, contravenes classic Islamic doctrine as well as the counsel of twelfth-century jurist al-Ghazali that: "The sin of sparing the lives of a thousand unbelievers is less serious than that of excommunicating a Muslim and shedding his blood."[54]

In so doing, it likewise openly refutes a tradition deeply embodied in a history that reveals that the Prophet Muhammad did not take to the sword to rid the world of unbelievers, but rather to defend his newly created society in al-Madinah—thereby rendering the House of Saud quite right in its claim that the notion of *takfir*, as now practiced, in reality, issues from deviant behavior rather than religious rescript.[55]

The challenge to any fundamentalist religious movement, of course, is that it is, both by definition and nature—reactionary—and as such, cannot remain tied to a dynamic, forward-looking political power base. Instead, it becomes a counterbalance to all vestiges of modernity and progress and a prime progenitor of social stasis. Accordingly, it was not surprising that in 1991, during the Gulf War to expel Saddam Hussein's Iraqi army from Kuwait—which cost the kingdom in excess of $55 billion in direct capital outlays—a group of Saudi dissidents calling themselves *al-Qaeda fi al-Jazirah al-'Arabiyah* (the "base" within the Arabian Peninsula), would amalgamate radical new dimensions onto traditional Wahhabi ideology and turn it against the state.

It is equally not surprising that in 1991, it would then join with the Advice and Reform Committee, also known as the Saudi Reform Movement, and other reformists of the New Islamic Awakening (*al-Sahwah al-Islamiyah*) movement in presenting the government with a Letter of Demands calling for reforms within the nation's political, economic, and defense sectors, and for the immediate establishment of an autonomous Consultative Council.[56]

Soon following up, this same coterie of vocal dissidents in 1992 would lodge with the government a formal Memorandum of Advice for governance. This memo—endorsed by an assorted collection of dissident *'ulama'* including such radical clerics as 'Abd Allah bin Jibrin, Safar al-Hawali, and Salman al-'Awda—cited ten Great Issues perceived to be in need of immediate redress, issues that would also profoundly shape the ideology of Osama bin Laden.[57]

Curiously, one of their principal grievances—that the kingdom's ruling *'ulama'* are little more than rubber stamps for the political wishes of the ruling House of Saud—speaks directly to the previously described longstanding advice and consent traditions of classic Islamic polity. For traditionally, that juridical body's principal function has been to advise Muslim rulers on the guidance of Islamic law as defined by the *shari'ah*—and then, once consensus on a course of action has been reached, to issue a legal opinion (*fatwa*) justifying its execution, thereby solidifying the legitimacy of governmental action.[58]

Within Saudi Arabia, this formal judicial body is known as the Council of Senior 'Ulama.' Established in 1971 by Royal Decree, with its membership appointed by the king, its express purpose, as the decree specifies, is to render opinions on the *shari'ah* as it applies to religious matters submitted to it by competent authority (i.e., the *wali al-amr* = the king).[59]

The members are likewise charged with advising the king on major policy matters. In 1979, for instance, they issued a *fatwa* sanctioning the execution of insurgents who had participated in the takeover of the Grand Mosque in Makkah. During the Gulf crisis in 1990, they also issued a *fatwa* sanctioning the stationing of foreign troops on Saudi soil to defend it against possible Iraqi encroachment. In this instance, their *fatwa* justified their decision thusly:

> It becomes necessary in a situation such as this for the 'ulama' to clarify Islamic ruling on the matter so that the people of the country and elsewhere may be cognizant of the correct viewpoint. . . .
>
> For even though the American soldiers are, from a strict religious standpoint, equivalent to unbelievers as they are not Muslims, they deserve support because they are here to defend Islam. . . .
>
> The Council of Higher 'Ulama' therefore approves the steps taken by the Ruler, may God grant him success, to invite forces equipped with arms to deter anyone who would contemplate invading this land.[60]

The price extracted for this *fatwa* is said to have been a promise from the king that American troops would respect Muslim customs and depart immediately once the threat had passed.[61] Resonating off this background, then, among the demands of the signatories of the 1992 so-called Memorandum of Advice were to:

- immediately review all of the kingdom's laws and replace those found not to be "Islamic" with *shari'ah* ones;
- establish a "high court" to ascertain the compliance of existing laws with the *shari'ah*; and
- require that all academic institutions focus only upon Islamic teachings; and to apprise *graduate students only* on the scope of Western traditions, and that solely for the express purpose of undermining them (!)[62]

Amidst this intellectual ferment, then, in March 1992, on a date coinciding with the tenth anniversary of his accession, King Fahd countered with a sweeping package of internal reforms. It consisted of three fundamental elements: (1) a 60-member (raised to 150 members in 2005) Consultative Council; (2) a Basic Law of Government, which drafted the kingdom's governmental framework while defining the rights of citizens; and

(3) a law governing its provincial administration.[63] Notwithstanding such semblance of progress, however, in mid-May 1993, several prominent Saudi Islamists proceeded to establish what they called the Committee for the Defense of Legitimate Rights—again designed to ensure full governmental conformity with the dictates of *shari'ah* law.

Thus, political ferment continues—resulting in the consummate irony that in the name of legitimate rights, such self-professing *salafiyah* Islamists totally deny the existence of *secular human rights*—insisting that all rights issue from God. Indeed, to this end, in late December 1993, this group gathered signatures calling for the conversion of the kingdom into a constitutional theocracy.[64]

Accordingly, al-Qaeda's gradual evolution—curiously guised in the garb of the French Revolution—would inexorably unfold. In the evolutionary process—as with most revolutionaries who leave no stone unturned in their quest for an ultimate end that they believe to be inherently "good"—in full fashion of their seventh-century *khawarij* predecessors— the proponents again portray the Islamic world as comprised of bipolar camps: the Apostles of Heaven (themselves) engaged in mortal combat against the Apostates from Hell (everybody else).

It is precisely this threat that they pose to civilized existence that haunts the planet still. As they have knowingly embarked upon a promethean struggle couched within a surreal paradox that takes on the dimensions of an attempted "theocratic coup"—an unfolding that is the focus of analyses outlined in the chapters that follow.[65]

4

Jihad: Do Wahhabis
Get a Bad Rap?

If they are inclined toward peace, then incline you also to it and trust in
Allah.

—Qur'an, Surat al-Anfal 8:61

THE GENESIS OF WAHHABI DOCTRINE

Close exegetic analysis of the Qur'anic verses presented in chapter 2 reveals that there are few significant differences, none substantive, between commonly accepted traditional translations of the Qur'an and that of the so-called Wahhabi edition produced at al-Madinah in 1996. Indeed, their common prescriptions for peace and war are concurrently shown to constitute a martial system fully consonant with the dictates of modern Hague and Geneva Convention mandates.

Having established that the incipient basis for modern Islamic terror lies not in the faith's intrinsic doctrine, therefore, it is next critical to ascertain whether it derives from contemporary understanding, to wit, whether there are substantive differences in exegetical interpretations of the doctrine. Seeking answer to this seminal question, inquiry turns initially, and quite naturally, to the doctrinal progenitor of Wahhabism himself: Muhammad ibn 'Abd al-Wahhab. This is, in itself, a critical methodological departure.

For in the aftermath of September 11, 2001, great attention has quite naturally been focused upon Osama bin Laden and his shadowy al-Qaeda terrorist network. In the process, much of the world has likewise become

65

familiar with the term Wahhabi and the fact that fifteen of the nineteen 9/11 hijackers carried Saudi Arabian passports. For many, the linkage thus is clear—Wahhabi = Saudi, ipso facto = terrorist. Indeed, for some, this implication has stuck with uncommon durability.[1] The "logic algorithm" is simple:

Socrates was a philosopher;
Socrates and his disciples were mental giants.
Ergo, all philosophers are mental giants.

Or as deduced in the more convoluted present context:

Muhammad ibn 'Abd al-Wahhab was a Saudi;
Osama bin Laden is a Saudi;
Osama bin Laden masterminded 9/11;
Fifteen of the nineteen terrorists who perpetrated 9/11 carried Saudi passports;
Muhammad ibn 'Abd al-Wahhab read thirteenth/fourteenth-century jurist Ibn Taymiyah;
The Egyptian wing of al-Qaeda quotes Ibn Taymiyah to justify its terrorist activities;
Therefore, the Saudi Muhammad ibn 'Abd al-Wahhab was a "Wahhabi terrorist."

But is this presumption fair or accurate? Is it a justifiable pretext for agonizing over what went wrong religiously and fixing blame? Chapters 5 and 6 sketch in some detail the sinister evolution of al-Qaeda within the Afghani mujahidin resistance movement carefully constructed by the U.S. Central Intelligence Agency in the 1980s to repel the Soviet invasion of Afghanistan. This was a well-planned, well-executed, and well-funded operation.

Yet little did the principal players at the center of what was then called Operation Cyclone—America, Saudi Arabia, and Pakistan in particular—realize at the time that their insurgent war against the Soviet Union in Afghanistan had amassed and mobilized, however inadvertently, the nucleus of a virulent movement proclaiming the banner of Islam that would ultimately become their mortal enemy—one that they would soon have to fight forcefully from within—even in the face of Amnesty International and general world approbation.

For, as analysis shows, from Afghanistan, sizable portions of the erstwhile mujahidin went to Chechnya to pursue their insurgent avocations against the Russians. As many as 4,000 others went to Bosnia to support the insurgency operations being waged by Muslims there. Many others went to Algeria, Egypt, Sudan, the Yemen, Kashmir, and Indonesia, while still others simply returned to their homelands of Saudi Arabia, Jordan, and the Sudan, equally zealous to hone their newly won skills into further successes in the nations of their birth.[2]

The Gulf War, and the attendant lingering U.S. military occupation of the region, in turn, exacerbated much anti-Western sentiment throughout the Middle East. Though Muslim opinion was initially divided over the propriety of Iraq's invasion of Kuwait, the overwhelming view in the street ultimately crystallized into a pervasive belief that this was a war against Islam wherein the West had needlessly intervened in an intra-Muslim dispute.

The predictable results occurred: a rapid ratcheting up of anti-Western sentiment and street action; as well as countervailing sharp criticism in the global media of local failure to provide adequate internal security for foreign economic interests, creating ever-widening fault lines between East and West; and mounting Muslim sympathies for insurgent movements, such as al-Qaeda, willing to take on perceived decadent Western imperialism wherever it might be found.[3]

Islamic street sentiment has, of course, been further conpounded by the ubiquitous problem of thrice-promised Palestine—a seemingly unsolvable conundrum. Jews, on the one hand, lay claim to the Levant as a sacred grant bequeathed by God, as manifest in scripture, that no mortal leader has a right to give away:

> In that day, the Lord made a covenant with Abraham, saying: "Unto thy seed have I given this land, from the river of Egypt unto the great river, the Euphrates"(Genesis 15:18)

> Every place whereupon the sole of your foot shall tread shall be yours; from the wilderness and Lebanon, from the river, the river Euphrates, even unto the uttermost sea, shall your border be. (Deuteronomy 11:24–25)

> There shall no man be able to stand against you; the Lord your God shall lay the fear of you upon all the land that ye tread upon, as He has spoken unto you. (Deuteronomy 11:24–25)

Thus, in Jewish eyes, *Eretz Israel*, the "land of Israel," is inviolable. Doctrinally central to God's commitment to make them His chosen people, to fundamentalist Jews, its possession is integral to their Covenant with God—thus rendering its relinquishment a direct denial of Divine Will.[4] Never mind that their own sacred book, the Torah, the Old Testament, describes in vivid detail how Hebrew king David forcibly seized it from the Philistines, the Palestinians. Never mind that it is concurrently one of the most holy places of Islam as well—the sacred site to whence Prophet

Muhammad was one night miraculously transported by God to receive divine revelation.

No mind either that for two medieval centuries, it was the Christian Kingdom—Christ's Empire on Earth recrudescent in the East—or that the Wailing Wall on Temple Mount, the Dome of the Rock atop al-Aqsa Mosque, and the Castle of the Crusader King all cohabited the same site. Never mind that it is the thrice-promised land of Palestine. In Hebrew eyes, it is the fulfillment of God's promise to the Jews.[5]

And therein lies the irreconcilable crux of the Muslims' complaint. They find it supremely ironic that it is they—with a far better centuries-long track record of treatment of Jewish minorities than do Christians—are asked to pay the price for the suffering of Jews in the Diaspora at the hands of European states—to sacrifice their homelands to refugees from centuries of pogroms in the Christian West—capped off by a World War European holocaust that precipitated the modern wave of Zionism.[6]

Thus, they too, with equal cause and conviction, believe that they have been denied their lawful birthright—and in the manner of jihadis of all faiths who fervently hope to hasten the return of the Messiah by carrying out God's judgments on earth—like the Jews before them, since mid-twentieth century, have often taken recourse to force and violence in the name of God in their quest to get it back.

Their insurgencies have coalesced around two specific groups as, in their fervid quest, there have emerged two sets of warriors who claim to labor through jihad for the cause of God: (1) religious fundamentalists (*usuliyun*) who act as literalists in their interpretation of the Qur'an and Prophetic Tradition attributed to Muhammad; and (2) professional militant jihadis who operate as psychopathic opportunists inciting the fundamentalists to violence, most often, as shown, in direct contravention of Islamic doctrine and prescription.[7]

The latter are those whom the world has, to its great regret, come to know as Islamic terrorists. Indeed, evidence continues to mount that, in the current context, they are increasingly able to recruit, indoctrinate, exploit, incite, and mobilize some elements of the former to violent action in support of the perceived cause. This is particularly the case for young, aged fifteen to forty-five, politically marginalized Muslim males enduring perceptions of relative economic deprivation who turn to seeking their fulfillment in the fundamentalist promise of that "inevitable victory of the Righteous" that only the scriptures can provide. In the words of renowned terrorism expert Harvey Kushner, recruits

> are promised an afterlife replete with golden palaces, sumptuous feasts, and virgin brides. The students are also told that their martyrdom guarantees that seventy of their relatives and friends will be guaranteed entry into heaven. . . .

The suicide bombers leave for missions directly from their mosques, having completed many days of chanting the relevant scriptures aloud with their spiritual handlers. Their favored verse reads:
"Think not of those slain in Allah's way as dead. No, they live on and find sustenance in the presence of their Lord."[8]

It is in this supercharged milieu of incitement to violence, then, that the shadowy al-Qaeda network has clandestinely emerged. In the process, many unfortunately have attributed the militant extremism on the part of its secular leader, Osama bin Laden, to the teachings of Muhammad ibn 'Abd al-Wahhab who is perceived, wrongfully, as will be demonstrated, to have legitimized and sanctioned jihad against unbelievers to promote the so-called doctrines of Wahhabism.

THE EVOLUTION OF WAHHABI IDEOLOGY

In this erroneous interpretation, then, this eighteenth-century Muslim reformer becomes the godfather of both modern terrorist insurgency and contemporary fundamentalist resurgence. Yet the reality is that, based upon studied analysis, any seeming doctrinal affinity between the two would-be reformist movements issues almost exclusively from a mutual devotion to studying the legal pronouncements of thirteenth/fourteenth-century Damascene Hanbali religious reformer Ibn Taymiyah. A brief review of the doctrinal evolution of the teachings of Muhammad ibn 'Abd al-Wahhab at this point, therefore, is not merely illuminating but quintessential for full and accurate understanding.[9]

Muhammad ibn 'Abd al-Wahhab's dissatisfaction with traditional unquestioning of past interpretation of Islamic doctrine (*taqlid*) grew directly from exposure to what he perceived to be a qualitatively flawed exegetical approach to divining truth from Prophetic Tradition by the Muslims' longstanding religious establishment, the *'ulama'*.

Moving to strip *taqlid* of its persuasive power, he sought to restore that authority to God alone through revelation. Recognizing the fallacy of relying upon second hand interpretations of the scriptures, he launched a call for a return to studying them directly, thereby reopening the long dormant "door to independent reasoning." His rationale was circumspectly laid out in twin essays: *Kitab al-Tawhid* and *Kitab al-Jihad*—as well as in his assorted, assembled *Fatawa wa Masa'il*.[10]

Muhammad ibn 'Abd al-Wahhab's worldview focused intently upon education—firmly convinced that acquiring and sharing religious knowledge was a paramount responsibility of Muslims. He concurrently believed and taught that knowledge was necessary for preserving public order—and that only educated people are worthy and capable of providing effective leadership to the Islamic realm.

In his global vision, then, education and debate were to be the preferred means for winning religious adherents. Because of the supreme importance that he placed upon knowledge, among the overarching responsibilities of true Muslims, he maintained, was that the pursuit of education must be accompanied by scholarly debate among believers to ensure its fullest dissemination.[11] For educated debate, in his view, was an integral part of jihad—recognizing that heartfelt adherence won through the logic of intellectual intercourse was preferable to sword-point conversions predicated upon Islam's classic "convert, remit, or die" expansionist formula.

To this end, it is critical to note that Muhammad ibn 'Abd al-Wahhab uses the term *qital* rather than *jihad* when referring to conventional warfare (*harb*).[12] As for him, the *da'wah*, field missionary work, was a preferable form of jihad in winning converts to Islam.[13] Accordingly, his personal writings on jihad reflect a powerful Qur'anic focus upon the sanctity of life. His vision of jihad portrayed it as exclusively defensive in nature—and he legitimatized it only in those cases where Muslims became victims of overt aggression. As such, there is a sharp and distinct disconnect between the teachings of Muhammad ibn 'Abd al-Wahhab on jihad and the more passionate preachings of such contemporary militant fundamentalists as Sayyid Qutb and Osama bin Laden.[14]

Hence, though it is frequently posited that bin Laden's global ideology respecting jihad traces its origins to the writings of Muhammad ibn 'Abd al-Wahhab—because both are so-called Wahhabis—the reality is that the former's doctrine derives more directly from the sundry works of the medieval Syrian scholar Ibn Taymiyah, as interpreted by his modern day Egyptian exegete, Sayyid Qutb, than they do from any ideological contribution of the eighteenth-century Najdi reformer. Indeed, the sole nexus that links the three is a shared affinity for differing aspects of convictions articulated within the exegetical works of Ibn Taymiyah.[15]

Because the teachings of Muhammad ibn 'Abd al-Wahhab stand at such significant variance with the violent, virulent preachings of Osama bin Laden, both ostensibly in the name of Wahhabi Islam, it becomes critical to revisit Wahhabi doctrine respecting the sanctioned causes for jihad and its prescribed conduct, as defined by the eighteenth-century reformer who lends to the doctrine his name—as the question of the validity of its alleged justification for the conduct of modern terrorist insurgency merits careful contemplation.

To this end, analysis commences with what is generally acknowledged to be the "Wahhabi Manual for War." At the onset of his *Kitab al-Jihad*, quite revealingly, Muhammad ibn 'Abd al-Wahhab clearly stipulates that the mandate for jihad is a "collective obligation" (*fard kifayah*) that must perforce be initiated by a spiritual leader (*imam*), and must not be an individualistic undertaking (*fard 'ayn*) pursued on an ad hoc basis by a random few.[16]

In his discourse on jihad, he must, of course, inevitably wrestle with the so-called paramount sword verse—

> Then, when the sacred months have passed, slay the polytheists wherever you find them, and take them captive and besiege them, and prepare to ambush them. But if they repent and establish worship, and pay jizyah, then leave their way free for them. Lo! Allah is Forgiving, Merciful. (Surat al-Tawbah 9:5)

—concluding that (1) it can only be fully understood when taken in conjunction with the Qur'anic verse "Muhammad 47:4," which calls for mercy and ransoming of prisoners; and (2) contends that jihad's sole and ultimate objective is to bring peoples to divine unity within the ummah, the Community of God. It is then no more than a call to conversion and adherence to the tenets of Islam.[17]

For jihad can concurrently be many things primarily defensive in both intent and effect—the "daily struggle against the devil," verbal jihad, written jihad, educational jihad, "missionary jihad," and personal jihad—commitments well beyond, and far more pacific than, the conventional "jihad of the sword," war.[18]

While jihad is indeed primarily a "defensive weapon," he contends, there are nonetheless three Qur'anically sanctioned circumstances wherein it can be engaged in combat. To wit:

1. Whenever you meet an army, be firm and think of Allah, that you may be successful. (Surat al-Anfal 8:45),
2. When you meet those in battle who disbelieve, do not turn your backs on them. (Surat al-Anfal 8:15), and
3. Whenever directed to do so by the *imam* (i.e., the communal *religious* leader, not its political one.)[19]

In the latter case, Muhammad ibn 'Abd al-Wahhab simultaneously constrains an *imam*'s ability to declare jihad by expressly forbidding him to incite people to it—again an admonition in direct contravention of so-called contemporary "Wahhabi jihadi practice."

Not only must jihad be pursued with piety and devotion—with faith providing the intent that lends it legitimacy—but according to Muhammad ibn 'Abd al-Wahhab, it must be preceded by a clear call to would-be adversaries to peacefully join Islam, asserting: "It is not permissible to commence invading or killing them prior to their being made aware." Only if they overtly reject "the Call," then, may recourse to jihad be legitimately pursued as stipulated by Surat al-Tawbah 9:12; whereas, if they accept, they are not to be militarily engaged but instead welcomed into the ranks of the Community of Believers.[20]

Even in cases of forcible subjugation through jihad, Muhammad ibn 'Abd al-Wahhab determines, the vanquished populace is entitled to remain in full possession of its properties in exchange for payment of requisite land and poll taxes, thereby placing them in a protective treaty (*aman*) relationship with Islam.[21] Though such taxes, by juridical prescription, are directly due to the Islamic realm (*Dar al-Islam*), they are not to be excessive, nor are they subject to increase—for the express purpose of jihad is not to enrich Muslims but rather to encourage would-be aggressors to either accept Islam or enter into protected treaty status.

In the conduct of jihad, the needless or wanton destruction of collateral property also is explicitly forbidden. So is book burning—as books are used to convey knowledge—and the demolishing of weaponry, as it can be employed to serve the cause of the mujahidin.[22] Contrary to contemporary jihadi representations depicting the endeavor as a noble quest for martyrdom through suicide, moreover, Muhammad ibn 'Abd al-Wahhab clarifies that amicable peace must always be the mujahid's first option, observing that the Qur'an stipulates:[23]

> If they are inclined toward peace, then incline you also to it and trust in Allah. (Surat al-Anfal 8:61)

> Freedom from obligation is proclaimed by Allah and His Messenger toward those with whom you have made a treaty. (Surat al-Tawbah 9:1)

The conditions for declaring such a truce are equally Qur'anically explicit. All truces must be fully consonant with the prescriptions of Islamic law. Only the *imam* or his sanctioned representative may proclaim them, whereupon he alone assumes full responsibility for enforcing them.[24] Truces declared by anyone else, even the nominal secular ruler (*amir*), therefore, are not binding. But once the *imam* has concluded a truce, it remains binding upon the ummah even in the event of the *imam*'s subsequent deposition or demise, predicated upon the Qur'anic verse:[25]

> And fulfill your treaty with them till its term. (Surat al-Tawbah 9:4)

Finally, when a treaty has produced a guarantee (*aman*) placing a subjugated people in protected (*dhimmi*) status, two irrevocable requirements are made incumbent by the subsequent relationship. The dhimmi must (1) acquiesce to paying the poll tax and (2) accept the jurisdiction of Islamic law.[26] Accordingly, such Islamically sanctioned treaties are represented to be consummately fair and equitable in that (1) they are entered into either voluntarily or as a prescribed condition of a negotiated truce; and in that (2) they are mutually binding upon the contracting parties. Muslims are thus obligated to honor their contracted conditions so long as their truce partners do the same. Thereby, an equitable peace is preserved.[27]

Given this firm commitment to the sanctity of treaties in the pursuit of equity and peace, then, it is not at all surprising that, contrary to most conventional depictions of Wahhabis, the writings of Muhammad ibn 'Abd al-Wahhab are strikingly absent of fervid calls to violence in God's name. His master, "Manual for War" (*Kitab al-Jihad*), does occasionally call for fighting unbelievers (*kuffar*). But a *kafir* is defined as only someone who upon exposure to the teachings of Islamic doctrine, first accepts them, then subsequently rejects them—in other words, backsliders, apostates who renege on their promises to God. Only in such cases can the use of force in God's name (*fi sabil Allah*) be justified.[28]

In stark contrast, of course, many contemporary fundamentalist practitioners of the arts of terror, who claim to proceed with the sanction, and indeed the mandate, of Muhammad ibn 'Abd al-Wahhab, emphasize militant jihad as the doctrinally prescribed means of expanding the territories of Islam—and thereby, its message. In their view, then, jihad has been ordained as an ongoing and permanent duty of the Muslim community executed for the purpose of eradicating unbelief through use of force. Envisioned equally as an individual and a collective obligation, its goal is represented as one of repelling any and all encroachment upon Islam's sacred domain—be it ideological or territorial.

The prime targets of modern Muslim fundamentalist terrorists, therefore, tend to be their own secular governments, which they perceive to be in league with the enemy—non-Muslim powers. Citing Ibn Taymiyah, they contend that any state that does not apply Islamic law in its entirety is guilty of apostasy and deserves deposition.[29] Their prescription: its overthrow in favor of an "Islamic state"—by them, defined as one wherein the *shari'ah* is exclusively applied. For in their unique cosmology, it is only by restoring Islam to power that Muslims can live in true accord with their faith and be restored to their rightful positions of power. Thus, their perception of jihad evolves as more offensive than defensive in its character.[30]

As readily evident from preceding analysis, it is clear that such unleashed political violence in relentless pursuit of global jihad does not issue from the teachings or writings of Muhammad ibn 'Abd al-Wahhab—which vary quite significantly, both in methodology and content, from those of modern Muslim militants. From whence, then, does the historic variance arise—and more important still, from whence does the modern propensity for violence derive?[31]

The foundations for contemporary misunderstanding are multiple. First, many traditional perceptions of Wahhabism have been projected primarily through the prisms of its opponents—an opposition that has claimed that Wahhabis, like their presumed seventh-century extremist *khawarij* ancestors before them, perceive the planet to be divided into two distinct bipolar spheres: (1) a world of believers, *Dar al-Islam*, the exclusive domain of the Wahhabis; and (2) a world of unbelievers, the *Dar al-Kuffar*, the domain of everybody else—a dichotomy then used as a pretext to declare jihad against them for their ostensible unbelief (*kufr*).[32] Concerned with the potentially messianic religious implications of such a message, the Ottoman Empire contributed materially to this stereotype, stirring up popular fear of the Najdis, even coining the term Wahhabi and claiming that their creed was innovative; and hence, heretical.[33]

Part of the confusion, as noted, arises with an all-too-frequent tendency to equate the doctrinal views of Muhammad ibn 'Abd al-Wahhab with those of someone whose early works he often consulted: the thirteenth/ fourteenth-century Islamic scholar Ibn Taymiyah. The latter clearly did condone violence—turning to the *khawarij* as a prototypic model to be emulated in his frenetic ongoing call for a militant jihad to defend the Dar al-Islam from the then ever-encroaching invasion of the Mongols.[34] As the foremost Hanbali jurist of the age, his determinations thus set strong historic precedent, coming to be echoed by generations of would-be successors—including such self-professing modernist "Islamic reformers" as Hassan al-Banna, Sayyid Qutb, Ayman al-Zawahiri, and Osama bin Laden.

Indeed, contending that the weakness of the empire was due to laxity in religious practice, Ibn Taymiyah's avowed expressed purpose was to employ Islamic law to justify an overpowering military defense of Muslim lands against incoming invaders—employing coercion and violence if need be—asserting that:

> Since lawful warfare is effectively jihad, and since its religious aim is that of Allah's will exclusively, and His word is uppermost, therefore, according to all Muslims, those who would impede His aim must be fought.[35]

And therein lies the great ideological divide. For Ibn Taymiyah's proponency of coercion and violence is uncompromising, standing in stark contrast to the advocacies of Muhammad ibn 'Abd al-Wahhab, who convincingly argued that such matters are acts of inner faith that issue from the heart—and hence, must never be coerced. In essence, then, the distinctive ideological difference lies in the reality that whereas Ibn Taymiyah maintained that anyone who heard "Islam's Call" and rejected it must be fought, Muhammad ibn 'Abd al-Wahhab rejected such unequivocal endorsements of jihad, contending that it applied only to those who moved aggressively against Islam, and though offered ample opportunity, proceeded to repudiate "the Call."[36]

But though Ibn Taymiyah's militancy was rejected outright by Muhammad ibn 'Abd al-Wahhab, such was not the case for others. Among them, Egypt's Sayyid Qutb endorsed it unequivocally, asserting that secular political, socioeconomic, and racial factors were far too powerful to be repelled by moral suasion alone—that to be successfully subdued, their proponents perforce must be physically engaged.[37] Contending that "submission to God's will" (*islam*) is a universal truth binding upon all mankind, he argued that the faith should be either accepted in its entirety or rejected. But if someone does not elect to accept it, then he, at the same time, must not oppose it or hinder the will of others to accept it. If he does so, it is then obligatory upon Islam to fight him until he is killed or declares his loyalty and submission.[38]

Drawing heavily upon past militant scholarship justifying holy war against non-Muslims in general, as well as their governments and institutions, Sayyid Qutb thus made jihad a global enterprise—a foremost tool of Qur'anic revolution—turning to armed struggle as the last best hope for drawing mankind to the message of Islam, a viewpoint fully consonant with his aforesaid vision of a bipolar planet sharply divided between the wisdom that embodies the Dar al-Islam and the ignorance that characterizes the House of Ignorance (*Dar al-Jahiliyah*).[39]

Like Ibn Taymiyah, then, Sayyid Qutb believed that the bifurcated world was not merely a reflection of conflicting ideologies but likewise constituted a necessary hostile relationship that invoked jihad as a quintessential instrument for ensuring that God's will prevails on earth. Asserting that, by its very nature, jihad is a dynamic, active force that Muslims possess both the right and the responsibility to unleash, he concluded, "Islam is not prepared to abdicate this right at any cost."[40]

WAHHABI IDEOLOGY AND THE CONTENTIONS OF BIN LADEN

This conclusion sets the planet upon the cosmic course on which it proceeds today. For Sayyid Qutb's avowed disciple, Osama bin Laden, whose views are documented in forthcoming chapters, first loomed large on the global horizon as the prototypic Islamic terrorist subsequent to al-Qaeda's cataclysmic 9/11 attack. Being previously a Saudi citizen—having been stripped of his citizenship by Saudi authorities in 1994—media presumption, ipso facto, has been that his extremist militant tendencies are, in some way, a byproduct issuing from some esoteric and ethereal Wahhabi doctrine. But such is clearly not the case.[41]

For though his world vision likewise is "bi-spheric," it is distinctly not Wahhabi in its roots but rather stands as a modern reflection of the medieval teaching of such scholars as Ibn Taymiyah and Ibn Qayyim al-Jawziyah, as synthesized and retooled by Sayyid Qutb and Ayman al-Zawahiri. And like Ibn Taymiyah and Sayyid Qutb before him, his global view too has been shaped in a surging sea of political turbulence.

For as documented in chapter 5, bin Laden's involvement in Afghanistan commenced in 1980 when the Afghan mujahidin implored the Saudi royal family to dispatch one of its members to lead the incoming Saudi armed contingent—then consisting primarily of militants, dissidents, and other lower-class Saudis perceiving economic deprivation in their homelands—to lead them in jihad against the Soviet invasion of their country.[42]

Because no one from the Saudi royal family was willing to participate, the mujahidin turned to bin Laden—a logical fall-back choice in that he was both wealthy and the scion of a family with well-known close royal family ties—having been selected to build much of the religious infrastructure that today supports the Islamic Holy Places in Makkah and al-Madinah. This experience, later combined with his emerging role as a vocal political dissident, would thereafter powerfully and profoundly shape his political outlook.[43] Indeed, as will be shown, the Soviets' ultimate defeat and forced withdrawal at the hands of his ragtag band of warriors of God would lead bin Laden to the messianic conclusion that his victory's movement was a sign equally of Allah's favor and of the righteousness of both its mission and its message.

Hence, while in the aftermath of the Afghan war, most Africans, Arab-Afghans, and other mujahidin from throughout south central Asia went home to pursue personal agendas, al-Qaeda, initially consisting largely of Saudi remnants, coalesced in 1989 to continue the Lord's work of global jihad against the infidels who dwelled far beyond the borders of East Afghanistan.

It was buttressed by this residual militant infrastructure, then, that bin Laden offered to the Saudi royal family his perceived capacity to defend Makkah and al-Madinah against the onslaught of Saddam Hussein in the fall of 1990. Believing that the defense of Islam's homeland was the rightful prerogative and duty of Muslims, not foreigners, he was convinced that he had found his cause and calling—and when the Saudi leadership refused his offer, inviting in America's military might instead, he actively engaged.

For the Gulf War's aftermath concurrently made clear to bin Laden that his jihad against the infidels must continue—and that to prevail, Sayyid

Qutb's vision of cosmic conflict between good and evil must be both re-lentless and unending—as at its close, armies of the unbelievers still oc-cupied the Arabian Peninsula, home of the most sacred Islamic Holy Places. To this end, upon returning to Saudi Arabia, he proceeded to es-tablish an Advice and Reform Committee as an umbrella organization for religious opposition groups. Devoted to the classic teachings of Ibn Taymiyah and his disciple, Ibn Qayyim al-Jawziyah, its proclaimed goals were to:

- eradicate all forms of *jahiliyah* rule;
- install true Islamic justice;
- reinstate the traditional *hizbah* tribal system of governance under the auspices of the *'ulama'* whereby citizens could directly bring charges against their rulers; and thereby to
- radically reform the Saudi governmental system.[44]

Though divested, as noted, of Saudi citizenship in 1994 as a result of his recurring criticism of its royal family, bin Laden's focus nonetheless sub-sequently broadened quite markedly from a concentrated focus on Saudi internal issues to international ones—most specifically to U.S. foreign pol-icy within the Middle East.[45] Concurrently, his critiques shifted from in-kingdom issues to targeting the United States everywhere—though his criticism of the Saudi government as "secular agents of the infidel" for their complicity with, and continuing support for, America, which he equated to an unholy alliance with godless *kuffar*—continued unabated, charging in an open letter them: "In foreign policy, your government ties its destiny to that of crusader western governments."[46]

His grievances? His perception that the Saudi government was unable to defend the Holy Places of Islam in 1991, inviting in the Americans in-stead—and now not only are the Americans unworthy occupiers, they have likewise maintained artificially low oil prices—and even from their proceeds, have squandered Islamic resources on purchases of expensive and needless weapon systems. Thus, his global jihad carries forth un-ending.

In attendant inflammatory tirades, influenced by al-Qaeda's ubiquitous spiritual advisor, Ayman al-Zawahiri, bin Laden relies most heavily upon the writings of Ibn Taymiyah in his unending calls to jihad because, in his own words, "Ibn Taymiyah was the original source of inspiration for jihad against a corrupt regime."[47]

In all of this, of course, Muhammad ibn 'Abd al-Wahhab is strangely lacking—but this comes as no surprise—as the sole nexus of ideology between him and bin Laden is that both he and bin Laden studied the various teachings of Ibn Taymiyah. But whereas Muhammad ibn 'Abd

al-Wahhab gleaned from Ibn Taymiyah's writings his precepts on economics, social conduct, monotheism, and how a righteous Islamic state
should conduct itself, bin Laden cherry-picked from them their most
strident militant passages written as he strove valiantly to rally the Dar
al-Islam against the horrific invasions of the Mongols that were unfolding in his thirteenth-fourteenth–century lifetime.

In sum, then, bin Laden's vision of global jihad is clearly rooted not in
Wahhabism but in Ibn Taymiyah, as synthesized and accentuated by his
modern day apostle Sayyid Qutb—and both are present in his perspective
of an ever-clashing world divided equally Muslims and *kuffar*—a perception made readily evident in a statement attributed to him in the aftermath of the 1995 Saudi National Guard and 1996 al-Khobar bombings:
"What is important in Riyadh and al-Khobar is that no Saudis were hurt
or killed in them, only Americans."[48]

He cites, for instance, the authority of Ibn Taymiyah and Ibn Qayyim al-
Jawziyah in his charges that most contemporary Islamic regimes are not
truly Muslim—and in his calls for the removal of the late Shaykh 'Abdul
'Aziz bin Baz as Grand Mufti of Islam on charges of being a mere puppet
of the Saudi government.[49]

His expressed goal of purifying through reformation Muslim governments that he deems unworthy simultaneously reflects a curious admixture
of Ibn Taymiyah's call for the violent-if-need-be overthrow of un-Islamic
governments blended with the "eradication of ignorance" prescriptions
of Sayyid Qutb under whose brother, Muhammad, bin Laden studied in
Jiddah in the mid-1970s—having come there after his release from an
Egyptian jail in1972.[50]

He likewise shares with Ibn Taymiyah and Ibn Qayyim al-Jawziyah a
reveling in the "glories of martyrdom." Asserting that "there is a special place in the hereafter for those who participate in jihad," his open
prayer for the 9/11 perpetrators, as faxed to the al-Jazirah television
network, was:

> We pray that these brothers are only amongst the first of martyrs in this new
> Jewish-Christian crusade led by the great crusader Bush under the banner of
> the cross. This is one of Islam's greatest battles.[51]

He concurrently echoes Sayyid Qutb's fears of Zionist and Crusader
conspiracies to destroy Islam, and thereby justifies the creation of a righteous society that, through militant activism, is capable of repelling
them—all themes strikingly absent in the voluminous writings of the
eighteenth-century Saudi reformer Muhammad ibn 'Abd al-Wahhab. To
the contrary, in fact, absent an imputed Najdi "Wahhabi influence," the
direct ideological linkages that constituted the Hijazi bin Laden's intellec-

tual evolution—via disciples of Egypt's Muslim Brotherhood—could not be more clear:

- the Egyptian-born Sayyid Qutb studied Ibn Taymiyah;
- fellow Egyptian Ayman al-Zawahiri was his immediate clone;
- whereas, in true medieval Islamic fashion, Ayman al-Zawahiri is today the doctrinal leader (*imam*) of al-Qaeda, of which bin Laden serves as commander (*amir*);
- yet apart from the fact that he too studied the works of Ibn Taymiyah, largely to glean his contributions on monotheism, Muhammad ibn 'Abd al-Wahhab is nowhere to be found within this tangled ideological loop of modern hate-inspired terror
- except to the extent that he belatedly fell victim to a predominantly Egyptian-orchestrated coup that hijacked a fragment of a religious movement that still bears his name.

Accordingly, in seeking incipient causes of modern Middle East terrorism, inquiry may productively start by examining indigenous *Egyptian*, rather than Saudi Arabian, radical Islamic movements, reflecting the convergence of multiple geographic and ideological realities previously noted:

- Osama bin Laden was raised in the western part of what is modern day Saudi Arabia that the Muslim Brotherhood had deeply penetrated;
- He commonly reads and quotes the works of its chief theorist Sayyid Qutb;
- Some of the organization's most prominent members, including Sayyid Qutb's brother, Muhammad, and Dr. Abdullah 'Azzam, were among his foremost college mentors;
- Egypt's "blind sheikh," 'Umar 'Abd al-Rahman, later implicated in the 1993 World Trade Center bombings, and his two sons, served with bin Laden in Afghanistan;
- Ayman al-Zawahiri—a disciple of Sayyid Qutb and the head of his own "Egyptian Jihad" group—is concurrently al-Qaeda's doctrinal leader and chief spokesman;
- Muhammad 'Atif, al-Qaeda's chief military commander until his death in a U.S. air strike in the Afghanistan War in November 2001, was Egyptian;
- Abu Muhammad al-Misri, general manager of al-Qaeda's erstwhile Afghan training camps, also is Egyptian;
- Muhammad 'Atta, al-Qaeda's lead 9/11 hijacker who died in the World Trade Center disaster, likewise was Egyptian; and

- The linkages go on ad infinitum, as much of the modern infrastructure of al-Qaeda has been built upon the foundations of Egyptian jihadist groups.[52]

At the ideological bottom line, then, it is the toxic preaching of such radicals—that of Sayyid Qutb in particular—that surreptitiously infiltrated into southwest Arabia and therefore onto bin Laden's radar screen in the 1960s–1970s via Egypt's exiled Muslim Brotherhood—and where they now remain compliments of Ayman al-Zawahiri—that is too often associated with what is today called "Wahhabism."[53] For the doctrinal reality is that though, in modern times, Wahhabis have often been depicted as out-of-control fanatics wreaking death and destruction upon anyone whom they considered unbelievers, this depiction finds no foundation whatsoever within the writings of Muhammad ibn 'Abd al-Wahhab. In the confirming findings of modern Arabian Peninsula historian David Commins:

> It emerged that 15 of the 19 hijackers on September 11 were Saudi nationals and that Osama bin Laden's organization was responsible for the attacks. This association with Saudi Arabia made it quite natural for many to see an intrinsic connection to the kingdom's long affiliation with Wahhabism.[54]

But the ideology of bin Laden and of al-Qaeda is not Wahhabi. It is instead part of the contemporary jihadist tendency that evolved from the teachings of Sayyid Qutb and took shape within the Egyptian militant groups that appeared in the 1970s and then spread in the 1980s thanks in large measure to the Afghan jihad. Indeed, the differences in the worldviews of Muhammad ibn 'Abd al-Wahhab and bin Laden are momentous and profound. Whereas the former prescribed a more localized message of jihad aspiring to the spread of Islam through education within a political framework that strove for an amicable coexistence, the latter preaches uncompromising global militancy to advance an "Islamic cause" cosmic in its perceived dimension.

While Muhammad ibn 'Abd al-Wahhab called for the curtailment of war, bin Laden invokes it constantly in a relentless quest for destructive results at any cost. While Muhammad ibn 'Abd al-Wahhab stipulated that jihad must be undertaken only as a collective obligation, bin Laden incessantly invokes it as an "individual obligation." While the former deemed it strictly defensive, bin Laden treats it as offensive—and while he sanctioned peaceful treaties with Jews and Christians, bin Laden preaches unending war against them. For precisely this reason, then, it comes as no surprise that this three-centuries-old Najdi Wahhabi doctrine was not accused of spawning terror until the emergence of al-Qaeda two decades ago.[55]

In short, unlike Osama bin Laden, Muhammad ibn 'Abd al-Wahhab clearly was not an advocate of "victory through violence," though his followers, at times, were. To the contrary, though he taught that adherence to monotheism (*tawhid*) should be upheld, recourse to violence and murder were not his prescribed methods for its achievement. Instead, he advocated that missionary outreach and learned debate were more appropriate means for invoking God's people to "the Call." His was, therefore, a mission of winning people not through the sword but through the heart—through dialogue, not destruction. Within his overarching vision, then, jihad would find no place as an offensive action. To the contrary, it must always remain a last, not a first, resort—a option to be exercised only in defending the ummah from overt aggression so that God's sublime business of winning souls through peaceful means can continue undeterred.[56]

Accordingly, his pervasive preaching in a persistent quest for peace flies directly in the face of modern charges that Muhammad ibn 'Abd al-Wahhab was, in reality, little more than a "histrionic, quasi-literate, backwater preacher" with no real appreciation for Islam's long history and tradition, as some of his detractors are wont to claim. For though he did evaluate classic tradition critically, he did not abandon it but instead refined it—functioning as a methodical analytic scholar well versed in its tradition.[57]

But though the writings of Muhammad ibn 'Abd al-Wahhab find neither echo nor resonance within the militant Islamic preachings of Osama bin Laden, because both are popularly perceived as Wahhabis, it is in the former's name that the latter's radical militant movement is too often unfortunately portrayed and defined by the media today.

Indeed, his teachings have, of late, become so convoluted in their purported message—supposedly in the name of Wahhabism—as to conjure up the image of an aging Shaykh articulating in his final days a disclaimer not unlike that invoked by Karl Marx in his dotage, when the latter was ruefully moved to conclude that if it has truly come to this, then,

I am not a Marxist!

5

Eastern Designs
and Holy War

And you shall know the Truth, and the Truth will make you free.

—John 8:32; etched into the Entrance Portal, Main Lobby, Original
Headquarters Building, U.S. Central Intelligence Agency

HOLY WAR: A CLASH WITH GLOBAL COMMUNISM

Al-Qaeda, quite naturally, did not get there by itself. It instead had powerful allies and enjoyed powerful assistance from unlikely sources—not the least of which was the United States. Indeed, imbued with its customary presumption of proprietary, globally exportable moral righteousness, the United States readily paved the way for al-Qaeda to spread throughout the Islamic world and beyond.

The crescendoing of events commenced in the mountainous and desert wastelands of 1970s south central Asia. The target nation, Afghanistan, had long been ruled by a monarchy until 1973 when a military coup d'état, led by Muhammad Da'ud and backed by the People's Democratic Party of Afghanistan, a communist organization, overthrew its long-ruling king and proclaimed the country to be an Islamic republic.

In 1978, it fell further to communist rule when the military overthrew Da'ud, and installed in his stead a self-proclaimed Marxist, Nur Muhammad Taraki, who, in turn, was overthrown and killed in September 1979 by another fellow socialist, yet neo-Islamist, with reported CIA backing, Hafiz Allah Amin. In response, fearing that the insurrection would spread to its own adjacent Islamic areas, the Soviet Fortieth Army on Christmas

Day 1979 mounted a full-scale invasion of Afghanistan. Entering Kabul two days later, elite units of the Soviet Special Forces (*Spetsnatz*) proceeded to storm the presidential palace, kill Amin, and install a Russian political puppet, Babrak Kamal, as president.[1]

Now at the height of its policy of the military containment of Soviet expansionism, America's government quite naturally could not stand idly by and let this incursion stand. It was the CIA, then, that first encouraged and armed Muslim militants—known as *al-mujahidin* (those who engage in jihad)—from the Middle and Far East, the Indian Subcontinent, and North and East Africa—to join up with the indigenous Taliban in forging a 1982–1992 jihad resistance against the Soviet occupation of Afghanistan.

The formula was simple. The CIA—with a global mandate and agenda of stopping Soviet Union expansion—knowingly baited the hook for Muslim fundamentalists. Meanwhile, in radical jihadist eyes, as this was the first time that an infidel had occupied an Islamic country since the Crusades, with a natural antipathy to godless communism, and possessing sufficient doctrinal malleability as to be able to cut a deal over Afghanistan with another ideological archenemy, the United States, Political Islam took the bait.

Accordingly, while between 1982 and 1986, there had been only around 200 Arabs engaged in the counterinsurgency, in 1986, there began a sudden influx of them as Saudi Arabian Airlines commenced granting "75% of cost" discounted tickets to citizens going to Peshawar to join the mujahidin—a total later to exceed 25,000—and as a consequence, the Pakistani Embassy in Riyadh started granting up to 200 visas per day to the young recruits.[2]

When the young jihadi wunderkind from Saudi Arabia, Jordan, the Yemen, the Sudan, Egypt, and elsewhere throughout the Middle East arrived in Afghanistan, they would be greeted by then well-known erstwhile Jiddah professor and Muslim Brother of Palestinian origin Abdullah Azzam—known in local political circles as the "jihad's poster boy" as well as a participant in some of its earliest and most significant successes, together with his prized pupil Osama bin Laden.

For upon graduating in 1981 from King Abdul Aziz University in Jiddah, where he had enjoyed Azzam as a mentor, this wealthy scion of a construction magnate who specialized in building roads, palaces, and religious facilities, proceeded to Pakistan to pursue jihad against the Soviet invasion of Afghanistan—there to catch up with his erstwhile college professor. A scholar as well as an activist, with a doctorate in Islamic studies from al-Azhar University in Egypt, Dr. 'Azzam would come to exert a profound influence in shaping the revolutionary ideology of the young bin Laden.[3]

Accordingly, within but brief weeks of the December 25, 1979, Soviet invasion of Afghanistan, they went to Pakistan where, working together, financed equally by direct and indirect contributions from Arab governments, Islamic charities, and wealthy associates, they established in February 1980 the Afghan Service Bureau (MAK = *Maktab al-Khidamat*)—an organization later implicated in the 1993 World Trade Center bombings—to serve as a training and logistics center supporting the Arab mujahidin who had come to fight the Soviets. To finance and supply it, bin Laden made repeated trips between Saudi Arabia and the Afghan front in the 1980–1982 period. Concurrently, an affiliated magazine promoting the insurgent cause, called *Jihad*, was initiated.[4]

As the war reached its peak in 1986, bin Laden and 'Azzam then moved from Pakistan to Paktia Province inside Afghanistan itself, where, in 1989, the former founded al-Qaeda (literally meaning "the base"), an organization explicitly structured to channel the energies of the mujahidin into worldwide jihad—an Islamic "rapid deployment force" designed to "pursue the *cause*" globally at short notice.[5] Indeed, the lessons that they now learned in establishing and funding insurgent training camps would later come to serve bin Laden well when the Taliban took over Afghanistan and encouraged him to likewise establish such bases under their auspices, as then front line journalist Mark Huband asserts:

> Arab recruitment to the Afghan mujahidin, the fighters of the jihad, was transformed when the fledgling Arab force defeated a major Soviet operation to seize a small Afghan mountain village, Jadji, in early 1986. Both bin Laden and Azzam were in the village, and with a group of fighters, they sustained a forty-five day siege by the Soviet forces, who were eventually forced to withdraw.[6]

Thenceforth, the jihadis learned that with a clearly identified, formally deployed external enemy of Islam, they could effectively apply military force, in this case, against the Russians. Thus, this curious American-directed, Saudi-funded, Pakistani-trained Islamic jihad against the Soviet "Evil Empire" dug in—and it is here that the consummate ironies of war mutate to gargantuan portions.

For it was the intelligence apparatus of one of America's foremost allies in the war on terror—headed by HRH Prince Turki al-Faisal, who later became the Saudi ambassador to the United States—that was the intermediary. It has been widely reported that Prince Turki financed the dispatch of many mujahidin, to be trained in terrorist tactics and indoctrinated with a militant combination of radical political ideology and puritanical theology by another U.S. ally, Pakistan—and then outfitted and sent to Afghanistan to fight its Russian invaders—all under the supervision of then CIA director William

Casey. It was, undeniably, a classic case of parties with ultimately conflicting ambitions joining in near-term common cause.[7]

For the Saudis, with the Russian invasion of Afghanistan coming just three weeks after the uprising at the Grand Mosque in Makkah—and coinciding with a Shi'i uprising in its Eastern Province inspired by the rise in Iran of coreligionist Ayatollah Khomeini—the timing of this jihadi cause was particularly propitious for diverting the attention of their fundamentalist core political support. In support of these activities, in fact, Shaykh 'Abd al-'Aziz bin Baz, grand mufti of Saudi Arabia, issued a *fatwa* declaring jihad in Afghanistan to be a "collective obligation" (*fard kifayah*). It was in this convoluted ideological petrie dish, then, that the political philosophies of Osama bin Laden began to coalesce. To quote one studied analysis:

> The United States had long considered Wahhabism to be an important ally in the "Great Game" then being played out against godless Communism. In fact, to solidify Saudi support, the United States took the extra step of drafting a wealthy Saudi student with ties to the royal family, Osama bin Laden, to finance and oversee the insurrection in Afghanistan.[8]

Called freedom fighters by the CIA and compared to America's founding fathers by no less than Ronald Reagan, the combined force of foreign mujahidin fighters and Afghani/Pakistani religious students not only forced the Soviet Union to depart Afghanistan, they ushered in the collapse of the Soviet Union and the end of the cold war.

Thus, this was no mere inconsequential or improvisational operation. For the grand "Afghan experiment" represented a confluence of disparate interests that traced its roots as far back as the Carter administration, when National Security Advisor Zbigniew Brzezinski proposed to Saudi Arabia to match, dollar-for-dollar, funding of an anti-Soviet counterinsurgency operation in Afghanistan. In his own words: "We are now going to have the opportunity to give the USSR its own Vietnam!"[9] Indeed, a CNN documentary showed Brzezinski delivering a speech to insurgents at the Afghani-Pakistani border exhorting them to fight for their religion, and for Allah (!). In this manner, then, Jimmy Carter, the most pacific of all American presidents, unwittingly jump-started al-Qaeda.

In Pakistan, the accession to power of the military regime of General Zia ul-Haq, which was attended by a religious backlash against the socialistic secularism of deposed President Zulfikar Ali Bhutto, lent further impetus to the rapidly burgeoning Islamic counterinsurgency operation. In the process, a $3.2 billion U.S. assistance package sanctioned by President Ronald Reagan in 1981 to empower Islamabad in pursuing its internal security interests was locally translated into achieving them by promoting instability among its neighbors—most notably Afghanistan wherein a covert effort to promote Pashtun dominance was intended to dilute recurring calls for a Pashtun state in West Pakistan. In 1984, in turn, President Reagan signed a National Security Directive calling for efforts to drive the Soviet Union from Afghanistan employing "all means available."[10]

Consequent Pakistani efforts to support Afghanistan's so-called freedom fighters coincided directly with American efforts to actively confront the Soviet invading forces through surrogates. Accordingly, when President Carter's master strategy of "punishing" American wheat farmers through grain embargoes and boycotting the 1980 Olympics failed to deter the determined encroaching Soviets, Operation Cyclone was conceived.

Pursuant to it, U.S. military aid for weapons purchases to the mujahidin—which was matched dollar-for-dollar by the Saudis pursuant to the aforesaid Brzezinski-Saudi bilateral understanding as implemented by the Reagan administration and sealed by a U.S. commitment to sell five AWACS surveillance aircraft to the Kingdom—was funneled through the Pakistani intelligence corps, Inter-Services Intelligence (ISI), which also contained elements of the indigenous *Jama'ati Islami* religious political party that followed the radical ideologies of its founder, Abu al-A'la al-Mawdudi.

Saudi aid, in turn, was channeled through preexisting relationships between the *Jama'ati Islami* and its principal religious charity, the Muslim World League, which concurrently recruited members of the Muslim Brotherhood—who supported the Islamist opposition to the Soviets—to Peshawar where the ousted Afghan parties had their joint headquarters in exile. Osama bin Laden was an early member of the contingents sent. A purpose-built conduit called *Al-Ittihad al-Islami* formally channeled the Saudi funds.[11]

In cash, between 1984 and 1986 alone, the Saudis contributed over $525 million to the Afghani resistance. In 1989, they agreed to add $436 million, or 61 percent, of a total of $715 million, with the rest coming from the United States. In all, Saudi Arabia's capital contribution matched or exceeded the $3.2 billion provided by Washington. In kind, between 250,000–300,000 Muslim volunteers—as many as 35,000 of whom were radical Islamists and 25,000 of whom were "Afghan Arabs"—a diverse forty-three–country multinational corps, the vast majority of whom were from Saudi Arabia—participated in the war, all trained by the Pakistani ISI, which provided an external operating base for the resistance as well as for its logistical support. The process, as described by the ISI's Afghan Bureau director Brigadier Muhammad Yusuf, was integrated thusly:

> The CIA's tasks in Afghanistan were to purchase arms and equipment and their transport to Pakistan; provide funds for purchasing of vehicles and transportation inside Pakistan and Afghanistan; train Pakistani instructors on new weapon systems and equipment; provide satellite maps and photographs for operational planning; provide all radio equipment and training; and advise on technical matters when requested. The entire planning of the war, all types of training for the mujahidin, and the allocation and distribution of arms and supplies were the sole responsibility of the ISI.[12]

At the height of its operation, the Afghan Bureau reportedly included 50 officers, 100 warrant officers, and 300 NCOs engaged in training more than 85,000 mujahidin in the 1984–1987 period alone.

The zealously anticommunist Reagan administration thereby bought openly into the Carter strategy as American military financial aid to the mujahidin mounted rapidly—from $30 million in 1980 to $250 million in each of 1984 and 1985 to $470 million in 1986 to $630 million in 1987. Indeed, by 1989, as noted, total aid to them had reached $3.2 billion. Among the high tech weapons provided were sniper rifles, timing devices for C-4 explosives used for urban sabotage, antitank missiles, and other sophisticated military hardware. They likewise provided the rebels with intercepted Soviet tactical intelligence and satellite reconnaissance data.[13]

In September 1986, the United States also started supplying the Afghan counterinsurgents with advanced shoulder-held, laser-guided Stinger missiles—portable, antiaircraft guided weapons with infrared seekers—the first such provisions outside of NATO. Other principal sources of U.S.-purchased weapons on behalf of the Afghani insurgents were China, Egypt, Turkey, and even the Russians' professed ally, India.[14]

Stinger missiles were a particularly inspired choice of weapon. These state-of-the-art projectiles—operationally as convenient as a crossbow—brought together Stone Age and digital technologies. So simple to deploy, in the words of one trainer, that "any near-sighted, illiterate Afghan could readily bring down millions of dollars of Soviet aircraft," they enjoyed the quite remarkable "kill rate" of 89 percent, destroying an average of one Russian plane per day. Indeed, operable by unskilled foot soldiers, they could paralyze an entire army—and soon the Afghan air force was effectively depleted.[15]

With this state-of-the-art technology, then, Afghanistan's curious collection of mujahidin—unkempt Stinger-wielding, bearded peasant freedom fighters—would ultimately force the withdrawal of the Russian Army from their country and, with it, the subsequent collapse of both the

Soviet Union and that bipolar global superpower balance that had dominated global politics for near half a century.[16]

Though Saudi Arabia and Egypt would occasionally be used as transit points for weapons flights from the United States, most such loads were transported by ship to Karachi. From there, they were transported to warehouses near Peshawar and Quetta in northwest Pakistan where that country's principal intelligence service, the ISI, would distribute them inside Afghanistan. About 75 percent of the weapons were allocated to insurgent Islamist rebels, the rest to other parties.[17]

While the requisite bank accounts were nominally controlled by the ISI, they were replenished monthly by the CIA and then used to pay for transportation, storage, and expenses of the Afghan parties. Matching Saudi funds, in turn, went directly to the seven in-country Islamist parties. In bin Laden's own words:

> To counter the infidel Russians, the Saudis chose me as their representative in Afghanistan. . . . I thus settled in Pakistan in the Afghani border region. There, I received volunteers who came from the Kingdom of Saudi Arabia and from all over the Arab and Islamic world. I then set up my first camp where these volunteers were trained by both Pakistani and American officers. The weapons were supplied by Americans, the money by the Saudis.[18]

Thus, support for the Afghani mujahidin became one of the CIA's foremost covert operations—and success stories—in the 1980s, with the Soviets formally withdrawing from the battlefield on February 15, 1989—due, in no small part, to the consummate battlefield success of America's surface-to-air Stinger missiles. As in Vietnam, a modern superpower had again been defeated in an asymmetric war—all quarterbacked by the irrepressible CIA Director William Casey and abetted by then Saudi director of intelligence, HRH Prince Turki al-Faisal—and in their wake, upon that battlefield, bin Laden's training ground operation now coalesced.[19]

UNHOLY PEACE: A CLASH OF CIVILIZATIONS

Such success, of course, lent self-validation to the Arab mujahidin insurgents, as in their own eyes, it was they and their military prowess—with the divine intervention of Allah and not their Saudi-financed, Pakistani training on precision-guided U.S. military instruments—who had brought the mighty Soviet Union down, and thereby ended the cold war. Not content with the perception that it was Washington that had won the cold war, they sought the admiration of and support of the Muslim world for their achievements in Afghanistan—convinced that it was their struggle that had defeated the invincible Red Army—thereby freeing them now to focus upon the sole remaining "infidel superpower": the decadent, capitalistic United States.[20]

Indeed, their consummate success had merely made more success all the more imperative. In the past, Muslims fighting the West could always turn to its enemies for comfort, encouragement, and aid. But now, in this altered new reality—with the demise of Soviet Russia—if al-Qaeda genuinely wanted to vanquish America, it would have to do so unilaterally. In the analysis of their doctrinal leader, Abdullah 'Azzam, speaking of the moral imperative to continue to individually pursue jihad:

> This duty will not lapse with victory in Afghanistan. The jihad will remain an *individual obligation* until all other lands which were formerly Muslim come back to us and Islam reigns in them once again. Before us lie Palestine, Lebanon, Andalusia, Bukhara, Tashkent, Chad, Eritrea, Somalia, South Yemen, the Philippines, Burma.
>
> Our presence in Afghanistan today, which is the accomplishment of the imperative of jihadi and our devotion to the struggle, in no way, means that we have forgotten Palestine. Palestine is our bleeding heart. It comes even before Afghanistan in our minds, our hearts, our feelings, and our faith.[21]

Indeed, for many expatriate Arab jihadis, returning home was not an option: they would return to ungrateful societies that did not value them particularly highly, and in which there were no real job opportunities waiting. Central to their frustrations was a genuine disconnect between the fervent rhetoric of jihad that had originally beckoned them to Afghanistan and the now grim lack of appreciation that they subsequently experienced when they concluded. Expecting to be euphorically revered as heroic vanquishers of godless communism, they were instead, when not actually deemed to be security risks, pretty much ignored.[22]

Thus, much like America's Vietnam veterans of the 1970s, they felt betrayed—and as social misfits in the world that they had left behind, began to cast about for new wars to fight. Indeed, for the Saudi Afghan jihadis, their frustration with their government intensified further still when it rejected Osama bin Laden's offer to defend the Islamic homeland against possible Iraqi incursions in 1991, opting instead to bring in foreign troops. After this rejection, bin Laden commenced his planning to relocate to the Sudan to launch an anti-Saudi campaign from there.[23]

Concomitantly, deeply disillusioned with what they perceived to be less-than-ideal, even apostate expressions of Islamic rule within their own countries, many other jihadis elected to remain in Afghanistan in the role of self-proclaimed Muslim Robin Hoods—readily taking on the infidel whether he be found within godless communism, the decadent Christian West, or in the doctrinally errant Muslim East.

After Kabul's fall to local mujahidin in April 1992, therefore, while an estimated 4,000 of these "holy warriors" remained in Afghanistan, the rest dispersed to other regions, particularly to Algeria, Sudan, Somalia, the Yemen, Saudi Arabia, Bosnia, and Kashmir.[24] Islamic scholar Gilles Kepel describes these developments thusly:

> The international brigade of jihadi veterans, being outside the control of any state, was suddenly now available to serve radical Islamist causes anywhere in the world. Since they were no longer bound by local political contingency, they had no responsibility to any social group either. They became the free electrons of jihadi professional Islamists trained to fight and to train others to do likewise.[25]

It is here, then, that bin Laden's personal agenda would take on yet another of those strange twists of fate that have symbolized his professional terrorist career. For returning home in 1989, he immediately found that his Saudi passport had been confiscated, forcing him to remain in the Kingdom until his surreptitious departure to the Sudan in 1991. While there, he witnessed the arrival of hundreds of thousands of American-led coalition troops dispatched to expel Saddam Hussein's Iraqi army from Kuwait.[26]

When his offer to engage 100,000 of his mujahidin in defense of the Islamic holy places was declined by a skeptical Saudi leadership, bin Laden was shocked and chagrined for a variety of reasons. As for him, the defense against Saddam Hussein was a battle among fellow Muslims, not between Muslims and infidels. Hence, the consequences were clear. By inviting in 540,000 American and other infidels to defend the holy places against Muslims, then, the Saudi ruling family, in his eyes, had conceded inability to defend the faith—and in so doing, had ceded its legitimacy.

Thus, the animus of bin Laden for the House of Saud, and its perceived American protectors, was born—which, in subsequence, has given birth to the evolution of al-Qaeda as a small coterie of radical neo-Wahhabis seeking to seize control from the Wahhabis themselves—thereby making the classic term Wahhabi fundamentalist and contemporary al-Qaeda jihadist not at all synonymous as oft portrayed in Western media. For while many jihadists may be, to some degree, Wahhabi, only a very small portion of Wahhabis are jihadist. As such, they are often at direct counterpurposes and even mortal enemies—with the former's objectives being:[27]

- To seize control of Islam's two most holy places: Makkah and a-Madinah;
- To then lead Islam in the reestablishment of a caliphal theocratic empire;

- To exploit the wealth of Saudi Arabia's petroleum resources to obtain weapons and secure political advantage; and
- To use the Arabian Peninsula as the launch pad for projecting global jihadist ideology.

As for bin Laden, his cause was therefore now becoming clear. America—with the vast military might of its soldiers, battle tanks, and military bases—was desecrating the sacred lands that housed Islam's most revered sanctuaries, making it an enemy that Muslims must perforce destroy. With this realization, the political destiny of the young multimillionaire construction magnate from Jiddah was forever joined with that of his Egyptian-born physician cum cleric companion, Dr. Ayman al-Zawahiri.[28]

Accordingly, departing Saudi Arabia in late 1991 on the pretext of a business trip, following a brief jaunt to Pakistan at the onset of 1992, Osama bin Laden and al-Zawahiri, his newly appointed deputy, accompanied by their families and closest followers, arrived in the Sudan where they were welcomed by Dr. Hassan al-Turabi—its de facto leader (as opposed to its nominal president, Omar Bashir) since a June 1989 coup d'état—on the condition that bin Laden would invest several hundred million dollars in the Sudan, a country then under strict boycott by many Western powers for human rights violations. In exchange, he offered open sanctuary for al-Qaeda's jihadis, a base wherein they could openly train for, and execute, their contemplated international operations.[29]

Indeed, bin Laden's 1992–1996 sojourn in the Sudan would prove to be an auspicious one, firming up his burgeoning ideological relationship with al-Zawahiri—with the former "chairman of the board" and the latter CEO of the now burgeoning al-Qaeda terrorist enterprise. Already, in their 1980s insurgency experiment in Afghanistan, they had commenced to develop a notion of global jihad which they now fine-tuned and tested during their mutual five-year exile in the Sudan—in the process, forging strong ties with counterpart jihadis in Chechnya, Tajikistan, the Philippines, Bosnia, and elsewhere.

By 1996, however, the initial warm welcome afforded to bin Laden and al-Zawahiri in the Sudan was clearly beginning to wear thin. Embarrassed by a failed attack on Egyptian president Hosni Mubarak while on travel in Ethiopia on June 26, 1995, attributed by some to them, their cash-short Sudani hosts now contemplated "selling" them to the Americans or the Saudis in the manner that they had delivered the infamous Marxist-turned-Islamist international terrorist known as Carlos the Jackal to the French authorities in the preceding year. But curiously, neither Washington nor Riyadh responded with an interest to "buy" bin Laden and his shadowy terrorist network, with the U.S. Justice Department contending that it lacked the statutory basis to charge and hold them.[30]

Hence, for political reasons that, at this writing, remain murky and complex, on May 16, 1996, after subtle pressure from the United States, bin Laden and al-Zawahiri were smuggled out of Sudan's capital, Khartoum, by private jet to Kandahar, capital of Afghanistan's "Islamic Emirate." There, fanatic young Taliban-led reformers educated within Pakistani religious schools (*madrasahs*)—wholesale supermarkets for "spiritual warriors" operating with Pakistani military support and tacit American approval—were leading a counterinsurgency that in September 1996 would wrest political control of Kabul from now corrupted erstwhile mujahidin commanders.[31]

Accordingly, learning from their successes achieved while resident in the Sudan, bin Laden and al-Zawahiri were afforded an opportunity to implement and execute their finely tuned militant theories and tactics of jihad on an even more grand scale when they returned to Afghanistan under the sponsorship of the Taliban between 1996 and 2001. For there, and in that period, the territory surrounding Kandahar would serve as the principal incubator and training center for would-be combatants throughout the Muslim world who now came specifically to train with al-Qaeda. Indeed, according to Western intelligence sources, an estimated 11,000 al-Qaeda recruits were trained in its camps in the five years up to September 11, 2001.

"Afghanistan reborn" would prove to be a brave new world for bin Laden. For in the seven years that he had been away, first in Saudi Arabia and then in the Sudan, the Taliban had done much to radically transform the country. Essentially comprised of young Afghani males who were graduates of strict Islamic schools, they were determined to convert their country into an Islamic caliphal state whose sole basis of law was the *shari'ah*—and now set out to pursue that goal with a decided vengeance. Accordingly, in areas that they seized, they installed a ruthless fundamentalist regime that rigidly enforced repressive moral standards.

With growing powerful support from the country's largest tribe, the Pashtun, the Taliban insurgency steadily progressed until, by 1994, they controlled nearly one-third of the country. Well supported in this quest, beside their heavily indoctrinated followers and al-Qaeda, they enjoyed direct support of the Pakistanis who viewed them as the only force capable of creating a stable country on their northern border, as well as the covert support of the United States who appeared to view them as a source of stability within the country.[32]

Upon his arrival in Afghanistan, bin Laden thus allied himself with the Taliban, and with his erstwhile allies in the Pakistani Inter-Services Intelligence (ISI) Agency which had backed the Taliban in their counterinsurgency to ensure the installation of a friendly government to the north and had also supported them in their final successful drive to take

Kabul in September 1996, there ostensibly to establish "God's caliphate on earth."[33]

Once settled in Afghanistan, bin Laden likewise established a close relationship with Afghanistan's new Taliban ruler, Mullah Muhammad 'Umar, whom he publicly acknowledged as commander of the faithful, titular head of the reestablished caliphal state. In response, the Taliban government afforded bin Laden a freedom to move about and conduct operations that he had never enjoyed in the Sudan.[34]

For al-Qaeda, Afghanistan thus represented a unique opportunity to seize and run a secure base. When bin Laden departed the Sudan, he needed a new place to train and initiate a campaign to establish his own caliphate. Afghanistan fit his design perfectly—as ruled by the Taliban, it would provide the sovereign territory needed to protect his operations from external attack. Hence, with the support his troops provided to the Taliban, both sides would benefit from the alliance.

Once installed, bin Laden quickly made Afghanistan the headquarters of his worldwide terror network. There, protected by a sovereign government, he increased his training of terrorists as well as planning and supporting attacks by affiliated terror groups. He likewise operated aggressive religious outreach programs that were an integral part of the training of al-Qaeda members.

Thus, al-Qaeda's grand alliance with the Taliban was spawned—creating a deadly Afghani training ground for jihadis—and though the West and moderate Islamic states have for a decade labored mightily to put the "genie of terrorism" back into its bottle, with Saudi Arabia even freezing bin Laden's assets and revoking his citizenship in 1994, as noted, it will seemingly not be rebottled. For as one astute observer of the American jihadist experiment in southwest Asia aptly, but bluntly, put it in 1994, "Once you program such people, you have to either find a way to reprogram them or kill them. There is no middle ground!"[35]

But, as subsequent analysis will reveal, the United States and her jihadi allies did neither. And thus it is today that a world has evolved that, failing to have reprogrammed al-Qaeda, is compelled to kill them—and wherein even otherwise well-meaning millions on each side of the current East-West cultural divide believe that the Christian and Muslim hemispheres are now foreordained to battle each other to an ultimate bitter end.[36]

6

How Western Jihad Created Al-Qaeda

The genius of you Americans is that you never make clear cut "stupid moves" in the Middle East; only *incredibly complicated* stupid moves that make us wonder at the possibility that we are missing something.

—Egyptian President Jamal Abdul Nasser, 1957

THE ENEMY OF MY ENEMY IS MY FRIEND

There is a famed proverb within the Arab East holding that: "The enemy of my enemy is my friend." Western governments have too often fallen into the trap of that assumption as well—in a notorious instance, failing to make a radical reprogramming of al-Qaeda an immediate policy imperative in the aftermath of the Soviet retreat.

For after the victory by the mujahidin over the Soviets, Pakistan and Afghanistan had been left together to confront residue of the war's seamy aftermath of refugees, criminal enterprises, and jihadis looking for new jobs—as parties to the erstwhile jihad took advantage of the chaotic, rapidly deteriorating circumstances to forge new alliances and coalesce into new multinationally composed "Armies of God"—now armed with automatic weapons and Stinger missiles—armies and armaments that still haunt the world today.[1]

Indeed, a semistructured, albeit half-hearted and ultimately unsuccessful, effort to deconstruct the rudimentary organization later to be known as al-Qaeda did take place following the Soviet Union's withdrawal from Afghanistan in late 1989. The initiative took on many forms; for instance, with Arabs continuing to drift to Afghanistan even after the Soviet retreat, the parties directing Operation Cyclone desperately sought ways to extricate themselves from the intricate infrastructure of logistic support that they had provided.

For its part, having achieved its primary goals, the United States rapidly lost interest and withdrew its front line physical and financial resources from Afghanistan—even attempting to buy back residual Stinger missiles from Afghani militias for as much as $400,000 each. But providing ongoing potentially lethal assistance to Afghanistan's perpetually fractious warlords, to whose diverse factions many of the incoming Arab jihadis had become attached, was likewise a function that Washington no longer wanted left to Pakistan's intelligence service, the ISI. Pakistani authorities, in turn, became more active in tracking down the Arab Afghans whom they had assisted in the 1980s. The arrest and subsequent extradition to the United States of 1993 World Trade Center bomber Ramsey Ahmad Yousef was one such example.[2]

This postwar clampdown on Arab Afghans by the Pakistani security forces—at the encouragement of Washington, London, Cairo, and other governments—was a key reason, in fact, why many chose to leave Afghanistan, relocating instead to Sudan, the Yemen, Chechnya, Bosnia, Tajikistan, Kashmir, Djakarta, and Riyadh—and London, Paris, Berlin, Madrid, and New York—to pursue their avocations there.

At the same time, Saudi intelligence commenced internal crackdowns to suppress the covert subversive activities of those jihad remnants returning to their homeland. Notwithstanding, within Afghanistan itself, covert U.S. and Saudi support continued to flow until in 1992 as yet another curious dimension to the American and Soviet governments' ongoing posturing of a "mutual symmetry of deterrence"—a zero/sum approach positing that "any good for Washington is bad for Moscow and conversely."[3]

Such on-the-ground geopolitical realities, of course, now make doubly ironic the reality that Prince Turki al-Faisal should be subjected to recurring, baseless allegations that he had some connection to terrorism when nominated two decades later, in July 2005, to be the Saudi ambassador to the United States—or that Saudi Arabia should be deemed less than a steadfast ally when terrorism has surreptitiously evolved on America's internal watch as well—or that the political activities for which it is now condemned originated at the express behest of the United States. Such are, perhaps, the occupational hazards inherent in sometimes being too good an ally.

As Prince Turki's predecessor, long time Saudi ambassador to the United States Prince Bandar bin Sultan, lamenting the notoriously ambivalent double standards that characterize the bilateral relationship, famously observed after the November 13, 1995, Saudi National Guard and June 4, 1996, al-Khobar U.S. barracks bombings:[4]

> When these things happen, you accuse us of being lax in our security. Yet when we crack down on these people, you accuse us of human rights violations.

Yet little did the West, and America in particular, discern the true dimensions of the leviathan that had been unleashed. For now, the battle lines were clearly drawn with Osama bin Laden's call for "a rain of bullets" to hasten U.S. troop removal from Saudi soil—an invocation punctuated with devastating consequence by the 1996 al-Khobar Towers barracks bombings killing nineteen American soldiers.[5]

In escalation, from his new hiding place deep within the Tora Bora Mountains of east Afghanistan, bin Laden followed two months later with his opening proclamation of jihad against the United States issued on August 23, 1996. The text, some ten pages in length, redefined his jihad as one of liberating Saudi Arabia from its would-be American protectors.[6] One and a half years later, moreover, bin Laden and al-Zawahiri broadened their call for jihad to a more global front in a London-based Arabic daily newspaper, *Al-Quds al-'Arabi*, on February 23, 1998, with a manifesto titled "Declaration of the World Islamic Front for Jihad against the Jews and the Crusaders."

According to the newspaper, it was faxed to them above the purported signatures of bin Laden and leaders of allied jihadi groups within Egypt, Pakistan, and Bangladesh. Curiously making no reference to al-Qaeda, the document called for the "killing of Americans and Jews wherever they may be found."[7] Commencing with a lengthy exordium that invoked a multitude of Qur'anic verses, it asserted:

> Since Allah created the Arabian Peninsula, laid out its deserts, and surrounded it with seas, no calamity has ever befallen it like these Crusader hosts that have spread over it like locusts, crowding its soil, eating its good fruits, and destroying its verdure.[8]

It proceeded by defining manifest challenges posed by the invasion and prescribing their remedy, stipulating that:

> *First*, for over seven years, the United States has now occupied the land of Islam in the holiest of its territories—Arabia—plundering its riches, overwhelming its rulers, humiliating its people, threatening its neighbors, and using its bases on the peninsula as a spearhead to fight against neighboring Arab peoples.

Though some in the past have disputed the true nature of this occupation, the people of Arabia in their entirety now recognize it. There is no greater proof of this than in the continuing American aggression against the Iraqi people, launched from Arabia despite its rulers who oppose the use of their lands for this purpose but are subjugated.

Second, despite the immense destruction inflicted upon the Iraqi people at the hands of their Crusader-Jewish alliance, and despite the appalling numbers of dead now exceeding a million, the Americans, despite all this, are trying once again to repeat this terrible slaughter.

It seems that Iraq's prolonged blockade following the war and its dismemberment and destruction are not enough for them. So they now come again to destroy what remains of this people and to humiliate their Muslim neighbors.

Third, while purposes of the Americans in these wars are both religious and economic, they also serve the petty state of the Jews to divert attention from their occupation of Jerusalem and their killing of Muslims in it.

There is no better proof in all of this than in their desire to destroy Iraq, strongest of the neighboring Arab states, and their attempt to dismember all of states of the region including Iraq, Saudi Arabia, and the Sudan, into sundry petty states whose division and weakness will ensure the survival of Israel and continuation of their calamitous occupation of Arab lands.[9]

Charging that these crimes thus represented "a clear declaration by America of war against Allah, His Prophet, and all Muslims," making jihad incumbent upon all of them, it concluded that:

In compliance with Allah's order, therefore, we issue the following fatwa to all Muslims: this ruling—to kill the Americans and their allies—civilians and military—is an *individual duty* for every Muslim who can do it, in any country in which it is possible to do it, to liberate al–Aqsa Mosque [in Jerusalem] and the holy mosque [at Makkah] from their grip, and in order for their armies to move out of the lands of Islam. . . .

This is in accordance with the words of Almighty Allah to "fight the pagans all together as they now fight you," and to "fight against them until there is no more tumult and oppression, and there prevails justice and faith in Allah."[10]

In this 1998 *fatwa*, then, bin Laden presented four principal grievances against the United States:

1. That it is solely responsible for its invasion of the Arabian Peninsula and the plundering of its wealth;
2. That Saudi Arabia was a mere "staging ground" for an aggression which its rulers were powerless to resist;
3. That working in tandem with Israel, it has inflicted great devastation upon the Iraqi people; and

4. That it has only done so to divert world attention away from the fate of Jerusalem and the plight of the Palestinian people being wrought daily at the hands of Jews.[11]

Hence, for bin Laden, his declaration of war against the United States marked no less than the resumption of Islam's struggle for world dominance that had commenced in the seventh century—and now stood as a golden opportunity for the faith's redemption.

For America, like ancient Rome and Byzantium before it, to bin Laden epitomizes the modern day leadership of the House of War. It is decadent—and as such, is both deserving of, and ripe for, overthrow. In so doing, he invokes a timeless anti-Islamic American-Zionist conspiracy theory worthy of Sayyid Qutb from a half century before. For in his stated view: "Pushing out this occupying American enemy is our most important obligation after our belief in Allah."[12]

In the process, the concept of jihad thus has been semantically transformed in bin Laden's eyes from one of effort or struggle to that of violence. For irrespective of all explicit, clearly defined classic Islamic prohibitions against collateral damage to noncombatants in jihad, he seeks to destroy the United States civilian-wise, militarily, and financially.

Indeed, for him, such mayhem is not collateral damage at all—because the United States Constitution proclaims a government "for and by the people." Hence, all Americans are, as her citizens, by definition, in his eyes implicated—and no one is to be spared because all are actively engaged by statutory inclusion in this cosmic clash of good and evil, as he vividly makes clear:

> The American people are the ones who pay the taxes which fund the planes that bomb us in Afghanistan, the tanks that destroy our homes in Palestine, the armies that occupy our lands in the Arabian Gulf, and the fleets that ensure the blockade of Iraq. Their tax dollars are given to Israel for it to continue to attack us and penetrate our lands. So the American people are the ones who fund the attacks against us, and they are the ones who oversee the expenditure of these monies in any way they wish through the candidates whom they elect.[13]

In his own words in invoking the need for a more global type of jihad in a post-9/11 world, in turn, he continues:

> These events have divided the entire planet into two parts: the side of the believers and the side of the infidels . . . and every Muslim must now rush to make his faith victorious.[14]

The specific triggers now invoking such recourse—

- America's occupation of Saudi Arabia during the Gulf War; and thereby, by implication;
- Its deprecation of Islam's holy places in violation of Caliph 'Umar b. al-Khatab's mid-seventh century "edict of 641 A.D." that they not be defiled by the presence of infidels[15]

—are predicted upon traditions attributed to Prophet Muhammad that there:

> "not be two religions in Arabia" and that "Christians and Jews be expelled from the Arabian Peninsula so that only Muslims live there"; and
> America's continuing use of Arabia as a staging ground for launching attacks upon Baghdad—seat of the Islamic caliphate for more than a half a glorious millennium wherein the religion had recorded many of its most magnificent achievements—and therefore, after Makkah, al-Madinah, and Jerusalem, also a most holy of places for the faithful.[16]

This stentorian proclamation, in turn, was followed in November 2002 by an open "Letter to America" posted on the Internet wherein bin Laden purports to enumerate the country's "manifest sins" and articulates seven principal demands. To wit, it must immediately:

- cease its "oppression, lies, immorality, and debauchery";
- admit that it is "a nation without principle or manners";
- withdraw support for Israel in Palestine, India in Kashmir, Russia in Chechnya, and the Manila government against Muslim rebels in the southern Philippines;
- desist in its support of Israel;
- end its commitment to corrupt leaders in Muslim countries and Muslim lands;
- withdraw support for UN sanctions on Iraq; and
- evacuate at once from all its present Muslim-occupied lands.[17]

These actions must be taken, it advises, so that America "does not force us to send you back to your homeland as cargo in coffins."

Lest there be residual doubt as to al-Qaeda's ultimate motives or intent, they were effectively dispelled in a strident memorandum justifying its attacks on its "faraway enemy," the United States, on September 11, 2001, issued in mid-December 2001 in the name of Osama bin Laden's mentor-successor to Abdullah 'Azzam, Ayman al-Zawahiri titled, *Knights Under the Prophet's Banner.*[18]

Al-Zawahiri's global view was clearly grandiose—interpreting the consummate success of al-Qaeda's jihad against the Soviets as a reenactment of the opening salvo of the nascent Islamic Empire's dramatic seventh century irruption from the Arabian Peninsula—the Battle of Ctesiphon in 637 wherein the embryonic Muslim army—"knights under the Prophet's banner"—utterly destroyed the longstanding ancient Persian Sasanid Empire before then focusing its attention on Byzantium.

Al-Qaeda's new project thus was to be a fulfillment of divine revelation—made manifest in the lifetime of Prophet Muhammad and his four immediate successors, the Orthodox Caliphs, in the four decades between 621 and 661, the Golden Age of Islamic Conquest. Since then, in the global view articulated by al-Zawahiri, the debauchery of the world has divided itself into two distinct, undesirable parts—backsliding Muslim-ruled states operating within the *Dar al-Islam* and corresponding corrupt and decadent unbelievers presiding over the *Dar al-Harb*.

This, then, was the inevitable outcome of the Islamic jihad initiated in South Asia by President Jimmy Carter and National Security Advisor Zbigniew Brzezinski in the 1970s, as executed by the CIA-led indomitable William Casey in the 1980s. Like their glorious ancestors, Afghanistan's jihadis had tangible reason to believe that they proceeded with divine blessing. Having brought down the Russian "godless superpower," as noted, their mandate now became to similarly topple the remaining decadent one.

With this master vision, then, the ragtag radical mujahidin now gathered around Kandahar sought to replicate the original winning political paradigm incarnated in their Prophet's lifetime—taking on, without discrimination, both infidel foreign nations and deemed apostate Muslim states.[19] To these ends, in his missive, al-Zawahiri argued compellingly that the movement needed a decisive strike to galvanize undecided Muslims into support by convincing them that it had become an irresistibly powerful force arrayed in mortal combat against a decadent and ever-weakening superpower that was aligned with, and protected, apostate governments within the Dar al-Islam.

Al-Qaeda's strategy, therefore, must be to strengthen its grip upon coreligionists by co-opting their support for the requisite armed struggle to create a countervailing Islamic empire. In his own words, in invoking the Qur'anic prescription to fight the enemy at its distant borders:

> The masters in Washington and Tel Aviv are using the regimes to protect their interests and to fight the battle against the Muslims on their behalf. But if the shrapnel from the battle reach their homes and their bodies, they will trade accusations with their agents about who is actually responsible for this.
>
> In that case, they will face one of two bitter choices: either to personally wage war against the Muslims, which means the battle will turn into clear-cut jihad against the infidels, or they will reconsider their plan after

acknowledging the failure of their brute and violent confrontation against the Muslims.

Therefore, we must now move the battle to the enemy's ground to burn the hands of those who ignite fire in our land.[20]

With this sequence of manifestos, then, the battle lines were indelibly drawn, and the tragedy of September 11, 2001—soon to be followed by those of Madrid and London—clearly could not be far behind. In the process was likewise set in motion a Washington-generated chain reaction of apocalyptic proportions, as the terror masters of al-Qaeda today periodically reemerge from the far wastelands of the Pakistan-Afghani border in *diabolos ex machina* mode to claim more victims still.

Al-Qaeda—the illegitimate birth child of Western-inspired jihad, nurtured by Egypt's Muslim Brotherhood as midwife, a threat now both mortal and global—pursues a lethal course in defiance of the whole of civilized mores as the world has come to know them and utterly without appreciation for the value of human life. That it was perhaps unwitting and inadvertent since the $3.2 billion in 1980s U.S. aid was targeted to aid Afghanistan's mujahidin in general and not its Arab-Afghani component in particular, and since al-Qaeda and its allies fervently deny any direct CIA connection, does not erase the devastating consequence.

Forewarned being forearmed, then, the West today painfully knows that the tranquil 1990s interlude between a longstanding cold war and a new War on Terror has ended. Because of an ostrichlike lack of foresight and political understanding, an age with stark new political realities has begun. To quote that famed character of the cartoon page, Pogo:

We have met the enemy . . . and it is us![21]

BUT THE ENEMY OF MY ENEMY
IS NOT INVARIABLY MY FRIEND

Yet the American diplomatic machine, and the CIA in particular, should have known better—having benefited from lengthy hindsight. Instead, it missed entirely the lesson offered by its British counterpart MI6 a half century before. As then, a perceived symbiotic relationship with Egypt's Muslim Brotherhood lent substance to the formation and evolution of the first so-called Islamic terrorist group global in its vision and regional in its outreach.

London's relationship with the Muslim Brotherhood was complex. Hassan al-Banna's autobiography indicates that it was established in

March 1928, in part, with a 500 pounds sterling grant from England's Suez Canal Company, used to create its first mosque which would serve as its headquarters and base of operations in Isma'iliyah at the northern end of the canal, according to the foremost Western expert on the organization, Richard Mitchell.[22]

Despite an outward semblance of hostilities between the Brotherhood and the British, however, this sub-rosa relationship would nonetheless continue on a variety of fronts. With the impending threat of Nazism at the onset of World War II in 1941, for instance, al-Banna would meet with operatives of the British Embassy in Cairo whereat further contributions from the Exchequer were pledged.[23]

Indeed, Egypt's royal court of King Farouk, MI6, and British diplomats in the second quarter of the twentieth century, from 1928 to 1956, would assiduously court Hassan al-Banna's subterranean organization as an Islamic political counterbalance first to confront Egypt's Wafd Party nationalistic, and later latent communistic, proclivities, including the Free Officers Movement of Colonel Jamal Abdul Nasser. In Mitchell's words:

> For the moment, the palace, the conservative heads of government and the Muslim Brotherhood shared common foes: communism and the Wafd. . . .
>
> In 1944, the secret apparatus also began to infiltrate the communist movement which during the war had taken on new life and which the Muslim Brotherhood considered to be one of their principal enemies. . . .
>
> The "intelligence" of the Society passed on information useful to the government in its continual roundup of real and suspected communists, especially in labor and university circles.[24]

To better position itself politically, the organization moved its operations to Cairo in 1932. With al-Banna promulgating the pan-Islamism of Jamal al-Din al-Afghani, Muhammad 'Abduh, and Rashid Rida, the global enterprise that would give birth to the Islamic political right—including its modern terrorist elements—thus was born. Organized into cells of five to seven members, to qualify for membership, its ranks would undergo doctrinal and guerilla warfare training often funded by the Arab governments themselves.[25]

Yet, though the British were aware of the Muslim Brotherhood's evocative political appeal, and though its underground paramilitary wing sometimes duplicitously turned against them, London was not at all hesitant to employ its services when it suited its political designs. Indeed, its Embassy, and later the American Embassy, in Cairo both maintained regular contact with it.[26]

The Arab-Jewish War of 1948 greatly strengthened the Brotherhood's base. The defeat of formal Arab armies by Jewish paramilitary units, and the creation of its own paramilitary units which—like the Afghani Arab ji-hadists' 1980s insurgency against the Soviets in Afghanistan—comported themselves respectably in the war efforts, not only discrediting the traditional Arab regimes but creating sizable cadres of seasoned guerilla veterans while adding for itself a new imprimatur of legitimacy as both a political and paramilitary organization—the propaganda value of which it did not hesitate to exploit throughout the Islamic world.[27]

Meanwhile, the United States, too, came to increasingly look to Political Islam in countervailing terms vis-à-vis a perceived rising threat of global communism. Indeed, as early as 1945, strategic planners began to incorporate a role for Muslims in their planning to contain the Soviet Union at its southern border. Among such efforts, the CIA reportedly replicated sundry tracts antithetic to Islam that were attributed to the Soviet embassy in Cairo, while also attempting to develop and identify a "Muslim Billy Graham" to evangelize anticommunist sentiments within the Islamic world.[28]

In this quest, they were buttressed by several prominent orientalists. Among them, Bernard Lewis—then at the University of London, now at Princeton—in a 1953 essay titled: "Islam and Communism," maintained:

> Communism is not, and can never be, a religion, while Islam, for its great mass of believers, still is; and that is the core of Islamic resistance to Communist ideas. . . .
> Pious Muslims—and most Muslims are pious—will not tolerate an atheist creed that violates their traditional moral principles.[29]

Kenneth Cragg, editor of *The Muslim World*, in 1954 would similarly add:

> We in religious resistance to communism understand that the Muslim world must develop an intellectual response to the challenge of communism on a level that is spiritual, metaphysical, and moral in order to combat the Marxist eschatology that looks forward to a communist Heaven on earth.[30]

Prominent Arab leaders chimed in to support the mounting anticommunist crusade as well. As reported in 1951 by Colonel William Eddy, a senior U.S. embassy consular officer in Saudi Arabia:

> While in an audience with the King of Saudi Arabia, Abdul Aziz al-Saud, the King addressed himself strongly to the same point. He affirmed that both Christianity and Islam are threatened by communism, their common enemy. . . . Muslims in the East, and Christians in the West, therefore, should be allies in this effort to defend their historic faith.[31]

It was in this context of surging anticommunist sentiment, then, that mid twentieth-century America deployed the tool of political Islam from within her diplomatic workbox. The successful CIA–MI6 orchestrated 1953 coup d'état—executed in league with Iranian clergy and street-rabble-rousing Muslim fundamentalists—against that country's prime minister Mohammed Mossadegh, would be the first salvo in the campaign. And while the shah was ultimately restored to the Peacock Throne, as a byproduct, political Islam was reignited—paving the way for the ascendance to power of the fervidly anti-Western Ayatollah Ruhollah Khomeini in 1978.[32]

In 1973, Anwar Sadat's initial success crossing the Suez Canal in his brief Ramadan War against the Israelis, ostentatiously figuratively fought under an Islamic banner, likewise led to a revival in the interests of the Muslim Brotherhood in Egypt. Yet, though a dangerous current in its own right and despite—

- the rise of the ayatollahs and the takeover of the U.S. Embassy in Iran and the insurgent occupation of Makkah's Grand Mosque in 1979;
- Islamic Jihad's assassination of Anwar Sadat in 1981 and Hezbollah's bomb-killing of 241 U.S. marines in 1983;
- the Muslim Brotherhood's successful spin-off of its Hamas affiliate with active Israeli assistance in 1987 as a counterweight to the PLO; and
- Israel's general courting of fundamentalist Islam in their engagement in Palestine

—Eastern and Western intelligence alike persisted in their infatuation with the Islamic political right.[33]

Yet the past seven-decades-long history of Western-wielding of the double-edged sword of political Islam proves that this can be a precarious, even lethal, course. Presiding analysis has documented how the arrival in Saudi Arabia of displaced elements of Egypt's Muslim Brotherhood in the second half of the twentieth century created a milieu propitious for al-Qaeda to be spawned—as well as the CIA's debacle of both training and arming it through its $3.2 billion "experimental jihad" against the Soviet Union in Afghanistan in the 1980s.

For electing the "Muslim option" on "the Great Chessboard," as Brzezinski described his ill-advised and ill-fated "arc of Islam" incursion into Central Asia in the late 1970s, can produce seemingly initially innocuous, but ultimately deadly, knights and pawns. As in discerning friend from foe within the disparate region can involve tough choices, as many options must be preserved and factored in. To quote Winston Churchill in 1944:

> Were Adolph Hitler to invade Hell, I would at least make friendly reference to the Devil in the House of Commons.[34]

America's subsequent support of the ascendancy to power of the Taliban in that same country in the 1990s to provide a secure base for al-Qaeda global terrorist operations leading up to 9/11 likewise further proves either (1) that there have been few lessons learned in the conduct of her half century of Middle East "cowboy diplomacy"; or (2) that the region has too many "moving parts" for prepackaged political solutions; or (3), that irrespective of locale, two wrongs still don't make a right. Indeed, the level of political naiveté that then prevailed was well articulated by a contemporary State Department official in asserting that:

> The Taliban will probably develop like the Saudis. There will be Aramco, pipelines, an emir, no parliament, and lots of *shari'ah* law. We can live with that.[35]

Yet in the post-9/11 world, the American Middle East policy course has become more enigmatic still. Bringing democracy to Iraq has been used as the *raison de guerre* for bringing down the regime of Saddam Hussein in its ongoing war on terror against the so-called Axis of Evil—Iraq, Iran, and North Korea. But once again, the challenge has not been so simple and has reverted yet again to the quest for more effective means of discerning friend from foe.

As paradoxically, Hussein was a determined *anti-Islamist* diametrically and irrevocably opposed to America's avowed regional enemies—the types of Shi'i theocratic governments that replaced him and in Hezbollah, that aspire to replace the democratically elected government of Lebanon and elsewhere—and that are concurrently implicitly aligned with the radical regime ruling Iran, a place where al-Qaeda insurgents are often given succor and refuge.

Indeed, Muslim anger at the 2003 U.S. invasion of Iraq itself could well create multiple waves of new jihadists for such antiterror U.S. allies within the region as Pakistan, Saudi Arabia, and Egypt that could even bring them down, as Western powers attempting to sort through the inscrutable political enigmas of the Middle East again constantly continue to revalidate the cogency of President John F. Kennedy's insightful admonition that "those who would ride the back of the tiger too often instead wind up inside."[36]

For in sum, original sources unequivocally prove that it was the impetus and funding provided by MI6 that led to creation of the Muslim Brotherhood in Egypt in 1928, an organization that, after its attempted assassination of President Nasser in 1954, took refuge in western Saudi Arabia where it won disenfranchised converts among its Wahhabi movement, who, in the mid-1980s, would flock to Afghanistan to participate in the American inspired, Pakistani-trained, and CIA-Saudi funded jihad against the Russian invasion of that country, creating the operating milieu wherein al-Qaeda was spawned and now threatens to bring down Western interests throughout the region.

Irrespective of the ultimate outcome, however, a series of interlinked political-military events unfolding within the Middle East over the course of the past half-century, at the least, stands in emphatic affirmation of Egyptian President Nasser's aforesaid prescient observation made as early as 1957:

> The genius of you Americans is that you never make clear cut "stupid moves" in the Middle East; only *incredibly complicated* stupid moves that make us wonder at the possibility that we are missing something.[37]

7

Is Western Democracy the Answer?

Democracy is a form of government that substitutes election by the incompetent many for appointment by the corrupt few.

—George Bernard Shaw

REFLECTIONS ON THE PORTABILITY OF ANGLO-AMERICAN DEMOCRACY

The politics of terror have broad branches that stem from deeply set economic roots. Both its political and economic dimensions are explored in the next two chapters. Commencing with its political extensions, inquiry begins by asking: Are democracy and Islam compatible? Is democracy an answer for the Middle East? Is it a viable antidote to terror? Is it, in its Anglo-American form, exportable unbundled to the world?

In early March 2004, before the death of Ronald Reagan—with Iraq moving toward its June 30 target date for self-governance, yet its security situation rapidly unwinding amidst mounting counterinsurgency and sectarian unrest—the author of this inquiry, in the satiric spirit of Jonathan Swift, penned the following tongue-in-cheek "modest proposal" addressed to the folly of "playing God" in deploying "democracy" as a prime tool of foreign policy ambition:

Iraq: Is Democracy the Answer?

It is today unfortunate that time has deprived the world of diplomacy of the vision and wisdom of Ronald Reagan. For there can be little doubt that were he still president, sometime on the evening of June 30, a C-130 would appear high above the "green zone" of Baghdad—and out would parachute Bud McFarlane and Oliver North bearing a cake, a Bible, working copies of the Constitution, the Federalist Papers, the Federal Register—authenticated copies of the Miami Dade County "butterfly ballot"—and a letter from Ronnie welcoming the Iraqis to the ranks of freedom-loving democratic peoples everywhere, whereupon . . . America would precipitously pull out!

But what about the vexing issue of leaving a stable working government in place? That too is readily resolvable by precedent. Appoint Dick Cheney to head the search committee to pick the next president of Iraq, an inspired choice who, after great mental angst and appropriate due diligence, would again doubtless conclude that only he was qualified to lead Iraq in this most critical of times—thereby giving America the *capo di tutti capi* needed to deal with the warlords of Iraq—while concurrently freeing up the vice presidential slot in the forthcoming November 2004 election for Rudy Giuliani, wherein, if Republicans can put New York into play by forcing a contest for its thirty-one electoral votes—there is no way the Democrats can get from here to there!

Absurd? Of course! But is it more absurd than present initiatives aimed at nation building in the Middle East? Is it more inane than to now attempt to reweld together with the solder of democracy three historic warring factions, Sunnis, Shi'is, and Kurds—first forged into an artificial "Iraqi" amalgam framed by the Sykes-Picot Agreement of 1916 as sanctified by the machinations of Britain's irrepressible Gertrude Bell in 1920—into a cobbled-up federal coalition wherein they co-govern, yet when they have no apparent desire or intent to do so, as the present groundswell of ongoing tragic carnage demonstrates. A noble aspiration, to be sure—but one that equally ignores doctrinal, historic, and real-time, on-the-ground realities, as a January 2007 National Intelligence Council "National Security Estimate" concludes:

> Even if violence is diminished, given the current winner-take-all attitude and sectarian animosities infecting the political scene, Iraqi leaders will be hard pressed to achieve sustained political reconciliation in the (18 month) time frame of this Estimate.[1]

Democracy is a precious, yet delicate, flower. Its provision of power—its source of moral suasion—lies in the notion that a nation's citizens are sovereign and that they exercise their sovereignty by electing "representatives." In a democracy, the people are the source of law—and that law, in turn, preserves those fundamental rights that protect the well-being of the sovereignty's individual members. For Islam, democracy thus poses formidable challenges, as theological historian Khalid Abu al-Fadl asserts:

> Many Muslim jurists have argued that law made by a sovereign monarch is illegitimate because it substitutes human authority for God's sovereignty. But law made by sovereign citizens faces the same problem of legitimacy.
>
> Within Islam, God is the only sovereign, and the ultimate source of legitimate law. How, then, can any democratic conception of the people's authority be reconciled with an Islamic understanding of God's authority?[2]

Many eminent Islamists believe that it cannot. Bernard Lewis contends that the cultures of Islam and democracy are fundamentally incongruent and that the choice that faces Muslims in the twenty-first century is between modernization and fanaticism; whereas economist Leonard Binder refers to "clusters of absence" within Islam that account for a "liberal democratic deficit" in many modern Muslim countries. To wit: the absence of a concept of liberty, the absence of a middle class, and the absence of autonomous governing institutions.[3]

The key question thus becomes: Is the amalgamated phrase "Islamic democracy" itself an oxymoron? As therein lies the latent inherent contradiction vis-à-vis the specific manner in which Islamic governance has historically evolved, creating new challenges that confront numerous incontrovertible realities. Foremost among them is the issue of what they posit for building that "modern governance with the consent of the governed" to which Islam and the West equally aspire—although with each viewing the range of potential solutions through slightly different prisms.

This is a conundrum that must be carefully contemplated. For today, while there is indeed a tendency to view unbundled Anglo-American democracy as a political paradigm aspired to, and usable, by all, there remain critical questions as to whether it is exportable to other cultures. Japan tried it, of course, but ultimately had to develop its own adaptation; it didn't succeed in Vietnam either; and it certainly didn't work within the erstwhile Soviet Union, giving birth to the Russian mafia whose only accomplishment has been to kill off the Sicilian mafia instead. When it comes to governance, therefore, it may well be that "one size does not fit all," as democracy is not, as some presume, a "natural and normal condition of all mankind."

The strains of this stark reality, in fact, run deep throughout the fabric of the Anglo-American democratic capitalistic experiment. To wit: it lacks portability, indeed manifesting an inexportability that defies ready remedy and belies Winston Churchill's keen insight that it is "the worst form of governance except for all the rest." As such, America cannot be the engine of democratic reform in the Middle East. It cannot transplant its concept of society to other nations—no matter how good its intentions or how strong its will. Top-down "do-gooding" and "trying harder" will not work, as indigenous institution building is a prerogative and right of those who live there.

The lessons learned: The United States cannot be the moral exemplar to Islamic world—nor to the world at large—nor should she aspire to be. For though the seeds of democracy were sown in ancient Greece and throughout history have reflected the evolutionary intellectual patrimony of all mankind, they flowered first in modern form in the West and it is upon U.S. soil that they have fully sprouted and taken root. Precisely for this reason, then, only within America is American democracy possible, for it cannot be isolated from America's traditions and her values.

Among other lessons learned: Democratization is the outcome of a process of acculturation. America cannot thus hope, or expect, to successfully airdrop working copies of the Federalist Papers, the Federal Register, and the Constitution—together with an acknowledgment from its president welcoming presumably eager Middle East peoples to the ranks of democratic nations—and anticipate pacific polling places to spring up in their wake. To succeed, Western-style institution building, if deemed desirable, must come first. To expect otherwise presumes a cultural arrogance that fails to comport with on-the-ground realities.

Small wonder, then, that the American democratic model has until now proven to be inexportable to Iraq. Small wonder that it has failed to produce a cohesive government as of yet. James Madison, meet Muqtada al-Sadr. . . . Thomas Jefferson meet Abu Mus'ab al-Zarqawi!

While to Western observers, then, the "problem with Islam" may appear to be a noticeable paucity of freedoms—freedom to inquire, freedom from indoctrination and constraint, freedom from pervasive economic corruption and mismanagement—therefore, the reality is that the road to the liberating democracy that they put forth as a panacea comes strewn with pitfalls, both ideological and institutional.[4]

Hence, the cherished dream of establishing "Islamic democracy" in a Western sense throughout the Arab East carries with it inherent irresolvable contradictions. For when Western politicians speak fondly of bringing democracy to the region, it is clearly a Western secular brand of democracy that they contemplate and intend, and not an indigenous Islamic one. As modern Islamic theorist Reza Aslan asserts:

> At the center of the debate over Islam and democracy is a significant struggle over who actually gets to define the Islamic Reformation that is today already underway in most of the Muslim world.[5]

The watershed question thus becomes: Can the principles of Western democracy be reconciled with traditional fundamental Islamic values?'

If they can, it will arise phoenix-like from the foundations of its unique religious mode. For unlike Catholicism, Islam does not have a pope—a single individual wherein reposes all responsibility for doctrinal conformity. There are no lords spiritual—no bishops, cardinals, synods, councils, or ecclesiastic courts. There are no Cardinal Richelieus. The state is church and church is state—with Allah the head of both and Prophet Muhammad and his caliphal successors His regents and earthly representatives.[6]

Indeed, the inherent difficulty with all such Christian-to-Islamic analogies lies at the fount from which all sources of reform flow and is an intra-Christian problem as well as an interreligious one. On the one hand, medieval Catholicism suppressed intellectual exegesis. It discouraged individual readings of the Bible lest they be misinterpreted. For that reason, God's revelations for man were preserved and presented to the masses largely in uncomprehendible Latin. As a consequence, the Church doctrine for centuries remained critically unexamined and in exegetic stasis.

On the other hand, Protestants do read the Bible—a reality that rendered Europe's Reformation intrinsically a protestant affair. They share a common symbolic set of unique politically activist religious tenets at work within a Christian culture. They can do exegesis. They can criticize the scriptures. They can criticize doctrine. They can be introspective. Thus, no one can accuse them of being "tools of foreign agents" seeking to undermine cause and creed.

Most Muslims, on the contrary, dwell within a different context. They more resemble Catholics in that they look to their "learned ones" (*fuqaha'*) for spiritual enlightenment. The Qur'an is inviolate. As God's creation and hence divine, it cannot be subjected to scholarly debate or constitutional exegesis in a critical sense—only top-down explanation and mass memorization. Though not an entirely homogenous civilization, then, Muslims are nonetheless enjoined against full freedom of expression and expected to conform to doctrine based on faith alone. Failing that, they are susceptible to the danger of being accused of being apostates or "importers of alien ideas." And therein lies the dilemma of democracy in the Islamic East.[7]

IS A "CONSULTATIVE DEMOCRACY" THE ANSWER?

All of these issues—a combination Mosque-State theocratic symbiosis harboring an intellectual environment wherein free thinking and debate are not open practices and are indulged at a premium at best—albeit wherein, certain modern Muslim countries have succeeded adapting and adopting certain functional democratic permutations. For Islam, as a doctrine per se, does not codify formal legal structure. It enjoys no legacy of administrative infrastructure, no case precedent, or apart from Prophetic Tradition, no common law.[8]

Rather, its ideological adaptation is a constant consensual process that synthesizes contributions of various fatawa derived from exegesis of the Qur'an and Prophetic Tradition into a rationale whole. It is to this extent, at least, paradoxically not unlike modern free market Protestantism wherein individual ministers may create their own interpretations of scripture within the confines of their own churches. Accordingly, it has evolved ad hoc in a paradoxical consensual way, as described by the renowned medieval Islamic jurist Ibn Qutaybah:

> Islam, the ruler, and the people are like the tent, the pole, the ropes, and the pegs. The tent is Islam, the pole is the ruler, and the ropes and pegs are the people. None can thrive without the others.[9]

Islam's rules for governance founded upon justice and the rule of law, as noted, are both explicit and Qur'anically prescribed. Its prescriptions are the evolutionary result of an ideological tripod buttressed equally by—

1. justice through popular cooperation;
2. decision making via consultation; and
3. justice applied with compassion

—all administered in a manner consistent with the dictates of a theocratic state as indicated in table 7.1:

These precepts are likewise clearly evident in the historic preconditions for accession to leadership of the ummah in that early on, in a precedent attributed to the renowned jurist Malik b. Anas, a modicum of representative governance was established on the condition that the leader selected—in that case, the caliph, currently the *amir*—is to be confirmed in the posting by the tribal elders through a postselection "pledge of allegiance" *(bay'ah/mubay'ah)* process conditioning that:

- To be legitimate, government must enjoy the consent of the governed, with such consent a binding contract between the ruler and the ruled;
- Such consent of the governed must be consensual and not coerced or obtained under duress; it can be abrogated for nonperformance; and

Table 7.1. Doctrinal Precepts Ensuing Equity in Islamic Economic Governance

Precept:	*Stipulation:*	*Verse:*
decision making via consultation	So pardon them and ask Allah's forgiveness for them and consult with them upon the conduct of affairs.	Surat al-Shura 3:159
	Those who harken to their Lord and establish regular prayer, conduct their affairs by mutual consultation; who spend out of what We bestow on them for sustenance.	Surat Al-i 'Imran 42:38
	And we sent not as Our Messengers other than men whom we inspired. Ask the people of the previous Scriptures if you know not.	Surat al-Anbiya' 21:17
justice through cooperation	We have created you male and female and have made you nations and tribes that you may know one another.	Surat al-Hujurat 49:13
	And if your Lord had willed, He verily would have made of you one nation	Surat Hud 11:119
justice applied with compassion	Your Lord has prescribed for Himself mercy that whosoever of you does evil through ignorance and repents afterward thereof and does right, for Him. Lo! Allah is Forgiving, Merciful!	Surat al-An'am 6:54
	He has prescribed for Himself mercy so that He may bring you altogether for a Day whereof there is no doubt.	Surat al-An'am 6:12
	This Qur'an . . . is a guidance and a mercy for believers. Lo! Your Lord will judge between them of His wisdom.	Surat al-Naml 27:77
	This is a clear indication for people, a guidance and a mercy for a folk whose faith is sure.	Surat al-Jathiyah 45:20

Note: On this, see K. Abu al-Fadl 2004, pp. 5 ff.

- The ruler must remain faithful to divine prescriptions for governance. Should he fail to do so, then those committed to fidelity through their act of *mubay'ah* are released from their obligation.[10]

Pursuant to Islamic law, at least as defined by Sunni jurists, therefore, there is explicit mutual agreement between the governor and the governed. The ruler presides pursuant to a social contract between him and those enfranchised with the power to contract (*ahl al-hall wa al-'aqd*) who pledge their fealty to the ruler in exchange for his promise to govern in accordance with the explicit terms of that contract.[11]

Who are these *ahl al-hall wa al-'aqd*? Juridical consensus is that they are those who possess the political power (*shawkah*) to ensure the compliance of the ruler and obedience of the public, that there thus must be a general consensus over each ruler, and that each individual must therefore give his consent. In this context, therefore, the weekly public session of the ruler (*majlis*) wherein issues are discussed and grievances are presented is the "ballot box." This is *Islamic democracy*—the Eastern variant—that must be incorporated into any realistic aspirations for the spread of "democratic capitalism" throughout the region.[12]

Indeed, there is a constitutional model established by Prophet Muhammad himself for laying the legal foundations for an Islamic democracy. For soon after migrating from Makkah to Yathrib (al-Madinah) in 622, he established the first Islamic state predicated upon a tripartite compact negotiated among those Muslim immigrants who had accompanied him from Makkah, indigenous Muslims of al-Madinah, and local Jews—a pact that established a federation of communities fully vested equally in rights and duties.[13]

So does the coalescing of these realities then mean that Islam and democracy are incompatible? To address this question, it is, at the onset, critical to bear in mind that all religions and their scriptures—Jews and the Old Testament, Christians and the New Testament, Islam and the Qur'an—have alike been used to justify monarchies (or caliphates) and elitist feudalism in the medieval past as well as democracy and capitalism in the present.

Thus, for all, it must be understood that while sovereignty may belong exclusively to God, to make it work, throughout history, it has invariably been delegated to human agency. Indeed, it is this defining difference between sovereignty in principle (de jure) and sovereignty in fact (de facto) that to effectively function on earth must perforce be executed by humans whether within a secular or theocratic state.[14]

That said, then—and despite its superficial trappings of "governance with the consent of the governed"—Islam, as conceived by its founding fathers, remains, in its basic doctrine, a theocracy, a legacy proudly proclaimed upon its money and its banners throughout history.

As such, at its roots, it is unlike Christendom whose founder bade his followers—

Render therefore unto Caesar the things that are Caesar's, and render unto God the things that are God's. (Matthew 22:21)

—a position wherein Christianity remained until the fourth-century conversion of the Byzantine Emperor Constantine and later, Christmas Day of year 800, when Charlemagne and his successors created, from the ether, the Holy Roman Empire and dramatically transformed the civilization and the culture of the Christian West into a feudalistic theocracy as well.

Islam, on the other hand, at its onset did not experience such a bifurcation of church and state. Its founder immediately proclaimed himself to be Constantine and founded his own sacred empire with no attendant need to create a parallel church—as for him, the dichotomy of *regnum* and *sacerdotium*, so vital in early Christian evolution, had no significant equivalent meaning. The Dar al-Islam was at once church and state with the Prophet and his *khulafa'*, his successor vicegerents, acting as Caesar at its titular head, and God as its sovereign and sole source of law.[15]

To paraphrase Bernard Lewis, whereas in Imperial Rome Caesar was God and in Christendom God and Caesar co-exist, in Islam God is Caesar in that he alone is the supreme head of state, the source of sovereignty, and hence, also of authority and law. The state is God's state, the law is God's law, the army is that God's army—and the enemy is God's enemy.[16]

From its inception, therefore, the Islamic polity was founded upon its religious roots; whereas its Christian counterpart, at its inception, was largely an unstructured underground movement, not an aspiring state, and as such enjoyed no formal polity. Thus, while the political foundations of secular jurisdictions are ostensibly predicated upon the separation of church and state, in the Islamic state, they are, in precept, unified. Yet taxonomically, is that reality, in actuality, a truly great divide?

The answer issues from their underlying doctrines. Islam envisioned itself as an inseparable Community of Believers established under God, and its leaders invoke the supplication: "God is Greatest" (*Allah huwa al-Akhbar*) in their speeches. America's Declaration of Independence in turn, proclaims: "One nation under God," whereas its Pledge of Allegiance honors "one nation under God, indivisible," and its political leaders close their pronouncements with "God Bless America."[17]

Islam pictured its caliph on its coinage, the gold dinar—proclaiming him to be "Commander of the Faithful," accompanied by Qur'anic verses, among them:

Trust in your Lord; so we have trusted. (Surat Al-i 'Imran 3:193)

America in turn, places pictures of her presidents on her currency issues, together with the words: "In God we trust."[18]

What is unconstitutional to Americans is un-Islamic to Muslims. Americans profess to be "one nation under God, indivisible," whereas Muslims are an indivisible Community of Believers. When wronged, Americans rush to their Constitution and common law. When wronged, Muslims seek remedy with the Qur'an as their constitution and turn to it and its attendant body of common law, *Sunna*, Prophetic Tradition. Muslims open their decrees with: "In the name of God, the Merciful, the Compassionate." The

U.S. Supreme Court opens its sessions with: "May God save the United States and this Honorable Court."

In approach and substance, then, there is no defining difference save in specific terms of reference. For in all of this can be found striking similarities shared between the Islamic and Western world views of being endowed by an omnipotent Creator who created all men equal with certain inalienable rights. In Muslim eyes, therefore, when government preserves these rights, its acts are legitimate ("Islamic"); whereas in American eyes, they are "constitutional." When desecrated, they are correspondingly "illegitimate"—"un-Islamic" in the Muslim East, "unconstitutional" in the Christian West![19]

IS AN "EASTERN REPUBLIC THE ANSWER?

Despite its veneer of theocratic autocracy, therefore, Islam, as observed, has also evolved and incorporated its own unique brand of democracy— as has issued from its processes of consensus (*ijma'*) and deductive reasoning (*ijtihad*) over time. That is why recourse to consultative councils (*majalis al-shura*) has been integral to Islamic rule practically from its inception—and why Muslim rulers seldom, if ever, historically have made major decisions materially impacting upon the Dar al-Islam without first consulting fellow tribal elders.[20] For instance, when 'Abd al-'Aziz ibn Sa'ud, founder of the modern Saudi dynasty—confronted with a revolt of his *Ikhwani* paramilitary force in 1929—temporarily abdicated, he was restored to power through a defined process of consultation with his *'ulama'* and fellow senior tribal leaders. Indeed, this practice has been perpetuated to the present day in Saudi Arabia with the establishment in 1992 of a then 60-member Consultative Council that has now grown to 150 members representing citizens from all walks of life.[21]

Islam's practice of popular consultancy thus enjoys strong doctrinal foundations. Though there have traditionally been within it little place for formal elections per se, its founding creed calls openly for a government of "advice and consultation" and for a ruler's openness to his people and to his responsibility to them.

The Qur'an itself, as noted, enjoined the Prophet to deal gently with believers and to consult them in public matters. It also employs the term "consultative" (*shura*) to describe the process whereby believers resolve their affairs in consultation amongst themselves. As a consequence, over three decades after Nasser's death, "the rickety monarchies" of the Gulf live on, their populations quite content with the "consensual" political systems that they have.[22]

At the other extreme, however, is the reality that since Nasser's death, no major Arab leader—save briefly for Saddam Hussein in his invasion of Kuwait in 1990—has been able to generate substantial support outside of his own country and internally, precious few have been readily willing to submit their current rule to plebiscite. Their reluctance is understandable—as their radical opposition is, at once, fractious and uncompromising.

For whereas democrats may perceive an obligation to extend voting rights to all, many fundamental Islamists labor under no such illusion or obligation as their principles implore them to suppress impiety wherever it occurs. And once God's will has been established, there can be no turning back, no precipitous rejection of His sovereignty as exercised through elected representatives.

For "electocracy" and democracy are not synonymous—and sharing power is not distinguishing feature of the prototypic *caliphal* theocratic state.[23] Unlike Western democracies, in Islam, once voted in, God cannot be voted out if the economy turns bad on His watch preceding a subsequent election. The "algorithm of electoral franchise" thus becomes one of: "one man . . . one vote . . . all male . . . just once!"—a challenge compounded by a religion consisting of multiple sects embracing a multiplicity of creeds each prescribing death for apostasy or reversion from Islam as they particularly view it.[24]

And therein lies the crux of the classic as well as contemporary, "traditional fundamentalist" versus "would-be reforming modernist" debate. For a viable Islamic democracy cannot perforce be a "theo-democracy" but instead must be a democratic system fitted within an Islamic moral framework at once committed to preserving the faith's traditions of religious pluralism and human rights, while concomitantly remaining open to the process of political secularization and change wherein the policy course of the theocracy can be reversed through popular plebiscite.[25]

These on-the-ground realities were made indelibly clear in a curious meeting in which this book's author participated immediately following the surprise showing of Austria's Freedom Party in that country's October 1999 elections. The occasion was the presentation of a replica of the battleship *Quincy*, upon which President Franklin Roosevelt and Saudi Arabia's modern founder 'Abd al-'Aziz bin Sa'ud met in Egypt's Great Bitter Lakes on February 14, 1945, to lay the foundations for the especially close bilateral relationship between the two nations that has since evolved.

The presentation was made to Riyadh's Governor Prince Salman bin 'Abd al-'Aziz, one of the most moderate, rational, and articulate members of the Saudi Arabian Royal Family, by U.S. ambassador Wyche Fowler, a consummate—if, at times, loquacious—diplomat. Fowler commenced:

> Your Royal Highness:
> This is not the first time that I have made a presentation to you. Two years ago, I presented to you other replicas from that historic meeting . . . and between us, we have now become famous. Ever since, stewardesses on Saudia have asked me to autograph our picture taken on that occasion that was published on the cover of that airline carrier's in-flight magazine: *Ahlan wa Sahlan.*

Had Fowler elected to stop there, the presentation would have concluded as an unequivocal, if uneventful, success. But, being the true Georgia politician that he is, of course, he didn't, continuing,

> You know, your Royal Highness, it is a good thing that you don't allow women to vote in your country . . . because if they did, they would have elected you the better looking.

Unfortunately, this latter remark lost something in translation. As after a brief pause for measured meditation and sidebar consultations with colleagues, Prince Salman responded in Arabic, as simultaneously translated by an aide:

> I am delighted that Austria's Freedom Party won last week's elections . . . not because I support them . . . in fact, I don't think that I even really know what they stand for.
> But I am delighted that they won for just one reason—you Americans and the British always go around the world preaching democracy as a cure for everything, including cancer. Yet now, when a party wins that you don't like, you try to block it from taking its elected seat of power.[26]

At this stage, of course, there were those in the audience doubtlessly reflecting in quiet unison: "It was on the Quincy that this special bilateral relationship began, and it is upon its replica that it now shall end."

Yet Prince Salman had delivered a compelling point: democracy cannot be spread unbridled and unbundled randomly around the world, a reality strikingly driven home by Saudi Arabia's first-ever municipal elections convened largely at the urging of the "democratic West" and its insatiable, if indiscriminate, human rights surrogates, in which *adult males only* participated in mid-spring 2005.

The results were reverberating, particularly in Jiddah, a city deemed unquestioningly to be among the most moderate in the country. The winners? Only long-bearded fundamentalist religious activists—those who view free elections as no more than a tool and precursor for reestablishing God's theocracy on earth as a formula for replicating an Iranian-like theocratic state—leading even the country's moderates, who would otherwise welcome free elections, to lament: "One Man, One Vote, One Time!"

For the winners in this instance are among those most deeply opposed to actual democracy but have learned to manipulate the democratic system to serve parochial ends, fully confident that such free elections are no guarantee of the long-term workings of democratic process. Hence, those who would externally impose top-down democracy must be wary of those who would use the democratic process to achieve power only to later abandon that process to retain political power and dominance, as there are few political interests in the developing world willing to leave quietly in compliance with the dictates of with popular will.

These examples in themselves would be mere curious political vignettes save that they have analogues more modern still. As New York Times columnist Thomas Friedman wrote in early 2006 in noting that Iran's hard-line president Mahmud Ahmadinijad had been popularly elected:

> So far, the democracy wave that the Bush team has helped to unleash since 9/11 has brought into power hard-line Islamic fundamentalists in Iraq, Palestine, and Iran, and has paved the way for a record showing by the Muslim Brotherhood in Egypt. If we keep this up, in a few years, Muslim clerics will be in power from Morocco to the borders of India. May God bless America![27]

Friedman's contentions are compelling. At the least, democracy has empowered a volatile axis of theocratic Shi'i Islamic governance that now dangerously arcs from Iran in the east westward through Iraq's Fertile Crescent centered on Baghdad down through Syria to Hezbollah in Southern Lebanon. Yet neither Islamists nor jihadists are, by nature, born-again democrats, thus framing the issue of whether it is cradles of democracy or incubators of insurgent terrorism that are being formed, as mere elections do not a democracy make.

For at the bottom line: a policy of good intentions must not be conflated with a policy of good results. As all democracies, both advanced and maturing, are *always* vulnerable to demagoguery—and political prudence does not dictate promoting democratic elections in which the victors concurrently proclaim eschatological hostility to the very precept. Democracy building requires democratic institutions, many of which are not present in much of the Islamic world. It also requires both propitious timing and the test of time. Though America declared her independence in 1776, for instance, she did not enact her Constitution until 1789 nor did she give women the right to vote until 131 years thereafter. In the cogent analysis of veteran Middle East political-military observer Anthony Cordesman:

> Elections do not mean progress unless there are national political movements that advocate practical courses of action. Electing Islamists and/or provoking civil war do not bring political stability and cannot defeat a religious and ideological movement.
>
> Democracy can only make things better if it is built on sound political and legal checks and balances that protect minorities and prevent demagogues and extremists from coming to power. Elections do more harm than good if they divide a nation in ways that encourage violence and civil conflict.[28]

Yet *carefully constructed* analogies to the workings of modern political process may not invariably be inappropriate in the pursuit of foreign policy. Iraq today, for instance, as noted, is an artificial entity issuing from the surreptitious Anglo-Franco Sykes-Picot Agreement of 1916—as subsequently blessed by Gertrude Bell and ratified by the Treaty of Versailles—producing an artificial and largely incompatible polity that only the totalitarian overwhelming use of force of a Saddam Hussein can govern, as America is today painfully finding out.

That said, there might nonetheless be ways of introducing pseudo-democratic adaptations by "thinking beyond the envelope" in the quest for productive federal governance. As is readily evident from ongoing on-the-ground realities, that goal will likely not be achieved by trying to export an unadulterated version of what is too often misrepresented as "the American democratic model"—looking perhaps instead, as America itself ultimately did, to republican, rather than ideologically pure democratic, governance at her inception.

Within Iraq, for instance, consternation amongst three mutually despising petty satrapies—the Kurds in the northwest, the Sunnis in the middle, and the Shi'is in the southeast—centers on the concerns of minority Kurds and Sunnis being politically dominated by the Shi'i demographic majority and by parallel Sunni concerns that the preponderance of Iraq's oil wealth is located in regions controlled by the Shi'is and the Kurds.

America's founders wrestled intently, yet ultimately successfully, with similar issues—particularly in response to the concern of the smaller states that they not be marginalized—creating a federal bicameral congress: with one house based on population, the other on geography, to preclude the rights of minorities from being subordinated to those of majorities.

This precept, promoted in tandem with a more general wealth-sharing implemented through a quasi-public General Stock Ownership Corporation—a new business development lending authority whereby a significant portion of oil revenues would be distributed without charge as shares to all citizens nationwide, thereby building an economy built not on petroleum wealth alone but concurrently upon a new form of entrepreneurial capitalism wherein all citizens are stakeholders—could likely more productively provide stable republican government bred of economic prosperity to Iraq.[29]

In the last analysis, however, the peoples of the world deserve the right to self-determination, absent gratuitous Western precedent and advice, in establishing their chosen forms of government and who will lead them. That choice may not invariably be Anglo-American–style democracy. The stark realities encountered in the pursuit of truly Islamic representative government are made the more poignant when, in pushing a nation forward toward democracy—as America has done with Palestine when its voters chose a government not of particular U.S. liking, as the Palestinians did in electing Hamas, the Palestinian branch of the Muslim Brotherhood, in January 2006—America then refuses to negotiate with the duly constituted government. Small wonder that many unaligned nations of the world often fail to fathom this approach to representative governance and find it difficult to distinguish between *Pax Americana* and colonial imperialism.

The bottom line, then, is that for democratic values to now genuinely evolve and spread throughout the Middle East on an enduring—rather than a force-fed "one shot"—basis, their prospects are likely more enhanced through time-tested and traditional processes of Islamic consultancy than through universal suffrage afforded to those not fully schooled in the etiquette of Western democratic process. That established, it is to reciprocal economic dimensions to the Middle East terrorist challenge that this inquiry now perforce turns.

8

Is Eastern Capitalism
the Answer?

Those who rehearse the "God's Book," establish regular prayer, and spend out of what we have provided; for them, hope for a commerce that will never fail. For He will pay them their full due. He will give them even more from His bounty.

—God's economic covenant with His
Community as reflected in Surat Fair 29:30

THE ECONOMIC ROOTS OF TERROR

Notwithstanding the political paradigms and their attendant parameters described, cursory review makes readily evident that the origins of so-called Islamic terrorism, at its nucleus, lie not so much with religion as with politico-economic dimensions to the modern Muslim world, as unrelenting poverty and economic inequality and continuing frustration at a seeming helplessness to rectify them run rampant throughout much of the modern Middle East. For in the last analysis, while deviant political actions can sow the seeds of terror, to take root they must fall upon fallow economic soil.[1]

In many places, the soil is extremely fertile. Today, many Muslim countries—the present Gulf Cooperation Council (GCC) states: Saudi Arabia, Kuwait, Qatar, Bahrain, Oman, and the United Arab Emirates excepted—have largely opted out of the global economy, an economic reality whose pervasive impact is revealed in the grim statistics. Within the 1990s decade, real per capita income in the world's twenty-two Arab countries averaged less that 1 percent growth, about one-fourth the rate of their population growths in that same period, and that trend continues to the present day.[2]

As a consequence, living standards within the Islamic world are coming to resemble more those of Africa than of the West. The facts of life are largely economic and the economics are not good. With its middle class, a vital bulwark between the *haves* and the *have nots*, rapidly eroding, an entire generation of disenfranchised unemployed, angry young people is exposed to the lure of extremist groups.[3]

To complicate such austere living conditions, the centralized economies now prevailing in most Middle East countries—invariably controlled by the state—too often leave many within the Islamic East feeling estranged from the benefits of national economic wealth and thereby deprived of the opportunities that it affords in their quests for what is known, and is seen to be, in the Western world as "life, liberty, and pursuit of happiness"—rights that in their region appear to be reserved for a privileged few.

Taken in aggregate, the Mid-East–North Africa regionwide economic numbers tell the story:

- Massive population increases are ongoing. The region had a population of 112 million in 1950. The population is now well over 415 million, approaching a fourfold increase. It is projected to more than double again, moreover, to at least 833 million by 2050.
- A "youth explosion," wherein those twenty to twenty-four—the key age group entering the job market and political society—has grown rapidly from 10 million in 1950 to over 36 million people today, and will continue to grow steadily to at least 56 million by 2050.
- Some 36 percent of the region's populace is under fifteen years of age, versus 21 percent in the United States and 16 percent in the European Union. Moreover, the ratio of dependents to each working-age man and woman is three times greater than those in a developed region like the European Union.
- The failure to achieve global competitiveness, diversify economies, and create jobs are phenomena likewise afflicting the region—manifestations in the GCC only partially disguised by the present surge in oil revenues. Direct and disguised unemployment rates range from 12 to 20 percent in many countries, and the World Bank projects that the regional labor force will grow by at least 3 percent per year for the next decade.
- A regionwide average per capita income of about $2,300 versus $26,000 in the high-income countries in the West continues to prevail.
- A steady decline in nonpetroleum exports as a percentage of world trade over a period of nearly half a century is mirrored in a parallel

pattern of decline in regional GDP as a share of its global counterpart.

- Hyperurbanization and a half-century-long decline in agricultural and traditional trades concurrently impose high levels of stress upon traditional social safety nets and extended families. The region's urban population was under 15 million in 1950. It has since more than doubled from 84 million in 1980 to 173 million today, and some 25 percent of that population will soon live in cities of one million or more.[4]

Thus, the already massive "rich vs. poor" gap throughout the entire Middle East–North Africa region is widening. Certainly, the great Islamist expansion of the mid-1980s was one key consequence of street perception of this disparity in wealth. Instead of responding to the surging frustration of disaffected Muslim youth at their perceptions of relative economic deprivation, therefore, funds that might otherwise have gone to economic remedy were instead channeled by their governments into efforts to engage them in jihad against the Russian military in Afghanistan.

Indeed, as noted, many initially responded. Young Saudis in particular had initially viewed the jihad as a unique opportunity not only to make a statement but to socially advance. Representing the first generation to grow up in the post-1970s economic boom, they seemed to be the vanguard of an emerging modern middle class—the Arab equivalent of baby boomers.

Yet raised in a bureaucratic theocracy whose economy was sharply nose-diving, they likewise often lacked many opportunities available to counterpart middle classes within industrial countries or even transitional Islamic countries such as Malaysia. Thus, jihad was not only an open door beckoning them but equally a convenient golden opportunity for more formalized Saudi society to shed itself of potential economic discontents and political dissidents at home.[5]

Economically, then, the world has clearly changed. For more than a millennium, the Muslim realm at large was the paragon of commercial prosperity. Today, it is rapidly falling behind in its frenetic quest to compete within the twenty-first-century global economy—with the products that it offers to the world, save for massive quantities of oil, not at all unique, and its manpower too often ill trained to fill meaningful, productive private sector jobs.

Thus, the reality that the world's quarter-of-a-billion Arab populace is growing four times faster than its income base is working in the jihadis' favor. For so long as Middle East economies perform poorly, radical theology will remain a viable—indeed, often attractive—alternative to the status quo. Indeed, in some quarters, it may already be too late, as while less than a fifth of the planet's populace today are Muslims, more than half of the 1.2 billion people living in abject poverty reside in the Islamic world—a phenomenon that may explain why economic malaise and political discontent are now endemic throughout much of its ranks.

It is such human reduced conditions, then, that terrorist organizations such as Hezbollah and Hamas deftly exploit by serving as self-appointed, quasi-nongovernmental organizations providing welfare, youth, shelter, education, medical, and other social services to the region's destitute and disillusioned. It is a role not unlike that of the Catholic Church in serving the poor of Latin America, including their common incessant criticism of capitalism as a force bereft of social conscience.[6]

These, then, are the factors that today precipitate the incipient flow of terrorism—an unfortuitous coalescing of socioeconomic conditions that create fertile breeding grounds for extremist philosophies and radicalism. As extremists have capitalized on the dissatisfaction of the Arab street and the majority of the Islamic world with their economic and political circumstance and what they perceive to be inequitable distributions of incomes.

Concurrently, they are abetted by powerful exogenous forces—as today, much of the Southwest Asian and African Islamic world, except for privileged ruling elites, is infested with endemic poverty, much of which is blamed upon Western economic exploitation, or alternately or in tandem, is perceived to be part and parcel of the ongoing process of "globalization."

The increasingly wretched economic situation pervading much of the traditional Dar al-Islam, together with the converse rising prosperity being won by the dynamic emerging economies of East Asia, has thus fueled mounting internal frustrations, as increasing numbers have come to discern sharp disparities between what is now stagnating *within* and what is dynamically evolving *without*.[7]

This combination of perceived Western economic penetration and subjugation, low indigenous industrial productivity, and inordinately high birth rates thereby coalesce to create a highly combustible socioeconomic mix which—when combined with high unemployment rates among the region's uneducated youth populace—has spawned new and ever-expanding breeding grounds for political disaffection.

These are on-the-ground realities that must be effectively addressed in the quest to stanch terrorism throughout the Muslim East—as in many of the region's key countries, highly complex internal political challenges are compounded by equally challenging economic ones—with perceptions of relative income deprivation rampant in many streets. A massive demographic explosion further amplifies the perception, as the mounting presence of large numbers of often unemployed Muslim males throughout the

Middle East region has become a natural source of instability both within Islam and against non-Muslims.

Again, the economic numbers tell the story, with Saudi Arabia an inspired choice as an illuminating case study. For with many of that country's and the region's most noteworthy terrorists having grown up within its less affluent districts, it is within them that the symptoms of unrest are most acute, yet wherein economic progress, if effectively achieved, can enjoy its most positive social impacts. Unfortunately, as analysis will show, much work remains to be done both abroad and at home.

Indeed, internationally, as noted in the analysis of chapter 5, Saudi Arabia has already inadvertently played a catalytic role in dispersing terrorist networks. For in the aftermath of the fourfold oil price increase the global embargo of 1974–1975, the country at last achieved the financial wherewithal to realize its aspired ambition of acquiring some modicum of spiritual hegemony over the global Islamic Community of Believers.

Accordingly, its prime objective became that of advancing Islam to the forefront of international attention—to substitute it for various competing nationalist movements within the Muslim world—and to refine the multitude of voices within it into a single creed. Its goal was global, extending beyond traditional frontiers of the faith even into the heartland of the West and its immigrant Muslim populations. To this end, a massive program of mosque-building, together with vast proselytizing (*da'wah*) missions and financial support, was put into place around the world.[8]

Concurrently, internally its huge petrodollar-financed and historically unparalleled program of infrastructure building attracted countless would-be workers from third world Muslim nations. While there, in growing relatively affluent from their Saudi salaries, many came to attribute its puritanical social milieu as the spiritual source of their own newly won material prosperity. Thus, upon returning home, social ascent became equated with an intensification of religious practice in a quest to spread the fundamentalist ideology to which they had become exposed.[9]

While in-kingdom, moreover, these expatriate laborers concomitantly contributed mightily to one of the economic miracles of the modern age, transforming the country from a relatively backwater nomadic society into a twenty-first-century economic dynamo industrially centered upon oil and petrochemicals.

As a consequence, at home Saudi Arabia has today become the largest free-market economy within the Arab East, and with a gross domestic product (GDP) approaching $400 billion per annum, generates well over two-thirds of the aggregate GDP formation among the GCC states—as well as approaching one-third of that within the Arab world as a whole. Indeed, its strategic location at the concourse of three continents has afforded it access to major markets throughout Europe, Asia, and Africa since ancient times.

Yet in many ways, despite noteworthy efforts aimed at industrial diversification, the country remains a "one crop economy," with oil its primary taproot, accounting for an average 35–45 percent of GDP formation, 85–95 percent of total exports, and 70–85 percent of total public sector revenues in recent decades. For like most GCC states, while oil has vastly enriched its public coffers, it has also frozen into stasis a more organic and diversified development, failing to create other independent economic sectors.[10]

This reality is, at once, a blessing and a curse, as when global oil prices are high, the country prospers; but when they become low, its economy plummets. In this sense, then, Saudi Arabia's physical security is a function of the price of oil. The vexing problems produced by this cyclic rollercoaster effect are concurrently compounded by a variety of endogenous economic factors. For in the Kingdom, as the heartland of modern political Islam as well as of classic Islam itself, the nation also confronts a multiplicity of development challenges demographic as well as industrial.

Macroeconomic data reveal, for instance, that at the onset of the 1980s, the U.S. and Saudi Arabia per capita GDPs in current dollar terms were approximately equal at $28,600. But whereas that of the United States today exceeds $40,000, Saudi Arabia's per capita GDP level generally hovered at or below $9,000 in the more than two decade period between 1981 and 2003. A prime reason: Until recently, a dramatically low oil market price structure, as Saudi Arabia's real per capita oil export revenues had precipitously declined from $22,174 in 1981 to $3,371 by 2003.[11]

A second major reason for this sharp decline in per capita GDP was that, with now nearly 24 million citizens, the country is experiencing one of the fastest population growth rates in the world, with an acceleration generally estimated at 3.5 percent nationwide and approaching 8 percent in its Riyadh capital.[12] As a consequence, the average Saudi family now consists of some 6.6 persons and the median age of the nation's populace stands at seventeen years of age and continues to descend rapidly, with an estimated 60 percent of the population below twenty years of age. Accordingly, because GDP growth does not proportionately create jobs, the nation's real GDP must grow by more than 3.5 percent a year merely to keep apace of population growth and sustain unemployment rates at their current levels.[13]

Examination of the economic ramifications of these disparate labor force trends upon industrial productivity also is illuminating. For today, while approximately 7 million foreigners constitute about one-third of

Saudi Arabia's slightly less than 24 million population, expatriate workers from across all occupations and skill levels now comprise about two-thirds of its total labor force, producing a serious negative capital outflow from the nation's economy estimated at over $15 billion annually.

Within this unique public-private job mix, moreover, the nation's governmentally owned enterprises and activities generate more than 60 percent of the nation's GDP—with 78 percent of its employees Saudi and 22 percent foreign. Key demographic and socioeconomic challenges to future national development thus are not inconsequential.

For today the unemployment rate among young adult Saudi males is rampant, with estimates running to as high as 15 percent of labor force and more, a phenomenon owing not only to a paucity of new jobs but to an unwillingness to accept less prestigious, lower-paying jobs now consigned to third world expatriates. These economic realities—high unemployment combined with an influx of militant refugees returning home from religious wars abroad—have thus coalesced to introduce certain dysfunctions within fractious elements of traditionally ultraconservative Saudi society.

Consequently, the mid-1980s witnessed the beginnings of sharp socioeconomic divisions and dislocations within Saudi society—a wealthy royal, tribal, and business elite coexisting side-by-side with economically marginalized urbanized Bedouin and traditional oasis peasantry. For the latter, moreover, rising literacy rates have often merely contributed to their awareness of the extent of their disadvantage.

Greatly complicating the Saudi economic scene has been the severe financial downturn that afflicted the nation as a result of the depressed oil prices of 1983–2003. As with the nation's population growing more rapidly, and hence demanding jobs at a rate far faster than a "single crop" oil economy could provide, the present generation has had to face the prospect of having to work twice as hard to earn half as much as did their parents in the 1974–1983 industrial "boom years."

Equally seriously, moreover, while their parents were born before the boom years into a less-than-buoyant socioeconomy—then experiencing an economic peak in the 1974–1984 decade, prior to gradually tapering off—the present maturing generation was born at the very peak of the boom years, thereby rendering what they have until recently financially experienced, graphically portrayed, to be nothing less than a straight line pointing down.

Further compounding the volatile mix of this boiling socioeconomic cauldron—one fueled by rampant demographic inequity—is a surging wave of xenophobia amongst the country's younger generation—explicitly those targeted by fundamentalists and terrorists alike as potential future ideological recruits. There is no question that they are vulnerable.

For whereas today Saudi Arabia is essentially governed at the administrative level by some 120,000 technocrats who were educated in the West in the 1974–1984 boom years peak, by 1985, with the opening of King Saud University in Riyadh and other major local universities already operating, most local educational infrastructures had essentially been put into place.

As a consequence, rather than benefiting from that cross-cultural fertilization that an international education can provide, most students today remain in-country to pursue their graduate and undergraduate studies at local institutions wherein they are constrained by curricula comprised of 75 percent or more of conservative socioreligious content—to the exclusionary detriment of those vital technology-intensive courses that can lead to meaningful, productive twenty-first-century jobs.

Adding to this cresting xenophobic tide have been the devastating internal social impacts of an occupying foreign presence during the conduct of the 1990–1991 Gulf War—which has, in turn, invoked shrill cries from, and afforded more voice to, the highly introspective conservative element of the country's citizenry. It is the convergence of these highly diverse socioeconomic trends, therefore, that has had the greatest emotional and intellectual impacts upon those rising generations of young Saudis who have of late endured perceptions of relative economic self-deprivation.

It is no accident, then, that within the past three years, within Saudi Arabia's capital city, Riyadh, the most potent hotbeds of deviant unrest have percolated up in some of its less-affluent districts situated along the city's defining outer "Ring Road"—prominent among them the "Badr District" located at "Exit 10 West" and the "al-Suwayd District" at "Exit 15 East."

For it is young unemployed male clusters located within such areas that the nation's 1985–2003 economic downturn most profoundly affected, making it not at all surprising that it is they who have responded most favorably to the Islamic preachers decrying society's creeping infestation of materialism, corruption, and consumerism, which they attribute to the West. What is happening there, moreover, can be extrapolated to not only the rest of the country but also to other economically less fortunate districts throughout the Middle East region—not only within the Gulf region, but likewise in Syria, Iraq, Egypt, and Sudan.

Consequently, a powerful theological rhetoric that promotes a return to a seventh-century "Islamic authenticity" is coming to attract many who are now growing increasingly frustrated with perceptions of a truncated pseudo-modernism, inordinate outside interference, and unequal access to economic opportunity—all phenomena today portrayed from raging pulpits as the prime source of all social and economic evils and ills.[14]

Within this mosaic of divergent socioeconomic blends, then, a clear division within society is continuing to emerge between those who cherish a return to tradition and a stricter application of Islamic values and morality and those who aspire to greater freedoms and outreach to the outside world and a fuller immersion into modernity. Often, such fissures are widening even within single-family units.[15]

As a result of the less-than-fortuitous coalescing of such rapidly cresting divergent geopolitical and socioeconomic currents, therefore, the shadow of Political Islam now casts itself across the stage of Middle East history with the elemental force of a cosmic cataclysm. For what was, prior to 9/11, impossible to contemplate has today struck with devastating impact, and as a consequence, civilization is compelled to confront its devastating fury.

SAUDI ARABIA: A CASE STUDY IN FREE-MARKET SOLUTIONS

Yet there remains real hope for remedy. In Saudi Arabia's case, the quest for economic regeneration is being abetted by powerful market forces—to wit, skyrocketing global oil prices. As a consequence, current economic numbers are highly promising:

- 2006 oil export earnings stood at a record $191 billion, up 18 percent from the 2005 record of $162 billion.
- A current account surplus of $95.5 billion was also realized in 2006, the eighth straight year of such surplus.
- GDP for 2006 came in at a record $372.7 billion, up from 2005's record $309.53 billion. GDP growth in nominal terms was 12.4 percent, which translated into 4.2 percent in real terms. This likewise as the fourth straight year of double-digit GDP growth—and this trend is expected to continue for the near term future. Meanwhile, the inflation rate remains below 1 percent.
- Per capita GDP reached $15,620 in 2006—up from $13,325 in 2005.[16]

With a $70.7 billion budget surplus realized in FY 2006, such buoyant revenue flows augur well for those relying upon government projects to sustain their corporate income streams—as the nation commences upon an upswing that may be sustainable for several years.[17] Major market indicators simultaneously remain strong as well as forward leaning. Between the onset of 1999 and the close of 2005, the Saudi stock market increased by over 550 percent in aggregate value (followed by a recent sharp decline resulting from market rationalization). Indeed, its capitalization over that period more than doubled its oil export earnings within that same period.

Notwithstanding oil-driven economic spikes, however, serious structural economic problems remain. For despite great progress within the past three decades and its ample resources cited, Saudi Arabia today remains an economy inordinately reliant upon a single "cash crop"—*oil* and its downstream derivatives—which, as noted, account for more than 10 percent of the world's daily consumption, roughly 90 percent of the kingdom's export earnings, 75 percent of its governmental revenues, and around 40 percent of its annual GDP formation. To this extent, then, the nation's political stability, founded upon its economic well-being, remains a direct function of its oil revenues.

To fully perceive the magnitude of the industrial development challenge that the nation thus confronts, it is useful to contrast its economic structure with those of other coexisting successful models, such as the pyramidal economies obtaining within the OECD countries. For in the prototypic, generic pyramidal free-market economy:

- Public/private interaction is ongoing;
- Private tax revenues fund governmental activities;
- Government serves as regulatory umpire between producer and consumer;
- The private sector is the economic engine driving commercial and industrial growth;
- Private economic activity produces those goods and services that comprise the nation's exportable goods and services flows; and
- Exports, combined with reverse investments, are the prime means of generating internal national economic wealth.

The key to generating jurisdiction-wide economic prosperity, then, is to develop a more economically diversified, fully integrated industrial base consisting of dynamic private sector producers that manufacture market-competitive, premier quality goods and services in high demand throughout the global economy.

But though Saudi Arabia does enjoy many valuable economic development assets, they are, in no small part, offset by certain industrial structural imbalances. As a consequence, unlike the pyramidal economies described that now exist in most of the Organization for Economic Cooperation and Development (OECD) countries, the nation has actually built an inverted pyramidal economy.

For though it has created a wide partial pyramid comprised of private small, medium, and large enterprises, they are dwarfed by overarching layers of *parastatal* industries—Saudi Aramco, Saudi Arabian Basic Industries Corporation (SABIC), Saudi Telecommunications Company (STC), and Saudi Electricity Company (SEC), etc.

- While these four huge parastatals, which are 79 percent Saudi-government owned, generate nearly two-thirds of the nation's total GDP (presently trending at 66 percent of total), they concurrently consume disproportionate shares of its natural and financial resources.
- Not only do such governmentally created entities use up vital, yet finite, resources, they simultaneously preempt balanced private sector industrial growth as they dominate the entire economy and establish its direction.
- As a consequence, while in a *pyramidal* economy, government serves as a "regulatory umpire," in the *inverted pyramidal* economy, such as that forged in Saudi Arabia, government is at once the nation's "regulatory umpire" *and* its principal economic player as well as its supreme legal authority.
- Government itself thereby becomes the nation's top-down industrial engine, widely distributing economic entitlements through targeted market baskets of public-sector service contracts and subsidies, while controlling most private-sector commercial and industrial performance through regulation.
- The net result is that Saudi Arabia has actually constructed a national entity that more resembles a public-sector-driven *consumptive* economy than a private-sector-driven *productive* one.
- Hence, the ultimate economic consequences of such highly disparate consumption and production trends pose serious challenges to its future economic well-being.

To "right side" its inverse pyramidal economy—while creating desired economic diversification—therefore, Saudi Arabia has properly turned to free-market-based solutions founded upon *privatization* of its monumental parastatals. Planned privatization of the nation's public infrastructural sectors alone, in fact, will invoke internal investments of $623.7 billion within the Saudi economy through the year 2020. Disaggregated by industrial sector, in one studied estimate, their projected capitalization is as indicated in table 8.1.

Accepting the commonly employed economic barometer that each $1 billion in exports creates 15,000 domestic jobs, this $623.7 billion in committed public-private investment capital can thus be demonstrated to equate to over 9.335 million employment man years in future business potential averaging 583,469 jobs for each of the next fifteen years.

**Table 8.1.   Value of Privatization Initiatives
Through Year 2020***

Sector	U.S. $ Billions
Infrastructure	$140.0
Electricity	$90.7
Water	$88.0
Telecommunications	$60.0
Petrochemicals	$92.0
Natural Gas	$50.0
Tourism	$53.3
Agriculture	$28.3
Information Technologies	$10.7
Education	$10.7
TOTAL	**$623.7**

*G. Heck 2005, pp. 1–5.

Saudi Arabia's approach for achieving balanced development through privatization, in turn, is founded upon building effective public-private partnerships. To this end, the aforesaid $623.7 billion in emerging privatization opportunities cited is supported by a targeted market basket of lucrative financial incentives enticing to investors with the objectives of the country's privatization strategy being to:

- improve national economic capacity and global marketplace competitive ability;
- encourage greater private sector investment both from within and from without;
- expand the inventory of national productive assets held by private citizens;
- upgrade the productive capabilities of the national workforce, while simultaneously increasing local employment opportunities; and
- rationalize governmental expenditures to reduce public sector budget burdens.[18]

These sweeping privatization initiatives have been attended by recent substantive economic policy reforms that also add materially to the nation's principal sources of competitive advantage. Indicative of the rapid pace of reform, they include:

- forming the Supreme Economic Council in 1999 to oversee national development;

- establishing the Saudi Arabian General Investment Authority (SAGIA) in June 2000 as a streamlined one-stop trade and investment center;
- passing the Foreign Direct Investment Law of April 2000;
- promulgating the Real Estate Law of October 2000 allowing foreigners to own in-country real estate;
- approving the Capital Markets Law of July 2003 to strengthen business and industrial finance by opening a new, structured, and more dynamic stock market;
- putting the infrastructure into place to privatize all of the major utilities—power, water, and telecommunications—pursuant to the Privatization Strategy of June 2002;
- forming the Supreme Tourism Council to promote the growth of recreation and travel;
- reducing corporate income taxation marginal ceilings from 45 percent to 20 percent pursuant to the Corporate Tax Law of January 2004; and
- lowering general import tariff rates from 12 percent and 7 percent to 5 percent on over 90 percent of all imported goods.[19]

Already these reforms have been an unqualified *business* success, establishing an atmosphere of improved efficiency, greater transactional transparency, more effective government oversight, and enhanced opportunities for foreign investment, thereby resulting in an enhanced ability to promote domestic investment and stronger overall economic performance.

Aimed explicitly at opening up the Saudi economy so that the nation's citizens can financially benefit to the maximum possible extent, the reform agenda is explicitly antiterrorist in its focus in ameliorating incipient sources of poverty and thereby reducing perceptions of relative economic deprivation. Indeed, already, by restoring popular economic hope, the reforms have been an unqualified *strategic* success as now that Saudi business prospects have dramatically improved in the 2004–2007 period, restoring economic hope, security incidents have concurrently dropped significantly.

These, then, are the very positive economic reforms that one crucial Middle East country, Saudi Arabia, has put into place to promote domestic stability through economic security—tabled as a solid blueprint for future industrial and commercial growth. Though critical questions remain both on their capacity for making perceptible near-term socioeconomic impacts, and on their exportability on a more regional Middle East basis to regions wherein poverty is pandemic and less enlightened economic regimes prevail, early results emanating from the reforms are promising, as an enlightened new leadership under King Abdullah appears committed to dispersing to the nation's populace the wide range of benefits that abundant oil wealth provides.

LESSONS FOR ISLAMIC SOCIETIES AT LARGE

Having reviewed a panorama of proposed *modern* solutions to systemic economic problems on a country-specific basis, therefore, it becomes equally critical to again look to the lessons of economic history—wherein Islamic global contributions have been seminal—for more *classic* regional industrial remedy. This is recourse with no alternative, as today, the economic conditions of many Muslim countries not blessed with oil wealth continue to erode within the backdrop of escalating social strain. This course must clearly be reversed.

For if the once legendary Islamic entrepreneurial instinct remains suppressed by lack of economic opportunity—that social cohesion, that consummate solidarity, that *'asabiyah* prescribed as quintessential for social progress by no less than the famed fourteenth-century Arab historian Ibn Khaldun—will inevitably continue to come unglued, carrying consequences horrific not only for the Muslim East but for civilization as it is now defined.[20]

The economic challenges, therefore, undeniably are many and bear repeating and include, but are not limited to, those of:

- promoting diversified economic growth;
- creating jobs;
- alleviating poverty;
- coping with urbanization;
- restraining population explosion; and
- attracting money for investment from domestic and foreign investors alike.[21]

Prescriptive remedy, in turn, requires a careful sort-through of Islam's historic economic roots. For paradoxically, though free-market capitalism initially sprouted into full blossom in the early Islamic Middle East, it is today viewed within many Muslim quarters with a modicum of suspicion as an imperial tool of parasitic external powers. Accordingly, while the creed does not, in principle, favor heavy state intervention in the economic working of *domestic* society, it often does tend to take a protectionist, even xenophobic, view of those *international* market forces that it suspects are manipulated by the capitalistic West.[22]

Thus, Muslim traditionalists frequently come off as ambivalent on the role of state within the economy. On the one hand, they support the concept of a liberalized industrial system, as classic Islamic theory contemplates the role of the state as limited to that of *facilitating* markets and merchants rather than *controlling* them. As such, they have also always objected to the founding precepts of both communism and socialism—communism not only for its atheism and socialism for its secularism, but upon their mutual insistence upon rigid control over free markets.

For Muslim theoreticians have traditionally supported modicums of individual autonomy to operate freely within an economy so long as they do not jeopardize societal welfare—and to these ends, they have no contention with unequal wealth distribution so long as basic principles of social justice are preserved.[23]

Accordingly, the crucial issue remaining to be explored centers around the applicability and utility for the modern Middle East of the Western free market model, which was itself, ironically, originally borrowed from the Muslim East in the later Middle Ages, reflecting the reality that the consummate economic success of the West today owes a monumental debt to its Islamic antecedents—a debt that it may now be well positioned to repay.

9

Epilogue: Reaping the Whirlwind

There is a tide in the affairs of men that,
Taken at the flood, leads on to fortune;
Omitted, all of the voyages of their lives,
Are bound in shallows and miseries.
On such a full sea, we now float;
And we must take the current when it serves,
Or lose our ventures.

—Shakespeare's Brutus

EXPLORING HISTORY'S COGENT LESSONS

What, then, are the lessons learned from this inquiry's exploration of Islamic doctrine and Middle East history in the quest to stanch global terror today issuing from the Middle East? Succinctly stipulated, they may be summed up in ten maxims synopsized in table 9.1.

Realization of these goals must, of course, perforce commence with a better understanding of the true nature of classic Islam and what its doctrine actually prescribes. For based upon the analysis of this inquiry, it becomes readily clear that the Qur'an aims primarily at instructing individual Muslims on how to attain individual inner peace. It is not primarily a cure-all for resolving social conflict, terror, and war, although it contains explicit prescriptions for war should that recourse become unavoidable. But overall, its prescriptions are defensive in tenor and intent. Indeed, as delineated in the Qur'an and Prophetic Tradition, Islamic principles for the conduct of war and peace are distinguished by the following characteristics:

141

Table 9.1.   Ten Critical Lessons Learned in the Quest to Stop Global Terror

1. Counter terror with decisive force.
2. Don't capitulate.
3. Don't negotiate.
4. Fix broken economies.
5. Downplay Anglo-American democracy as a carte blanche solution.
6. Promote indigenous capitalistic self-determination in its stead.
7. Don't stereotype—identify and support your friends.
8. Learn what true Islam stipulates.
9. Reach out to Muslim moderates.
10. Encourage reforms that restore Islam to its classic doctrinal roots.

They likely subscribe to the four basic modern principles of the Law of War as codified by the Hague and Geneva Conventions as demonstrated in table 9.2:

Table 9.2.

Legitimacy	as reflected in	Righteous Intent
Proportionality	as reflected in	Measured Response
Distinction	as reflected in	Discrimination
Humanity	as reflected in	Aggression Avoidance

As such, as demonstrated in analysis, the Qur'an:

- Explicitly directs its followers not to initiate hostilities;
- Requires them to accept peace overtures from would-be adversaries;
- Instructs them to engage in negotiated démarches with such otherwise would-be adversaries seeking peace prior to engaging in armed conflict;
- Mandates that they adhere to honorably concluded treaties;
- Forbids them from indulging in terror, torture, or attacking civilian populations;
- While extolling the virtues of "martyrdom" contracted in God's cause, prohibits suicide in its pursuit;
- Mandates fighting as units fully arrayed in battle formation. As such, modern terrorist operations organized into clandestine cells are essentially shown to be no more than rogue operations that directly contravene the doctrinally defined founding precepts of the Islamic Code of Conduct for War.
- Exhorts Muslims to engage in defensive warfare to preserve the territorial integrity of the Dar al-Islam; and

- Fully recognizes the status of Jews and Christians as Peoples of the Book—as monotheistic co-religionists—and preaches peaceful coexistence with them.

In delineating these interpretations, it is worth reiterating, no substantive differences between the so-called Wahhabi Qur'anic translations and those of traditional classical Islamic schools of thought are evident.

In short, at its roots Islam prides itself as a religion of tolerance, and there is little within its doctrine that suggests otherwise. As such, the practices of terrorist groups such as al-Qaeda may be seen as antithetical to its teachings. For in its prescriptions, Qur'anic doctrine directly discredits and refutes, rather than supports, the militant tactics of terrorist jihadi networks. Recognition of this reality is critical to any strategy that seeks to mitigate the spread of terror and spare future generations from its nihilism now perpetrated in Islam's name.

Such a quest, in turn, confronts numerous additional incontrovertible realities—some geographic, some political, some economic. On the one hand, within the heartland of Islam, the base where much modern terrorist ideology has been spawned, the inhabitants of the Arabian Peninsula cohabit a curiously insular world that is at once a blessing and a curse. On the other hand, an inherent sociological phenomenon issuing from that reality is that the Peninsula's traditional Islamic culture appears to be living proof that given relative stasis in a given physical environment and the exogenous factors that impact upon it, basic social values do not change rapidly over time.

Accordingly, a 1920s *Ikhwani* warrior could now likely integrate into Saudi society without substantive disruption and without losing the same certitude of conviction with which he once faced the onslaught of oncoming enemy tribesmen. By extension, it does not seem unreasonable to assume that the Islamic socioeconomic values of today's generation will likewise be shared by many descendants of that which emerges tomorrow.[1]

Yet another consequence of this relative isolation, quite remarkably, is that to this day, there is no term in Arabic for "Arabia," an expression that was coined by the ancient Greeks. The region is called instead *jazirat al-'Arab* (Peninsula of the Arabs)—not because the Arabic language lacks richness, for it truly is rich and variegated, but because Peninsula Arabs were never compelled to think in terms of fixed ethnic or territorial identities.[2]

On the positive side of isolation, in turn, since the death of Prophet Muhammad in 632, Muslim forces have never had to fight non-Muslim military forces in or around Makkah or al-Madinah. The Najd, in particular—because it makes no tangible claim to an abiding religious or commercial import that would subject it to the ambition of imperial design—has never been subjected to external conquest. Thus, its intrinsic values and beliefs, such as its introspective Wahhabi doctrine, have evolved as indigenously pure and unvarnished by colonial taint.[3]

On the negative side, its relative remoteness tends to isolate peninsula inhabitants from those currents of cross-cultural fertilization that empower civilizations to advance pulled forward by the tides of global progress, instead creating latent potentials for the evolution of an encirclement syndrome wherein outsiders come to be perceived as enemies.[4]

For this reason, then, it is likely not surprising that early medieval Islamic historians themselves do not self-identify as Arabs either but instead as Muslims and refer to their non-Muslim neighbors and opponents alike as simply infidels or, at times, by vague general terms such as Franks or Romans.[5] In such an insular milieu, it is not difficult to contemplate how indigenous thinking could readily mutate into delusional paroxysms of confrontation and self-righteousness, creating seminal breeding grounds wherein religious terrorism could be conceived and grow to flourish.

Ironically, this relative isolation has concurrently impacted profoundly *in a positive way* upon the nature of the reaction of Peninsula Arabs to such political issues as recurring pan-Arab and pan-Islamic movements. For there, Arab identity is based not primarily upon historic, linguistic, cultural, or religious issues but instead along tribal bloodlines. Hence, unlike much of the rest of the Arab Middle East, they have preceded forward with a unique self-assurance. For not having been subjected to colonial domination, they have never really lost their sense of Arab identity and hence have never had to rediscover it.[6]

This would all begin to change, of course, as the Middle Ages inexorably wound to their close—as Arabia was first briefly threatened by the Crusaders in 1182 on a foray led into the Hijaz by the irrepressible Reynald of Châtillon, then occupier of Kerak in present-day south Jordan, in direct violation of a pact existing between the Christian King of Jerusalem and his Muslim counterpart Salah al-Din (Salidin = Weapon of the Faith) al-Ayyubi.[7]

Six centuries later, in the eighteenth century, moreover, the next perceived infidel threat to the peninsula would come with the consolidation of European power in south Asia and the appearance of Christian ships off Arabian coastal shores. The resulting sense of outrage was at least one factor in the subsequent religious revival today known as the "Wahhabi movement" and the rise of the insular Saudi state accompanying it.[8]

Starting in the late 1930s, of course, the massive discovery of oil likewise gradually transformed Riyadh from a small oasis into a major metropolis affecting all aspects of Arabian life. But this rapid emergence from isolation is only an extremely recent phenomenon as evidenced by the twin realities that (1) as late as four decades ago, this now cosmopolitan capital city contained only two paved roads; and (2) where the holy places are concerned, many Muslims still see their struggle in religious terms and view the U.S. troops sent in to liberate Kuwait as occupying infidels.

Yet despite its millennia of highly concentrated isolation, as shown in chapter 1, the history of the brand of Islam that first sprung up upon the Arabian Peninsula has paradoxically demonstrated longstanding commitments to intellectual outreach to other cultures, and in the process, to quite prominent religious pluralism. As from the onset of the faith, Prophet Muhammad afforded special protected status to Christians and Jews.

This commitment issued from his belief in a common divine text (*Umm al-Kitab*) from which all Revealed Scriptures were derived and as well as from his dream of establishing an Islamic Empire of God consisting of a single unified *ummah* comprised of the three heavenly centered Abrahamic faiths as Qur'anically revealed. No other scripture, in fact, expresses greater comity with, and reverence, for its sister religions and their traditions than does the Qur'an.

Throughout the grandeur that is its history, Islam has thus nurtured tolerance, not terror. Throughout the majesty that is its history, Islam has been one of the world's great religions, lending dignity and meaning to lives impoverished of both. It has taught peoples of different ideologies and clans of different races to live side-by-side in brotherhood. It has inspired great learning with which it has enriched the world. What it is witnessing today, therefore, is not only anathema to it, it is wholly out of character.

Islam and Christendom are sister religions that grew out of a common heritage of Jewish revelation and Graeco-Roman philosophy and science. Thus, though often in militant combat throughout the ages, they share a certain coexistent kinship that distinguishes and binds them. Indeed, throughout much of history, Christian and Jewish physicians, financiers, and business people were among the foremost and most prestigious professionals at caliphal courts.[9]

ECHOES OF HISTORY IN THE MODERN MILIEU WORLD

It is thus doubly ironic, then, that today, while most Muslims are not fundamentalists and most fundamentalists are not terrorists, most present-day terrorists are intolerant fundamentalist Muslims and proudly offer themselves to the world as such. Hence, while their fellow Muslims understandably complain when modern media label certain terrorist movements and acts as Islamic, yet do not identify parallel Basque or Serbian terrorists as Christian or Orthodox Hebrew terrorists as Jewish, there is cogent reason. The latter don't openly market themselves in that religious context.

What is the most striking about modern pseudo-Islamic religious terror, though, is that it is almost invariably symbolic and executed in dramatic ways, as the telegenic nature of modern religion, as exemplified by Al-Jazirah TV, has lent an extraordinary twist to the practice of public terrorism, creating its own "electronic ummah" that now makes possible claiming near instantaneous Web site credit for depraved acts of barbarism. Indeed, in an extremely improbable marriage of "sacrilege and Silicon Valley," al-Qaeda, in particular, has grown accomplished in this infamous technique. As to quote television analyst Bryan Jenkins: "Terrorism is theater!"[10]

Moreover, its disturbing displays of violence are unfailingly accompanied by some sense of enduring, absolutist moral justification as characterized by the intensity of the participants' focused commitment and professed transhistoric scope of goals. Hence, while most decent Muslims' complaint about the subsequent stereotyped reportage is understandable, it is more justifiably addressed to those who are actually making the news than to those who cover and report it. For their faith faces a special problem wherein a bin Laden does more in defining Islam's image to the world than do its moderates.[11]

Are such narcissistic terrorists a genuine threat to civilization as mankind knows it? To such simple questions, simplistic answers have frequently evolved that, precisely because of their simplicity, have themselves often been misleading. Among them, many in the Muslim East have been raised to view the Christian West as an irreconcilable enemy of Islam. They concurrently have been taught that Islam's enemies must be destroyed. Hence many, though not all, would-be terrorists have become hostile and dangerous not because the West needs an omnipresent enemy but because *they* do—because they have become more obsessed with attacking perceived enemies of Islam than with defining and projecting the faith's historic noble image.[12]

It is in this context, then, that many in the Islamic world have come to blame American support of Israel and a perceived corresponding U.S. lack of enthusiasm for the Palestinian cause as the incipient cause of the region's angst and strife. Yet this too is a simplistic explanation at best, as Sayyid Qutb came to hate America in the late 1940s and early 1950s, a full decade before the United States formalized its support for Israel—a reality that suggests that the search for the source of terrorism must penetrate further still.

Indeed, in this quest it must extend to the extent of perceiving to perceive terrorism's actual goals. In confronting it, Muslims must define themselves. Do they really want the very name of Allah to terrify the world? Or do they want it to signify a supreme God of goodness and mercy. A religion is what a religion does. When militants incite masses by the millions to pour out in the global streets in blind rage because the pope randomly quotes the intemperate remarks of an otherwise nondescript fourteenth-century Byzantine emperor, Manual II Paleologos, in an otherwise uneventful speech at the University of Regensburg in Germany in September 2006, is this the face of Islam that most Muslims wish to portray—that "if you call Islam a religion of violence, we will kill you"?

Such public violence is undeniably powerful. It can be used to remind the populace at large of the underlying godly power that makes a religion's ideology potent. As such, it can be used to render "divine judgment." It can also be used to create manmade incidents of fear on God's behalf as if its participants have, in some mysterious way, discerned the mind of God, thereby creating one of history's ironies. For though religion can be used to justify violence, violence can conversely be used to empower the impersonation of pseudo-religion.[13]

Challenges of combating terrorism likewise confront several other incontrovertible modern socioeconomic realities. In the Middle Ages, as noted in chapter 1, Islam was the foremost global civilization, powered by dynamic industry and commerce and leavened by original creative arts and sciences.

But within the past half millennium, the Islamic world has lost no small measure of its erstwhile dominance and leadership, first to the modern West and now to the rapidly modernizing Far East. Concurrently, throughout much of the region, the pace of its own modernization has been slow as well as patchwork in its impact—with the results achieved often disappointing.

Its quest for modern militaries has brought a series of humbling defeats. Its quest for industrial development has frequently brought corrupt local economies inordinately reliant upon external aid. Its quest for political freedom from colonizers has likewise, at times in its stead, brought only dangerous new-style indigenous dictatorships—differing from their imperial predecessors only in their more modern instruments of repression and indoctrination.[14]

And improvement aimed at constructive remedy too often does not loom large on the near-term horizon. For after centuries of being the *leaders*—the most advanced, the richest, and the mightiest—commencing in the eighteenth century, the planet's Muslims have been forced to gradually relinquish that role to one of being mere *technological followers* of the West.

The twentieth century brought with it further humiliation still—as no longer being even first among followers, they found themselves falling even further back in the ranks of would-be modernizers, most notably, to the young dynamic entrepreneurs rising rapidly in East Asia and particularly, on the Pacific Rim.

To further add insult to injury, the proud heirs to the civilizations that built Babylon and the pyramids—creators of most of the Seven Wonders of the Ancient World—now find themselves compelled to hire not only Singaporean, Malaysian, and Indonesian, but likewise Japanese, Korean, and Taiwanese, contractors to meet requirements for which their own contractors are incapable, as a once mighty empire of builders has been increasingly laid low.[15]

These widening technological gaps have thus come today to pose increasingly acute challenges—both practical and psychological—for which rulers, theoreticians, would-be reformers, and regional rebels have yet to produce pragmatic solutions, as their attempts at modernization and reform have often not met with success. In the cogent words of Samuel Huntington, collectively today's Muslims "have become convinced of the superiority of their culture yet obsessed with the inferiority of their power."[16]

As for them, the overarching question has simply become: If Islam is indeed a true obstacle to science, to modernization, and to technological development, then how is it that in the early Middle Ages, when imbued with even greater fervor of the faith, Muslim societies were pioneers in all three domains. Its contemplation—reflecting the twin realities (1) that terrorism is a mental illness, not an ideology—a tool, not an end—a tactical gimmick masked in religious language; and (2) that while religions aren't inherently bad, adherents can be, and often are—concurrently invokes the questions initially raised in the introduction as one not of—

What has Islam done to Muslims?

—but:

What have deviants done to Islam?

This reality implies that the way to defeat terrorism conducted in religion's name from the outside is to distinguish between polemic and ideology, confronting the terrorist while leaving the devout free to pursue their faith. For in the last analysis, the problem isn't "What's wrong with Islam?" but it is getting self-professing coteries of Muslims to adhere to its classic precepts—as the real war on terrorism can only be won by Muslims pragmatically working within Islam itself.

As at its roots, the incipient problem is neither classic Islam nor its convictions. For, as analysis has concurrently made indelibly clear, a religion is defined in positive valence by its doctrine and that of Islam is defined within the Qur'an. Its verses are unequivocal in their intent. Islam is a religion not only of moderation but of progress. Historically, it produced momentous scholarly and scientific advance from algebra to the astrolabe, to astronomy, and on through the entire alphabet.

Some of the great progress being realized in East Asia today is, in fact, being forged by devout Muslims diligently at work in Malaysia, Indonesia, as well as elsewhere. Both are Islamic countries and both have generated high-tech, rapid growth economies that compete on a global scale. Is it sheer happenstance, then, that both are concurrently part and parcel of that spiraling prosperity that today characterizes the Pacific Rim?

In short, through its history, Islam has invariably been in the vanguard of economic and technological development as well as a religion of tolerance and coexistence seeking peace. These are positive realities that modern militant fanatics operating under its banner and seeking what they perceive to be a righteous return to the seventh century forever cannot change.

For at the religious bottom line: their handiwork is not Judaism, nor is it Christianity; it is not Islam. Civilization—comprised of all faiths: Buddhists, Christians, Hindus, Jews and Muslims—is instead dealing with an intrinsic evil, an "evil incarnate" emanating from the bowels of hell yet being perpetrated in Islam's name, and as Islam's sacred, scripturally defined formulae for holy war has, for some, devolved inexorably into the perpetration of "unholy terror" fraudulently proclaimed as creed.

What is today taking place within the Islamic world, then, is, in fact, far less a clash of civilizations between East and West, as Samuel Huntington would contend, than it is a continuing divisive conflict amongst Muslims themselves, as the longstanding debate of a century ago over imperial colonial occupation has now given way to a more introspective one of whether Muslims should be permitted to declare jihad against one another. The divisions remain the same—only the language of the dialogue has changed.

As a consequence, today the world of Islam stands at a moment of truth. For while Muslims take just pride in the reality that their religion is one of peace, the violence of just a handful of its radicals has dominated its popular perception and projection throughout much of the world—reflecting the reality that those who comprise the vast majority of decent Muslims may well have inadvertently ceded to the bin Ladens and Zarqawis the power to negatively impact their futures.

The stakes could not be higher. The outcome is not only important for the future of the *religious* East, it is equally important for the *political* West, whose policy makers must not yield to ready stereotypes but instead learn who genuinely represents historic Islamic values and not mere mutant ideological hybrids spawned to satisfy self-serving modern political ends—and then, carefully sort through the intellectual processes actively at work within both in the necessary quest to differentiate their friends.[17]

It is, moreover, an intensely internal struggle today playing out not only in the central Arabian heartland which was the birthplace of Islam, but also in the long developed capitals of the Middle East—Tehran, Cairo, Baghdad, Damascus—and the Orient—Djakarta and Manila—as well as in the cosmopolitan capitals of the West—London, Paris, Berlin, Madrid, New York, and Washington—wherein that message is being redefined and refined by successive generations of recent Muslim immigrants.[18]

Part of the challenge contributing to propensities for new solutions, as chapter 8 reveals, issues from mounting perceptions on the Muslim street of relative economic deprivation, making a compelling case for fundamental structural reform throughout much of the Islamic East. The facts of life remain largely economic and to fix an economic problem, one must attack it at its source—a reality that carries with it the knowledge that the quickest passage to people's hearts is through their pocketbooks.

To this end, then, it may well be that more dinars, dirhams, riyals, and dollars must be put into the pockets of average Muslims to enable them to feed their families if the spreading morass of despair that can emanate from perceptions of relative economic deprivation are to be effectively dispelled. Expensive gasoline, combined with internal wealth distribution reforms, may well be a price that the Christian West must pay to stanch the flow of political terrorism now seeping from the Islamic East. Such an economic course will not be cheap, of course, but it may make more sense than other options, particularly when viewed within the context of Winston Churchill's famed aphorism that "people will always do the right thing only after having exhausted all other possibilities."

Other options have been tried—and failed spectacularly. Among them, conciliation is ultimately a senseless dynamic. It is likewise likely a deadly one. For the ongoing struggle against terrorism, to quote Ephesians 6:10–17, is indeed against "the cosmic powers of the present darkness"— defined by Ezekiel 32:22–32 as one to be waged relentlessly against "those who spread terror in the land of the living."[19]

Christian theologian Lee Griffith cites Revelation 13:3 to push the point that terror cannot be fought with terror, that "the Beast cannot be killed with violence!" This view conforms to an all too common notion that "terrorism cannot be defeated—only reduced, attenuated, and to some degree controlled." But such a caricature does not comport with fact and instead once again invokes vague memories of echoes of Neville Chamberlain's cane on the cobblestones of Munich.[20]

For the reality is that the only times that Middle Eastern terror has been effectively suppressed has been accomplished by Muslims themselves when Jordan's King Hussein obliterated it in the Palestinian refugee camps in Black September in 1970—and again a dozen years later when Syria's Hafez al-Asad decimated Muslim Brotherhood fundamentalists who had holed up in Hamah in 1982, with the estimated killed in this latter action fixed by Amnesty International in excess of 25,000.

In short, the lessons of history of the war on terror unequivocally hold that to win, force must be met with force, or failing that, to quote seventeenth-century British poet John Milton, there will be "from the flames, no light, but only darkness, visible."[21]

IS THERE, THEN, HOPE FOR REMEDY?

That said, the convergence of these realities implies that, at the political bottom line, Western strategists cannot "fix" Islam. But modern moderate

Muslims can—and must. It is they who have the most at stake in their quests to live normal daily lives. It is they who must now act to create an impervious "religious firewall" between the would-be radicals and themselves if Islam's great cultural heritage and rich legacy to world civilization are ultimately to survive.

Who will win—moderate Muslims who want to recapture their faith or those who would use religion as a weapon to achieve self-serving political goals? The answer may forge the course of future civilization. While time remains, therefore, the moderates must act before an iron curtain of closemindedness descends with a terrible finality between Political Islam and the outside civilized world.

The stakes are extremely high—for the consequences of allowing the bin Ladens of the world to win are both clear and calamitous. The question of whether the Islamic community is willing take on the tough issues that fuel extremism in order to win space for the revival and reform of Muslim societies throughout the planet remains, at best, problematic. Yet the global consequences are immense.[22]

To date, this hasn't happened and part of the reason may well indeed be cultural. As this inquiry has shown, Islam has an untold story to tell. Yet today it isn't being told in the forthright manner that some of the causes of other world cultures enjoy. In the spring of 2005, for instance, the Frankel family of Detroit donated yet another $20 million to the University of Michigan to expand its Institute of Judaic Studies that they previously established.

The global Islamic community is certainly vastly larger than its Jewish counterpart. It too enjoys great wealth concentrated in the hands of individuals who could readily establish institutes of Islamic studies throughout the world to highlight those foundations of faith that their 1.4 million coreligionists cherish and hold dear.

Yet curiously, to date, that recourse hasn't been adopted, as wealthy Muslims appear reluctant to commit their capital to share the majesty that is Islam. Indeed, when such a course is even suggested, they look at the suggester as if he or she is mentally dispossessed. But why? Why not create a parallel Institute of Islamic Studies at the University of Michigan? Or better still, why not merge the two to create a new omnibus multireligious center dedicated to supporting original research into the shared histories of all of the Abrahamic faiths?

This is not a radical proposition. It is instead affirmation of the time-tested precept of "doing well" by "doing good."[23] But until that happens, on the whole, many Muslims today appear more willing to concede outright the global public-relations battle to other cultures than to actually take the requisite steps to win it, preferring to attack its perceived enemies rather than promoting its intrinsic values as relevant for future emulation, with the result that the present stasis of misunderstanding persists as a pandemic. This reality, of course, greatly complicates the task of would-be sympathetic policy makers in their quests to discern and promote their friends.

In tandem with a need for better religious understanding have come calls for religious reformation. Indeed, the very concepts of reform and renewal are intrinsic to the Islamic faith and are integral to its heritage. Both causes invoke a call to a return to the true fundamentals of Islam as manifest in the Qur'an and *ahadith*. Indeed, *islah* is a specialized Qur'anic term used to describe the reformist activities of rectifiers, as in:

> O Moses. Is it thy intention to slay me as thou slewest a man yesterday? Thy intention is no other than to become a tyrant in the land and not to be one who sets things right (*min al-musallihin*). (Surat al-Qasas 28:19)

Renewal (*tajdid*), in turn, is predicated upon a Prophetic Tradition holding that:

> Allah will send to His ummah at the onset of each new century those who will renew its faith (mujaddidin).[24]

In this vein, noted medieval Islamic scholar Richard Bulliett observes:

> A Muslim tradition holds that with every new century, there comes a "renewer" (*al-mujaddid*), literally a person whose mission is to remake Muslim religious life anew.[25]

Traditionally, the beginning of a new century is a ripe time for the renewer to appear. Of more relevance to present-day matters, the turn of the fifteenth Islamic century in 1980 brought with it not only the Islamic revolution in Iran but an enhanced feeling among Muslims and non-Muslims alike that something new and titanic was at hand.

Since then, scores of authors have argued that Islam is in need of a reformation, or more specifically, a Martin Luther, the Christian renewer par excellence. At the turn of the new millennium, explicit to the aspired objectives of reformation, then, have been recurring calls for a concurrent process of renewal—a revival of Islam's founding normative traditions combined with a relegitimization of the precept of deductive reasoning (*ijtihad*) to: (1) restore the faith; (2) remove accreted innovations from its practice; and (3) reexamine the continuing validity of current institutions as established by the religious hierarchy, the *'ulama'*.[26]

To these ends, some—often called "neofundamentalists"—have argued that the requisite reform invokes the need for an ideological reformulation not unlike the Protestant Reformation or its doctrinal counterpart, the Vatican II Council of 1979 within Catholicism. Others,

such as Sudanese jurist 'Abd Allah Ahmad al-Na'im, argue passion-
ately for an Islamic legal reformation. Iranian-born Islamic scholar Reza
Aslan, in turn, makes a compelling case that such a reformation is already underway:[27]

On the Enveloping Islamic Reformation

It may be too early to know who will write the next chapter of Islam's story, but
it is not too early to recognize who will ultimately win the war between reform
and counterreform. When, fifteen hundred years ago, Prophet Muhammad
launched a revolution in Mecca to replace the archaic, rigid, and inequitable
structures of tribal society with a radically new vision of morality and social egal-
itarianism, he tore apart the very fabric of traditional Arab society. It took years
of violence and devastation to cleanse the Hijaz of its "false idols." It will take
many more years to cleanse Islam of its new false idols, bigotry, and fanaticism,
worshiped by those who have replaced Muhammad's original vision of tolerance
and unity with their own ideals of hatred and discord. But cleansing is inevitable
and the tide of reform cannot be stopped. The Islamic Reformation is already
here. We are all living it.

—Reza Aslan, No God but God, 2005, p. 266

In a March 25, 2005, in a follow-up on the Sunday morning political talk
show, *Meet the Press*, Aslan continued:

I think that from an American perspective, we can look at the events of September 11 and its aftermath as perhaps initiating a sort of "clash of civilizations," to use Samuel Huntington's ubiquitous term.

But from a true Islamic perspective, what is taking place in the Muslim
world is actually an internal battle between Muslims—a standoff between
those who, for the past century, have struggled to reconcile their faith with
the realities of the modern world and those who have been reacting to those
stark realities by reverting to a more fundamentalist version of their faith.

We are living in the twilight of an Islamic reformation, and it is a reformation that is inevitable. Reform can be slowed down, but it cannot be stopped.
Obstacles can be placed in its way—and I think that since September 11, there
have been obstacles, as well as a galvanizing of fundamentalist forces. But
the tide of reform is inevitable.[28]

Such recurring reformer calls for a genuine return to the founding precepts of Islam are themselves undeniably genuine. Paradoxically, though,
in their quest, it may well be that Muslims who are truly serious about
their attainment *are not fundamentalist enough*. They may not need an ideological revolution—they may instead merely need to just take back the
foundations of their faith.

For at the bottom line, as this inquiry shows, Islam doesn't need a "New Testament." It doesn't need a "Reformation." What it needs is a genuine *salafiyah* movement that removes centuries of gross misperception that have accreted within its doctrinal formulae and prescriptions and restores it to its traditional ideological foundations. Muhammad Ibn 'Abd al-Wahhab aspired to this goal but never quite reached it, but it must be reached, as the time has come to write the book *What's Right with Islam!*[29]

In short, while Western political experience may be richly inspirational for some, Islamic political thought and traditions are likewise relevant and worthy of accommodation. To that end, Islam's moderate majority must seek the restoration of Muslim society by returning it to its historical roots, and they must act now to forestall that all-encompassing, impervious miasma of intolerance and hatred that now threatens to engulf the Islamic world. To quote a prominent Islamist slogan: "*Islam nafsuhu huwa al-Hall!*" (Islam itself is the solution!) At the bottom line then, Bernard Lewis notwithstanding, the problem is not "what went wrong with Islam," but is instead the challenge of co-opting self-professing deviant coteries of Muslims to adhere to the classic teachings of its doctrine.

The challenge will not be easy, as fundamentalism—be it Islamic, Jewish, or Christian—is, by nature, both literal in its interpretation and reactionary in its vision, and its back-to-basics solutions may not invariably be addressed to twenty-first-century challenges and concerns. As a result, religion building, like nation building, is invariably a complex process. But if peaceful coexistence between the East and West is to be restored, it is a challenge that must be met head-on.

The key political issue at stake, then, is not just a restatement of the longstanding "Eastern question." For what the West faces is a Muslim world rife with strife—with complex social grievances that are at once historical and modern, psychological and physical, political and economic—all coalesced into a challenge that is deep-seated and structural. And while cynics may say that: "It's the Muslims' problem—let them deal with it!"—the events of 9/11 made indelibly clear that the world is no longer all that simple, that it is irrevocably interrelated in an intricate aggregate of enveloping dilemmas that hold profound ramifications for all.[30]

Throughout history, every religious tradition has faced the perennial challenge of translating its creed into terms relevant to its time. This quest, in its most general form, is that of defining the eternal, essential principles of the faith and ascertaining how they may best be restated to make them cogent in contemporary terms. For each new era brings its own germane parameters for accomplishment and for determining how they are best understood, pursued, and met. This is the essential challenge confronting modern Muslims—the vast majority of whom deem themselves to be moderate—today. How effectively the challenge is met may well determine, in fact, if the quest to end global terror is to end in peace.

The course is laden with potential pitfalls and will definitely not be easy. For it bears repeating that within the past half century the *only* times that terrorism has effectively been stopped in its tracks has been with still greater terrorism—King Hussein of Jordan in "Black September" with the Palestinians commencing on September 16, 1971; and President Asad of Syria with the Muslim Brotherhood at Hamah in 1982. In each case, King Hussein and President Asad proved conclusively that terrorism can best be trumped through upping the ante by tabling even greater terrorism as its ace.

America missed a golden opportunity on September 12, 2001, when it then already knew that Osama bin Laden's al-Qaeda organization was responsible for the World Trade Center disaster that had occurred the day before. Indeed, within twenty-four hours of the attack, elite CIA units were already en route to Afghanistan and U.S. Special Forces would follow there within mere days. On October 7, in fact, bin Laden himself exulted in a televised message that:

> Allah has blessed a vanguard group of Muslims, the very spearhead of Islam, to destroy America.[31]

Had the nation acted decisively then, bin Laden and his followers could have been decimated in their hiding places at Tora Bora and the terrible "genie of religious terrorism" could well have still been put back into its bottle. The planet would have understood, cognizant both that political correctness does not win wars on terrorism and that terrorism manifests all of the symptoms of disease, not war—it cannot be won, it must be eradicated.

With all of world sympathy at its disposal and a wealth of weapons with expiring shelf lives, then, America could easily have transformed the imposing Parrot's Beak Mountains of Tora Bora into that great crater that forever glows in the dark—a spectacle at once so awesome that a thousand years from now, peasants of the Indian subcontinent would still tread with trepidation to the edge of its radiating vast expanse and peering in, conclude that global civilization, with equal determination on each side of the intellectual great divide, must never, ever play the game "My God is greater than your God" again.

Draconian, perhaps, but 'tis better than another wake-up call from hell! As even for terrorists, there is a tipping point whereas the price becomes too great. When President Harry Truman exercised a nuclear option at Hiroshima and Nagasaki, he did so with a moral conviction that his course of action would save thousands of innocent lives. Taking out al-Qaeda's command center and senior leadership on September 14, 2001, with ultimate extreme prejudice, could have, in this instance, been achieved with equal, if not greater, moral justification and with far less collateral damage.

CAN AL-QAEDA STILL WIN?

Fate seldom overlooks its opportunities missed. It was an opportunity unrequited wherein the world sought righteous redemption and cried out for revenge, yet one that likely will not again resurface. It was missed because of political trepidation, because American policy makers failed to discern that while a war on terrorism is not an attack on a religion, it must nonetheless perforce be a ruthless, persevering attack on the precept of terrorist jihadism, which is a mutant, cancerous outgrowth of religion. Accordingly, given these stark doctrinal and political realities, will the militancy of al-Qaeda in the long term succeed?

If it does, then al-Qaeda as a political movement will become utterly incorrigible if not unstoppable. Having defeated one great superpower in the wastelands of Afghanistan, should it now succeed in driving the other "great Satan" from Iraq, that success will be perceived as a clear sign to its metastasizing deviant subculture that political Islam is not only recrudescent but, with God's blessing, invincible—and with that conviction, the suffocating pall of a toxic cloud of terror falsely perpetrated in Islam's holy name will have been cast over the entire world.

But as with Afghanistan and the Soviets, should a violent expansionist Islam arise from the battlefields of Asia, it will again not be won by military power or prowess, but will instead issue in the form of a pandering pandemic bred and nurtured in the halls of Washington, by those who, determined to lose at all cost for self-serving political reasons, would cut and run in opting for an easy exit strategy—who, buoyed by cherished memories of Neville Chamberlain's cowardly equivocation in the face of danger, would again snatch defeat from victory's jaws—and not by those who today possess the moral courage to stay the requisite course for ultimate victory. This is a watershed in human history.

In reality, however, while al-Qaeda can in theory succeed, that probability is not likely. The reasons are two-fold. In the first instance, though like fascim and communism before it, it does draw its lifeblood from the "politics of victimization," it is nonetheless insular. Because it is parasitic upon a particular religious faith, it does not resonantly speak to those outside that faith's constituency. As such, it lacks the potent global appeal of fascism and communism which, given time, the West effectively defeated in the twentieth century.

Second, and equally important, it is unabashedly reactionary, offering no genuine alternative winning vision appealing to most Muslims for the future. It is likewise significantly weaker than its failed twentieth-century totalitarian predecessors, rendering it less likely to win—both intellectually and geopolitically. On this, the lessons of history are unequivocally clear.

Hence, if, on the one hand, Osama bin Laden can convince a significant portion of Islam to buy into his al-Qaeda view that the West is indeed both weak and decadent, a threat to Islam that must be perforce eradicated, then a long and bitter struggle may well lie ahead for America in particular, but equally for Europe as recent events in London, Madrid, and the suburbs of Paris make crystal clear. And to this end, he may find a modicum of encouragement in his perceptions of recent equivocation, as he asserts in a May 28, 1998, media interview:

> We have witnessed in the past decade the decline of the American government and the weakening of the American soldier who is ready to wage cold wars and unprepared to fight long ones. This was demonstrated in Beirut when the Marines departed after two explosions. It was repeated in Somalia. . . .
>
> Our soldiers are surprised at the low morale of American soldiers. . . . After a few blows, they run in defeat. . . .They forget about being the world leader and the leader of the new world order. They leave dragging their corpses and their shameful defeats.[32]

Indeed, this may well be bin Laden's end game—precipitating 9/11 to draw the United States into larger conflict within the Muslim world. Surely knowing that his al-Qaeda network cannot single-handedly defeat the United States, he may well instead merely be manipulating it as a catalyst to exhort the Islamic ummah to join his global jihad. Hence, his declaration:

> America is a power possessed of tremendous military might and a wide-ranging economy. But all of this is built upon an unstable foundation which can be targeted, with special attention to its obvious weak spots. A small group of young Islamic fighters managed to provide people with proof of the fact that it is possible to wage war upon and fight against a so-called great power. They managed to protect their religion better than the governments and peoples of the fifty-odd countries of the Muslim world because they used jihad as a means to defend their faith.[33]

According to this line of reasoning, then, once America is drawn into a major regional Middle East conflict, it can be worn down by the malaise of general attrition in a guerilla war—thereby precipitating a "civilizational clash" that would render the region essentially ungovernable and ripe for a takeover by his would-be caliphate. The strategy is not without its guile and is one contemplated in the abstract by Bernard Lewis in a more regional context:

> A possibility, which could even be precipitated by fundamentalism, is what has of late been fashionable to call "Lebanonization." Many of the states of

the Middle East—Egypt is an obvious exception—are of recent, artificial construction and are vulnerable to such a process. If central power is sufficiently
weakened, there is no real civil society to hold the polity together, no real
sense of common identity. . . . The state then disintegrates—as happened in
Lebanon—into the chaos of squabbling, feuding, fighting sects, tribes, regions, and parties.[34]

But while Osama bin Laden could, in precept, in the end, still be proven
right, recent Western success in the arrests and killings of key elements of
his al-Qaeda leadership and network suggests that the tide of history is
instead rising against him and that his prospects for success are accordingly growing increasingly problematic, if not dim.[35]
    Conceding that political movements and empires transit through se-
quential periods of emergence, rise, and decline, the ultimate answer as to
whether they will prevail thus must be sought in their intrinsic natures.
Geopolitical analysts tend to evaluate societies in terms of individualism,
pluralism, and the rule of law. These are the values that early on empowered the West to invent modernity, expand exponentially in technology,
and become the envy of the modern world.[36]
    But these are values unique to Western civilization yet alien to the East.
The critical question therefore arises: Are there corresponding distinctly
Eastern political values? Stated differently: Are religious zealots such as
the bin Ladens, al-Zawahiris, and Mullah 'Umars of the twenty-first century strikingly unique? How do they differ from the totalitarian Mus-
solinis, Milosevics, Maos, and Pol Pots of the twentieth century? Are they
true leaders of enduring ideological movements or mere transitory phenomena?
    In the twentieth century, as noted, both fascism and communism, in
their times, secured the dialectic integration of much of Europe's under-
privileged classes, invoking widespread political debate—a mobilization
that became institutionalized through participation in mass elections and
even access to government, as in the cases of Hitler's Germany, Mus-
solini's Italy, Stalin's Russia, and Tito's Yugoslavia. Yet today these ideologies have not only been rendered obsolete, they have been eradicated,
as the 1989 cave-in of the Berlin Wall to the forces of democracy indelibly
made clear.[37]
    Today, while classic Islam—being a religion and not a political ideology—
has never been doctrinally or operational fascist, terrorist jihadism invoked in its name far too often evinces many of those genes. As ideologically, fascism and communism shared much in common with the brand of
toxic terrorism now being perpetrated in the faith's good name, both in
their day being the ideological equivalents of Islamism in the politics of
"victim mongering." For all, violence becomes a first recourse rather than
a last resort. All share an "us vs. them" mentality—and a bipolar global

view—in the case of communism, a "class" dichotomy; in the case of Nazi fascism, a "racial" dichotomy; in the case of modern Middle East terrorism, a "religious" dichotomy.[38]

In each case, fanatics have sought to divide their societies between the forces of "good" and "evil," between the "virtuous" who are foreordained to rule and the "virtueless" who are condemned to disappear. In all three cases, an external enemy has been invoked as the epitome of evil—and in all three cases, proponents have emerged within these lesser developed societies highly jealous of, and seeking to surpass, more advanced, productive, and successful ones.

At the bottom line, then, and despite its superficial trappings of religious fervor, political Islam, Islamic extremism, is indeed remarkably similar to its now defunct precedent secular cousins, fascism and communism. It was sympathetic to the Nazis in World War II; and in its modus operandi, a quest to transform its jihad into a "clash of civilizations," in fact, is fascist in approach. For it is a shared expression not of spirituality, but of alienation and in particular, a seething rage founded primarily upon resentment of the democratic, capitalistic West and its prosperity and strength.

And like its fascist and communist predecessors, it too seeks a millennial redemption through politics. Animated by the pursuit of temporal power—the dual quests for the abolition of globalization and the destruction of the decadent, libertine West—it today calls for a recrudescent utopian "Pan-Islamic state" featuring an unconstrained centralization of God's authority at its disposal.[39]

Yet while fascism and communism were, in their times, sustained by powerful political bases within militarily formidable powers, Political Islam enjoys no such strategic advantage. For despite his focus on projecting a *salafist* image, apart from a few disaffected intellectuals and deranged, dispossessed suicide bombers, Osama bin Laden has been remarkably unable to unify poor urban youth, the Muslim middle class, and its merchants into a working coalition of the nature that the Ayatollah Khomeini did in his Iranian revolution of 1979.[40]

And time is definitely not on his side. For while in the late 1980s and early 1990s, Muslim mujahidin were able to exult in the reality that, with significant external support, they were able to drive the Soviet superpower from Afghanistan, two decades later any remote expectation that the movement could similarly bring down the United States has been effectively shattered by the fall of the Taliban and the scattering of its adherents into a global diaspora.[41]

Moreover, such projected imagery of political Islam as it does exist runs directly contrary and counterintuitive to the current tide of cultural invasion that Silicon Valley has wrought. For, while fundamentalists may still vehemently oppose the physical presence of foreign troops on their soil, they cannot prevent the cyberspace invasion of their airwaves, via the electronic "virtual ummah" of the satellite and Internet, of foreign global ideas and trends. As already, via them, the powerful lures of modernity and progress are generating striking resonance among large sections of trendy Muslim youth. It is a battle over the right to self-definition and self-determination—with the outcome of the war on terror hinging directly upon the outcome of that struggle.[42]

Certainly political Islam remains capable of wreaking great damage, as 9/11 left no doubt. Succeeding on a battlefield of terror arrayed against the menace of a ruthless, fanatic, heavily armed, tactically flexible, theocratically inspired neofascism unequivocally opposed to all those of values that civilized society holds dear will unquestionably be an overarching challenge. But as noted political economist Brink Lindsey also may well have accurately assessed:

> [T]heir destructive power is today undeniable. But in the end, I do not believe that they can avoid the fate of other radical movements of the "'Industrial Counterrevolution"': interment in what President Bush has stirringly referred to as: "history's unmarked graveyard of discarded lies."[43]

Mutual understanding is quintessential to this end. This work is dedicated to its promotion in the quest to ensure amity and peace. No nation on earth has provided more stability security, prosperity, and liberty to the peoples of the world than has America. Yet she endures a global joke, not entirely undeserved, regarding a United Nations survey that asked: "What should be done about food shortages in the rest of the world?" In the United States, so goes the joke, no one could answer because no one could understand the phrase: "the rest of the world."

Both sides of the ideological divide must fix that. Enhanced mutual understanding is a critical first step.

Appendix A

Islam's Code of Conduct for Engaging Foreign Policy

If they lean to peace, then lean thee also to peace.

—Surat al-Anfal 7: 63

REFLECTIONS ON THE ISLAMIC QUEST FOR JUST WAR

The rational bases advanced for terrorism today being perpetrated in Islam's name are perhaps best understood by placing the contentions within the ideological context from wherein they were first set. To this end, analysis commences by seeking fuller understanding of the doctrinally prescribed Islamic approach to foreign policy—as before "deviance in practice" can be determined, it is critical to comprehend what is the prescribed norm.

For though conventional portrayals of the Islamic Law for War and Peace have often cast the doctrine as invoking relentless effort by the *Dar al-Islam* (the abode of those who have submitted to Islam) "to militarily engage and subjugate the World of Unbelievers (*Dar al-Harb*)," the pragmatism of reality throughout history has more often prevailed over the perceived prescription of doctrinal mandate.

The reason for this reality has typically derived from longstanding universal traditions regarding the conduct of foreign policy as a function of state, as the medieval Muslims also referred to their empire as the *Dar al-Salam* (House of Peace)—a bifurcation that did not mean that war was the dominant political reality within the Dar al-Harb, but only that outside of Islam, there could be no genuine peace.

161

Yet here, semantic clarification may be in order. For while some may take issue with characterizing the early Dar al-Islam as a "theocratic state," the reality is that the concepts of state and society were then identical. The term *state*, in fact, is not to be found in the Qur'an nor was it in significant usage in Prophet Muhammad's time.

The term *ummah* (community) was in vogue instead—with the word and concept of *dawlah*, meaning *dynasty* or *state*, not truly popularized until early 'Abbasid times. Accordingly, some analysts have adopted the political term *divine nomocracy*—a governance by immutable law defined by the *Oxford Dictionary* as a "system of government based on a legal code; a rule of law of a community"—to define the early Islamic state.[1]

This is a crucial distinction. For, as noted in subsequent analysis, in Prophet Muhammad's "global view," each of the Peoples of the Book—Christians and Jews alike—had been sent their own prophets or prophet to communicate to them divine law which then came to constitute a covenant between Him and that people. This reality implied, therefore, that the world was foreordained not to be a monolithic hegemonic society but instead a composite, pluralistic community with each people conforming to its own covenant and to the guidance of its own prophet or prophets.[2]

Islam, in turn, was to be God's "final revelation" and Muhammad the "Seal of the Prophets." Hence, the term *Islam*, meaning "submission to Allah's will," itself reflected a covenant between God as Governor and the Community of Believers, the governed. Indeed, in his compact with the people of al-Madinah in 623, Muhammad described the Muslim *ummah* as one distinct from all others in which all loyalties, tribal or otherwise, were now superseded by Islamic brotherhood.

Within this shared community, Allah was the sole source of governing authority and Muhammad His vicegerent—directly instructed by Him and enjoined to rule with consummate justice. Pursuant to this process, while full submission to Islam qualified the individual for membership within the Islamic congregation, it concurrently conveyed an Islamic nationality representative of both a religion and a state.[3]

In this global view, then, the universal nomocracy of Islam, like its counterpart *Respublica Christiana* in the West, assumed that its adherents formed a supranational Community of Believers, bound by one law and governed by one ruler. Hence, Muhammad was at once, in a religious sense, God's legate on Earth serving as His overseer and, in a secular sense, Caesar, serving as secular ruler of His domain. His caliphal successors, in turn, as rulers of Islam, were at once popes and emperors whose functions were both as enforcers of divine law and administrative governors responsible for the security and expansion of Islam.[4]

Accordingly, the doctrinal foundations for the earliest sources of Islamic law were the Qur'an and Prophetic Traditions (*ahadith*), sayings or actions attributable to Prophet Muhammad that gradually came to form the embodiment of Muslim common law (*sunnah*). To justify its moral code, like the other heavenly religions, Islam represented that its jurisprudential ideals system issued from a divine source that encapsulated God's will and justice. Thus, in legal theory, divine law preceded both society and state—with the latter existing solely for the purpose of its enforcement. Its juridical basis was simple. That which was not prohibited by divine law was permitted by it.[5]

Given the secular complexities of governance, other sources of auxiliary juridical tradition also gradually came to be employed. To this end, the early caliphs and their jurists often resorted to personal opinion (*ra'i*) to supplement the jurisdictional coverage of divine and common law. In this process, over time, four separate and distinct schools of Islamic jurisprudence eventually came to be recognized: Hanafi, Maliki, Shafi'i, and Hanbali.

Analogy (*qiyas*), pioneered by jurists of the Hanafi school of legal thought of Iraq, likewise became prominent in usage. Consensus (*ijma'*), advanced by the Maliki school of legal thought of al-Madinah, became a primary source of common law as well. The juridical basis for consensus was a tradition attributed to Prophet Muhammad that "my people shall never be unanimous in error."[6]

Within this system, then, the Islamic law of nations, as articulated by Hanafi jurist Muhammad b. Hassan al-Shaybani in his *Kitab al-Siyar*—as well as by numerous ideological contemporaries—was not a separate body of law per se, but instead a comprehensive extension of existing legal precepts designed to govern the relations of Muslims with non-Muslims whether within or outside the Dar al-Islam.

Unlike conventional modern international law, which contemplates a "family of nations" each enjoying full sovereign rights and equality of status, however, Islamic international law more closely resembled those of ancient Rome and early medieval Christendom—predicated upon the basis of a "universal state" whereby, as "Divine nomocracies," they presumed that mankind constituted one community bound by one legal code which, through proselytizing, was ultimately destined to constitute one community, bound by a common law and ruled by a common ruler.[7]

Similar to other then contemporary international law, moreover, that of Islam was ordinarily applicable to individuals rather than to territorially defined groups—for like all ancient and medieval law, it was both universal and extraterritorial in its application and binding upon all Muslims, as individuals or groups, irrespective of whether they resided within the Dar al-Islam or without. Within it, moreover, formal recognition of the law of no other nation but its own was paramount—a polity whose ultimate goal was a single universal system of religious law to be administered exclusively by its ruler (*imam*).[8]

As such, its foreign policy, equivalent to "custom law," wherein rules expressed in treaties with non-Muslims fell within the categories of agreements, and *fatawa* (juridical decrees), as well as legal commentaries and opinions of caliphs and *imams* in both interpretation and application based upon analogy and logical deduction from authoritative sources, formed the basis of its corpus juris.[9] Within it, as described in chapter 2 and appendices B and C, jihad, the judicious exercise of a moral prerogative for imperial expansion was destined to be the primary instrument for propagation of the faith, with the ultimate goal of institutionalizing Islam as a universal religion.

This was an ambitious undertaking for the then perceived world, which, as noted, was bifurcated into a "world of believers" (= the Dar al-Islam) cohabiting with scriptuaries, Peoples of the Book (*dhimmis*), operating under the protection of a covenant (*aman*) within territories corresponding to Muslim rule and a parallel "world of the unbelievers" (Dar al-Harb = literally "House of War") encompassing all other communities lying outside the realm of Islam. Within this global political matrix, then, jihad against the Dar al-Harb need not perforce be martial; indeed, it was preferably accomplished through moral suasion.

The Arabic term *jihad*, in fact, directly derived from the triliteral root verb, *jahada*, meaning "to exert." Its juridical-theological meaning therefore mandated the exertion of one's efforts in the cause of Allah, thereby rendering His word supreme. It derived from the Qur'anic verses:

> O you who believe. Shall I show you a commerce that will save you from a painful punishment. Then you must believe in Allah and His Messenger and strive diligently for the cause of Allah with your wealth and lives . . . and He will give you another benefit which you love; help from Allah and a present victory. Give good tidings (O Muhammad) to the believers. (Surat al-Saff 10–13)

Hence, the precept of jihad, as observed, did not necessarily invoke war, since exertion in Allah's cause could be achieved by peaceful means as well. As such, it was a tool of religious propagation that could be employed either by the sword or through persuasion; but in its earliest Makkan revelations within the Qur'an, the emphasis was clearly on the more peaceful doctrine of voluntary acquiescence.

The pioneering Muslim jurists, as noted in chapter 2, had in fact, delineated numerous ways whereby jihad might be carried out by the heart, by the tongue, by the pen, and by the sword. Of them, "by the heart" was deemed foremost in preference and constituted the greater jihad.[10] Thereby,

Islam outlawed all other forms of war and violence except in self-defense or to preserve order. Only a war that had an ultimate religious purpose—to enforce Allah's law or to check transgressions against it—was sanctioned as legitimate. In the pursuit of jihad, therefore, medieval Muslims were trained and retrained constantly, reflecting a conviction that the best way to preserve the peace was to prepare for war (*si vis pacem, para bellum*).[11]

In this quest, the medieval Muslims, like their imperial Holy Roman counterparts, were committed to the precept of just war (*bellum justum*). In both approaches, for any war to be *justum*, it must also be *pium* (pious), within the sanction of religion and in accordance with the will of the worshipped Supreme Being. Indeed, St. Thomas Aquinas, deeply acquainted with Muslim writing and jurisprudence, formulated his own theory of just war along lines similar to the Islamic doctrine of jihad.[12]

Doctrinally, such jihad—unless the Muslim community was subjected to surprise attack, which then invoked all believers to fight, including women and children—was regarded by Muslim jurists of all schools to be not an individual but a collective obligation. As such, its imposition caused recourse to jihad to become a state obligation.[13]

Medieval Muslim jurists distinguished two separate species of jihad, that against unbelievers and that against apostates, dissenters, and other would-be seceders from Islam. Accordingly, beyond the general jihad prescribed against polytheists, al-Mawardi subdivided jihad against believers into three categories: jihad against the apostate (*al-riddah*); jihad against the dissenter (*al-baghi*); and jihad against the seceder (*al-muharib*).[14]

Predicated on the Qur'anic verse—

Make ready for them whatever force and strings of horses you can, to terrify the enemy of Allah and your enemy (Surat al-Anfal 8:60)

—other jurists frequently added a fourth category of just war: *ribat* (homeland security) defense of the borders of the Dar al-Islam; to wit, stationing forces within its harbors and frontier towns (*thughur*) for defensive purposes. Some Muslim jurists explicitly cite Prophetic Traditions, in fact, wherein Muhammad is reported to have said that deployment for service in *ribat* was preferable to the pursuit of militant jihad.[15]

Would-be jihadists had to meet several preconditions, including being:

• among the Islamic Community of Believers;
• mature and of sound mind;
• able-bodied;
• male in gender;
• without debt and economically independent;

- possessing parental approval and that of the *imam*; and
- fully committed in allegiance and obedience to the jihad commanders.

The jihad, when initiated as a public duty, was therefore a collective obligation that could only be declared by the head of state, the *imam*, or his designated deputy. According to the medieval Muslim jurist al-Mawardi, such delegation of authority to invoke jihad could also be made to regional governors, particularly those bordering territories of the perceived enemy.

Indeed, commanders of the homeland security border forces (*al-ribat*) were under permanent sanction to declare war against the "distant enemy" if attacked. Private citizens likewise could, and indeed were fully expected to, rally to such a cause as an incumbent obligation. The initiation of actual fighting, however—mandatory by martial doctrine—must invariably be preceded by a call to the would-be opposition to join the Community of Islam in accordance with the Qur'anic verse: "We never punish until We have first sent an Apostle."[16]

In the early Muslim conquests, military commanders would generally wait three days subsequent to issuing such an invitation prior to commencing fighting. Within this period of hiatus, therefore, negotiations could, and often did, take place. At times, such negotiations led to amicable settlements, as in the cases of the terms of surrender of numerous towns in Iraq and Syria during the early Islamic conquests.

Such also applied to negotiations of Muslim commander 'Amr b. al-'As with the patriarch of Egypt in 637, which brought the nation's Copts to peaceful terms with the Muslims. At other times, however, they failed and were cut short, with active war commencing thereafter, as was the case with Rustum, commander of the Persian Sasanid military, preceding the fateful Battle of al-Qadisiyah, which also took place in 637. Similar negotiations were likewise often undertaken with the Byzantines, and later the Crusaders, as precursors to war.[17]

As for termination of hostilities, having been promised victory by Allah, fighting could only come to a close with the capitulation of the enemy. The sole exception to this mandate under Islamic legal doctrine could come only in a circumstance of prospective defeat or other grave incidence of *force majeure*. Thus, the *imam*, as titular leader of the Community of Believers, was enjoined to abstain from war if his forces were insufficient; but if he elected to engage the enemy and faced imminent defeat, he was obliged to effectively withdraw in order to save lives of surviving followers. Such defeated commanders, nonetheless, were obligated to proceed on the presumption that such a setback was temporary, and that the battle would be resumed in a subsequent second round.[18]

REFLECTIONS ON THE ISLAMIC PURSUIT OF JUST PEACE

At the bottom line, however, as detailed in analysis in chapter 2 and appendix C, the ultimate goal of the Islamic consummate quest for just war was not violence but to achieve a just peace. For while in theory, the doctrinal objective of Dar al-Islam was a concerted effort to constantly reduce the Dar al-Harb until it would ultimately disappear, in practicality the dichotomy of the peace option persisted through the entire course of Islamic history.

Seeking to accommodate this lingering bifurcation, then, certain Muslim jurists—most noteworthy the Shafi'is—advanced a third temporary global division, a Domain of Peace (*Dar al-Sulh*), Domain of Treaty (*Dar al-Ahd*), or Domain of Neutrality (*Dar al-Hiyad*), thereby giving a measure of qualified recognition to a non-Muslim state either before a state of hostilities commenced or after initial resistance on the condition that it pay tribute, a poll tax (*jizyah*), or alternately, ceded at least a portion of its territory to the victorious Muslims. In the latter case, intended future jihad against it would be reduced to dormant status.[19]

The ruler of state, as noted, was the *imam* or caliph presiding over his imamate or caliphate. In Islamic legal theory, God—not the *imam*—was head of state. But in daily practicality, the *imam* served as its secular administrator. As described by noted Islamic scholar Majid Khadduri:

> The imam is under obligation to see that Islam's ultimate mission, namely, the supremacy of Allah's word over this world, is carried out by jihad. To achieve this end, the imam enforces law that regulates the relations of believers with nonbelievers during war and peace; he issues orders for the proper conduct of fighting, enforces the law in all newly occupied territories, and punishes Muslims and non-Muslims within his territory if they violate the law. He also decides when the jihad should be continued or stopped, and advises when Muslims should accept peace and reach terms with the enemy even on their own terms.[20]

In the conduct of the militant pursuit of foreign relations, the *imam* was likewise enfranchised to delegate his powers and authority to provincial governors or front-line commanders in the field. Indeed, they often were empowered to individually negotiate terms of peace and engagement with the enemy, conduct jihad, and to divide the spoils of war. In this quest, the territories coming to constitute the ever-expanding Dar al-Islam could be acquired either by force (*'anwatan*) or by peaceful negotiation (*sulhan*).[21]

Recognizing this distinction, Muslim jurists took great pains to define what actually constituted the domain of the Dar al-Islam. An early litmus test was whether the believer could freely fulfill the obligations of religion—

in particular, whether open public prayer could be held on Fridays and Islamic holidays. Indicative of the ultimate determination of this status was that a sword would be placed upon the pulpit of the speaker at Friday prayers in the case of the former; or a wooden staff if acquired through the latter. If, in turn, public Friday prayer could not freely be said within its confines, then a territory was not deemed to be an integral part of the Dar al-Islam.[22]

Additionally, though within the Dar al-Islam, no territorial divisions were in theory recognized, in practicality, Muslim jurists tended to distinguish between its more sacred and more secular properties. Al-Mawardi, for instance, singled out the twin sanctuaries at Makkah and al-Madinah (*al-haramayn al-sharifayn*) as foremost in reverence, then the *Hijaz*, and then the rest of Islamic-held territories. Indeed, the Islamic corpus juris, the *shari'ah*, also distinguished between these three land taxonomies in terms of tax levies, land ownership, and access by non-Muslims.[23]

In preserving the international interests of the Islamic polity, in turn, immigration policy traditionally was focused more toward the presence of foreigners, particularly merchants and emissaries coming to operate within the Dar al-Islam, than to sojourns of Muslims functioning outside its confines in the Dar al-Harb. In this process, though Islamic law recognized only Muslims to enjoy full legal rights within their homeland, non-Muslims too enjoyed certain legal protections if they entered with formal permission.

Levels of protection depended upon the nature of their entry status. Three separate categories of immigrants could be afforded limited legal rights: the true foreigner (*harbi*) who entered with or without sanctioned right of entry; the legal immigrant (*musta'min*) who entered pursuant to a prearranged security agreement (*aman*); and *dhimmis*—Peoples of the Book—scriptuaries and others who had surrendered peacefully to Muslim armies in exchange for limited civic privilege and acquiescence to the payment of a poll tax (*jizyah*).[24]

Hence, the *harbi* might legitimately enter to travel or reside within the Dar al-Islam for a limited period pursuant to a permit of safe conduct (*aman*) issued by Muslim authorities. As such, he was afforded a variety of legal safeguards by virtue of his acquired *musta'min* status. But the duration of his *aman* could not exceed one year. Were the *harbi* to wish to reside within the Dar al-Islam for a longer period, therefore, he could do so only by agreeing to pay the prescribed poll tax, thereby acquiring dhimmi status.

The *aman* was granted by the *imam* or his designated representative in accordance with a sanctioned truce (*muhadanah*) in effect between the Dar al-Islam and the *harbi*'s homeland, or alternately by individual believers acting the capacity of commercial agents. The former was deemed to be an official *aman*, the latter an unofficial one. When the *aman*'s prescribed purpose was achieved, the *musta'min* would perforce be repatriated to his country of origin.[25]

Once sanctioned, while within the Dar al-Islam, the *harbi/musta'min* was entitled to travel to any city within it except the twin Holy Cities of Makkah and al-Madinah in the Hijaz—and to reside permanently within it if he agreed to accept dhimmi status in exchange for payment of the poll tax. While enjoying the right of safe conduct in his movement, he was concurrently permitted to engage in business transactions within the limits of the law. The *aman* normally terminated after its one-year shelf life expired or if the *harbi* voluntarily departed the Dar al-Islam. Should he then later wish to return, he had to obtain a new *aman*.[26]

The *aman* thus filled a utilitarian purpose for Muslims and non-Muslims alike in the conduct of commerce by making possible the establishment of amicable relations among them, being a venue for the exchange of travel among countries. As such, it served as a visa whereby foreigners were permitted to visit the Dar al-Islam and without which no exchange of commercial goods was possible. In regularizing the crossing of frontiers, therefore, it facilitated the flow of ongoing productive trade of Muslim merchants with fellow merchants located beyond their immediate borders.[27]

The travel of Muslim merchants to non-Muslim countries, as noted, was rarer. But in the ongoing transit flow, Muslims entering non-Muslim countries were subject to restrictions analogous to those imposed upon the *musta'min* within the Dar al-Islam. They were, in principle, not expected to undermine authorities of the visited territory or country, and if they entered by means of an *aman*, they were expected and obliged to obey its laws as well as their own.

As for dhimmis residing within the Dar al-Islam, they likewise enjoyed certain rights beyond the pursuit of life, liberty, and property ownership. Such rights included an indefinite *aman*, though one that did not convey full citizenship. For though as Peoples of the Book, they believed in Allah, they were legally disadvantaged by virtue of not accepting Muhammad as His prophet, one of the preconditions for full membership within the brotherhood of Islam.

TREATIES AND THE QUEST FOR PEACE

Nonetheless, the prophet Muhammad, in his lifetime, did engage in negotiations with dhimmis, concluding treaties of coexistence with both Jews and Christians in the early al-Madinah period that offered them full religious autonomy and certain other rights including property ownership and other protections in exchange for both payment of the poll tax and their unqualified support of the early Islamic state.[28]

Muhammad also issued autonomous constitutional charters (*'uhud al-ummah*) of modus vivendi to Christian and Jewish tribal groups incorporating them as subjects within the Islamic state, stipulating that they were "one nation, separate from other peoples." Early Muslim rulers likewise frequently entered into bilateral treaties of sundry natures with rulers presiding within the *Dar al-Harb*. The legal sanction for such treaties, predicated on the Qur'anic verse "If they incline to peace, then incline thee also to peace" (Surat al-Anfal 8:61), was purported to be found in the verse:

> How can there be a treaty with Allah and His Messenger for polytheists except those with whom you have made a treaty at the Inviolable Place of Worship? So long as they are true to you, you must be true to them. Lo! Allah loves those who keep their duty! (Surat al-Tawbah 9:7)

This Qur'anic injunction was supported by popular tradition as well. Not only did the prophet Muhammad engage in treaties with Jews and Christians to consolidate his embryonic domain at al-Madinah, but prior to Makkah's capture, he concluded a ten-year truce known as the Treaty of Hudhaybiyah with the city's Qurashi tribal leadership affording his followers access to Islam's holy sites that would later become a prototype for future Islamic treaties. In other examples of diplomatic treaties, there also is a Prophetic Tradition related by al-Tabari that held: "The Byzantines will make a secured peace with you."[29]

Hence, based on both scripture and Prophetic Tradition, Muslim jurists, citing the Treaty of Hudhaybiyah as a model, generally concurred that if it served Islamic political interests, a peace treaty concluded by its leadership with the enemy could be a valid instrument binding upon all Muslims. Neutrality, a state of *Dar al-Sulh* or *Dar al-Hiyad*, with certain nations, likewise prevailed in Prophet Muhammad's time—with Habashah, (Ethiopia), Nubia (the Sudan), which paid an annual tribute called *baqt*, and Cyprus reported as having enjoyed this status.[30]

The process of signing treaties with the enemy was continued under later caliphs. The Umayyad caliph Abd al-Malik b. Marwan, for instance, signed various nonaggression treaties with the Byzantines in a quest to secure his external borders while he was putting down internal insurgencies fomented by the would-be seventh-century seceders known as *khawarij*. Early 'Abbasid caliphs likewise concluded sundry treaties with their Byzantine counterparts for multiple reasons.

One such treaty, to preclude border violations, active in the reigns of the caliph Harun al-Rashid and the emperor Nicephoros Phocas, compelled Byzantine emperors to pay annual tribute to the caliphs in Baghdad. Anti-Crusader chieftain Salah al-Din al-Ayyubi (Saladin) also contracted a treaty with the Crusader leader Richard Couer de Lion in 1192 that called for a cessation in hostilities to permit civilian travel for pilgrimage purposes.

Ransom treaties to exchange prisoners of war among combatants likewise were frequently negotiated. Predicated upon the Hudhaybiyah model, most Muslim jurists again held that a treaty with the enemy must be for the convenience of Islam and could be no longer than ten years in duration. They also maintained that such treaties, once contracted, became the same as religious obligations that must be steadfastly observed through their durations.[31]

International diplomacy was integral to the foreign policies of medieval Islamic rulers as well. Early on, it was resorted to as an auxiliary to, or substitute for, war—among other things, to herald the advent and ascendancy of Islam to other rulers and to provide for exchanges of prisoners of war after the termination of hostilities. In the 'Abbasid era, it also became a venue for conveying diplomatic messages and exchanging politically astute gifts. The purpose of such diplomatic legations was to make representations of the Islamic head of state to foreign monarchs in a quest to attain specific political or commercial objectives. Official titles of legates employed in this capacity often included those of messenger (*rasul*) or ambassador (*safir*).[32]

From the time of the prophet Muhammad, Islamic ambassadors were sent to foreign royal courts. Indeed, upon proclamation of his prophetic mission, he is reported to have immediately dispatched emissaries to Byzantium, Egypt, Persia, and Ethiopia inviting their rulers to embrace Islam. Such diplomatic intercourse continued during the reigns of the Umayyad and early 'Abbasid caliphates as well—as many diplomatic missions were exchanged with the Byzantines, in particular, for the purposes of signing peace treaties or exacting tribute.[33]

Diplomatic emissaries were usually permitted to enter into the Dar al-Islam without possessing an *aman*. As declared official emissaries, moreover, they were permitted to proceed directly to the seat of governance in the Dar al-Islam, often ushered in by formal guides. They likewise enjoyed certain political rights and privileges. Such rights included indefinite *amans* that conveyed full diplomatic immunity throughout their stays provided that they observed their duties and did not engage in prohibited acts such spying or buying weapons.[34]

During early 'Abbasid rule in particular, the exchange of lavish gifts often attended emissary missions, as ambassadors were dispatched between Islam and Christendom not only for public-relations purposes but to exchange prisoners of war, conciliate differences, convey congratulations and condolences, and facilitate trade. The Carolingian king Pepin the Short is said to have sent a delegation to the court of the caliph al-Mansur in 765, which then remained in Baghdad for three full years before returning to Europe bearing gifts for the king. Another delegation from Pepin reportedly met an Islamic counterpart team sent by al-Mansur in the city of Sellyus in 768, from whence each again returned to its sovereign bearing gifts.[35]

Medieval sources, both East and West, likewise wax eloquent about the exchanges of ambassadors and gifts between the Holy Roman Emperor Charlemagne and the 'Abbasid Caliph Harun al-Rashid commencing in 797. Indeed, three separate embassies were sent by Charlemagne to that caliph's royal court, and at least two 'Abbasid missions went to Europe in return. These démarches were often accompanied by an exchange of lavish gifts, perhaps the most noteworthy of which was Harun al-Rashid's present of various aromatics and fabrics, a clock, a chessboard, and an elephant, Abu 'Abbas, to Charlemagne. The caliph even reportedly offered to make Charlemagne custodian of Christian holy places in Jerusalem and initiatives were concurrently explored to establish a Carolingian-'Abbasid alliance against Byzantium.[36]

In conjunction with this initiative, in 799, the patriarch of Jerusalem likewise sent a mission to Charlemagne and the latter responded by sending alms and other offerings. In 800, another mission sent by the patriarch carried to Charlemagne the keys to the holy sepulcher and the site of Calvary, together with a Jerusalem banner.[37] Such exchanges of embassies are cited by medieval Muslim and Christian historians alike. Describing events transpiring in the years 787–801, Charlemagne's biographer Einhardus, notes:

> The Emperor went from Spoleto to Ravenna and stayed for a few days before reaching Fara. It was there that he was told that ambassadors from Harun (al-Rashid), King of the Persians, had entered the Port of Pisa. He agreed to meet them and they were officially presented to him near Vercelli. One of these two was a Persian of the East and envoy of the King of Persia; the other, a Saracen from Africa.
>
> The two announced to the Emperor that the Jew, Isaac, whom he had sent previously to the King of the Persians with Sigismond and Lanfred, was returning with great presents; but that both Sigismond and Lanfred were dead. The Emperor then sent the notary Erchinbald to Liguria to prepare a fleet to carry the elephant and other things that Isaac was bringing with him. . . .
>
> In the month of October of this year (801 A.D.), the Jew Isaac returned from Africa with the elephant, entered the port of Vendres, and passed the winter at Vercelli because he could not cross the Alps which were then covered with snow. On 20 July, he arrived and brought to the Emperor the elephant and other presents that the King of Persia had sent him. The elephant's name was Abu 'Abbas.[38]

A third and final mission sent by Charlemagne to the 'Abbasid court reportedly set out in 809, but arrived in Baghdad only to learn that Harun al-Rashid had died. The sources likewise indicate that in 831, his son and successor, the caliph al-Ma'mun, similarly sent an embassy to Charlemagne's son and successor, Louis the Pious.[39]

Almost a century later, moreover, Queen Bertha of Rome is said to have dispatched an embassy to her 'Abbasid counterpart, the caliph al-Muktafi, exchanging various gifts and proposing a treaty of friendship, and it appears, even marriage. This curious exchange is described by a contemporary Arab chronicler:

> Bertha, daughter of Lothar, Queen of Faranja and its dependencies, sent a present to al-Muktafi bi-Allah via 'Ali the Eunuch. . . . 'Ali the Eunuch brought the present and the letter of the Queen of Faranja to al-Muktafi bi-Allah and also a message not included in the letter lest anyone other than the Caliph become aware of it. . . . The message was a request for friendship and marriage.[40]

These various diplomatic missions between Charlemagne and 'Abbasid Caliph Harun al-Rashid were, in fact, concurrently prominently featured in the *Carolingian Royal Annales*, which focus upon the various "precious gifts" that were exchanged between them.[41] The legendary Monk of St. Gaul indicates, for instance, that Charlemagne dispatched to Harun al-Rashid sundry royal red fabrics which were greatly valued in Baghdad—a possible indication that Charlemagne was subliminally seeking to expand the exports of textiles from Gaul to the 'Abbasid domain.[42]

Charlemagne, as Holy Roman Emperor, appears to have been particularly concerned with, and committed to, his empire's foreign commerce with the Islamic world—with a number of emissaries being sent by him to Baghdad and Cordoba. Economic historian W. Heyd is of the opinion that the Carolingian monarch explicitly selected specific valuable goods as gifts to be borne by his ambassadors to the caliph Harun al-Rashid as enticements to develop new consumer tastes, and thereby, promote commerce.[43]

Indeed, it appears that the Dar al-Islam may have been a targeted prime beneficiary of Charlemagne's open-market economic policies, as medieval Arabic geographies likewise provide no small amount of evidence of contemporary trade between the Carolingian and 'Abbasid empires.[44] Such successful international commerce was, in fact, extremely critical to forging the early strong economic sinews of the Dar al-Islam—as trade with non-Muslims greatly influenced the expansion of Islam along trade routes that coursed Central Asia, India, and Southeast Asia, as well as East Africa.

In short, throughout the narratives of the sundry Arab geographers and the various exchanges of diplomatic relations of this era are distinct undercurrents of relative amicability, and certainly little, if any, indication of particular hostility on the part of the Islamic caliphate toward the "land of the Franks." To the contrary, political and commercial relations appear to have been maintained on a quite friendly and stable level, as Western Europe was subject to some lively scholarly interest on the part of contemporary Near East explorers and chroniclers.

Thus, the Islamic world greatly expanded through commercial and cultural contacts well beyond the political frontiers established by its military conquests. Reflective of the perceived importance of foreign trade, a Qur'anic verse held that:

> When prayer is ended, disperse ye into the land and seek of Allah's bounty; and remember Him greatly so that you may be successful. (Surat al-Jumu'ah 62:10)

To this end, as noted, Muslim jurists also paid special attention to juristically opening the doors of the Dar al-Islam to productive, mutual bilateral international trade. Among their rulings to incentivize such commerce, an *aman* four months in duration could be granted to a non-Muslim merchant. In addition, should his business not be completed within that period, it could then be renewed.

Foreign merchants transacting commerce within the Dar al-Islam were usually required to pay a 10 percent customs duty (*'ushr*) on all transactions that exceeded 200 dirhams in aggregate value. This flexible, rate, however, could be lowered by the *imam* if he explicitly wished to promote ongoing foreign trade or alternately raised if he was in specific need of revenue. It could not, however, be collected more than once per year. Moreover, if the non-Muslim merchant's home country did not levy a customs tax, a reciprocal toll-free trade taxing arrangement was frequently observed.[45]

This, then, in synopsis, was the doctrinal basis for the Islamic Code of Conduct for Engaging Foreign Policy—an international protocol that governed an early medieval global civilization wherein the Dar al-Islam was the brightest star within its firmament and that empowered it to become the premier commercial superpower of the age.

Appendix B

Islam's Code of Conduct for Waging "Just War"

Fight in the way of Allah against those who fight against you, but begin not hostilities. Allah loves not aggressors.

—Surat al-Baqarah 2:190

THE ISLAMIC RULES OF MILITARY ENGAGEMENT

Though early doctrinal commitments to the doctrine of "just war" were longstanding, and derived equally from Greek, Roman, and Christian antecedents, they also, as noted, enjoyed strong Islamic parallels. First articulated by the Greek philosopher Aristotle and the Roman orator Cicero, then developed by St. Augustine in the fifth century, the precept would later find vivid expression in the thirteenth-century writings of St. Thomas Aquinas.[1]

In precept, the concept strived to justify the use of force under carefully defined battlefield conditions including proportionality—the expectation that more lives would be saved by the use of force than would be lost—and legitimacy—the notion that the undertaking had to be explicitly approved by an established authority. Thus it was that Pope Urban II's initial proclamation of the Crusade at Clermont and all nine subsequent formal Crusades were punctuated by the battle cry: *"Deus hoc vult!"* ("God wills it!")

Just war theory is as old as warfare itself, possessing a lengthy legacy deeply rooted in church history. While parts of the Bible hint at an ethical behavior in warfare and concepts of just cause, the most systematic exposition is given by St. Augustine of Hippo (d. 430) in his masterpiece, *The City of God* (*De Civitate Dei*). While lamenting the destruction and loss of life that attend war, Augustine nonetheless believed that a just war might be preferable to an unjust peace. Accordingly, he stipulated that the use of force is necessary—though always regrettable—within a "fallen world" in order to restrain evil, but that its ultimate goal must remain to restore peace.

St. Thomas Aquinas (d. 1274), in turn, significantly contributed to the development of just war theory in his *Summa Theologica*. Discussing not only the justifications for war, but also the various activities that are permissible in war's conduct, he formalized three criteria for a just war: (1) "right authority" (a sovereign government rather than individuals); (2) "just cause" (to avenge wrong or restore what was unjustly seized); and (3) "good intention" (the advancement of good or the avoidance of evil).

In the Renaissance, Protestant reformers, as well as Catholic and Protestant natural law theorists, further upheld the just war tradition. In modern times, its principles, frequently divorced from their religious origins, have likewise often been incorporated into international laws governing armed conflict, such as those embodied within the codes derived in The Hague and Geneva Conventions as well as in modern military doctrine and practice.

Beyond the abstractions of medieval doctrine, there were powerfully pragmatic justifiable causes for recourse to war as well. In Islam, defending the Muslim homeland, the Dar al-Islam, at its distant borders, for instance, was formally defined in a fourteen part integrated sequence of Qur'anic verses as valid reasons for just war:

Precept 1: *Maintaining the territorial integrity of the Islamic realm is a legitimate pretext for the pursuit of just war.*
Verse:
Make ready for them all you can of horses tethered that thereby you may dismay the enemies of Allah and your enemy and others besides them whom you know not but Allah knows. (Surat al-Anfal 8: 60)
Comment:
The Arabic first measure verb rahiba, which means to "be frightened" or "intimidated," is employed in this verse.

Precept 2: *If recourse to just war is elected, doctrine holds that it then must be aggressively and decisively waged.*
Verse:
If thou comest upon them in war, deal with them so as to strike fear into those who are behind them, so that they will remember. (Surat al-Anfal 8: 57)

Comment:
The Arabic second measure verb *sharrida*, employed in this verse literally means "to frighten or drive away."

Whether or not this objective is to invariably be achieved through terror, as is suggested by Surat al-Anfal, however, requires further exegesis. 'Ali indeed does translate the verb in question, *rahiba*, to mean "strike terror"—

> Against them make ready your strength to the utmost of your power, including steeds of war, to strike terror into the enemies of Allah and your own enemies, and others beside whom ye may not know but whom Allah knows.

—whereas Pickthall translates it as "dismay" and the al-Madinah version conveys it to mean "threaten." Indeed, this is among the very few instances wherein the Qur'an may possibly be interpreted to directly encourage an infliction of terror per se by Muslims upon others—and that in pursuit of just war.

Four other verses within the Qur'an tend to connote the concept of striking terror into the hearts of unbelievers as well. As related by the translators analyzed, they are presented in table B.1:

Table B.1.

Verse	Term	Pickthall	Ali	Madinah
50:2	ru'b	terror	terror	terror
8:12	ru'b	fear	terror	terror
3:151	ru'b	terror	terror	terror
7:4–5	ba's	terror	punishment	torment

As may be seen, while evidence of employing the word "terror" may well appear in the Qur'an, the usage is not entirely unambiguous. Indeed, it is often deduced from different terms, and at times, the same word is translated differently by the same translator in different contexts. In each instance, however, it is critical to note, it is *Allah Himself* striking terror—to wit: literally the "fear of God" within the unbelievers for their apostasy without invoking the need for mortals on earth to serve as surrogates in its fulfillment. In this sense, then, it is not unlike the Judeo-Christian Jehovah's biblical proclamations:

> Vengeance is mine' saith the Lord. (Romans 12:19)

> I will send My terror before you and will throw confusion into all the people. (Exodus 23:27)

The Lord thy God shall deliver them unto thee and shall destroy them with mighty destruction until they be destroyed. (Deuteronomy 7:23)

Nor does the word jihad—the Islamic *bellum justum*—ever appear within the Qur'an as a concept connoting holy war (*bellum pium*). For Muslims, as shown, war is always "just" or "unjust," never "holy." This is a point emphasized by Muslim scholar Muhammad Haleem:

> Another term that is misunderstood and misrepresented is *jihad*. This does not mean "Holy War," as that phrase does not exist as a term in Arabic, and its translation into Arabic is alien. The term that is specifically used within the Qur'an to connote "fighting" is *qital*. Jihad can be by argumentation, financial help, or actual fighting. Jihad is always described within the Qur'an as *fi sabil Allah* ("in God's cause"). On returning from a military campaign, the Prophet said to his followers: "We have returned from minor jihad (*al-asghar*) to the major jihad (*al-akhbar*)—the struggle of the individual with his own self.[2]

Indeed, the very term *holy war* did not originate with Muslims at all but instead with the Christians of the Crusades in their quest to lend an imprimatur of theological legitimacy to their campaigns to seize Near East lands and secure access to new trade routes to the Orient. As such, it evolved not as a definition of a specific type of warfare nor does it determine whether it may be preemptive or strictly defensive.[3]

Accordingly, the classic Islamic concept of jihad in the sense of "warfare" does not issue directly from the Qur'an—wherein the term is often used to refer to a believer's inner struggle for righteousness—but from jurists of the early 'Abbasid period (e.g., the late eighth and ninth centuries), who developed it in a general effort to clarify the nature of the Islamic community, the proper leadership of that community, and the community's relations with the non-Islamic world.

Central to this conception as noted, was the legal division of the world into two distinct bipolar realms: the Dar al-Islam, "abode of Islam," and the remainder, the *Dar al-Harb*, "abode of war"—as characterized in the former by "faith" (*iman*) and in the unconquered latter by "unbelief" (*kufr*)—making its residents, in effect, "sovereign *kuffar*."

The Dar al-Islam, as Muslim jurists understood it, had existed since its creation by the prophet Muhammad himself who had served as its first head. It was a community at once religious and political, and thus its ruler, like the prophet, was understood to be supreme in both spheres. At any time, there could be only one right ruler who was understood to be the successor of the Prophet and inheritor of his authority.[4]

Operating within this context, then, the Arabic term *jihad* (as opposed to *harb*, general warfare, or *qital*, killing)—literally meaning "struggling" or "striving" for peace and social justice—in its Qur'anic context, is almost invariably followed by the phrase "in the way (or cause) of God." The definitive Arabic dictionary, *Lane's Lexicon*, describes it as:

> Exerting one's utmost power, efforts, endeavor, or abilities in contending with an object of disapprobation.[5]

Jihad, therefore, cannot be equated semantically with general warfare (*harb* or *qital*), as its meaning is much broader—for, as noted, taxonomically, there may be a broad variety of types of jihad, prominent among them:

- jihad of the heart: the struggle against one's personal sinful inclinations;
- jihad of the tongue: speaking out for good while opposing evil;
- jihad of the pen: writings that serve to propagate the faith; and
- jihad of the sword: (*jihad al-sayf*) religiously grounded warfare to defend or propagate the faith.

Based on these distinctions, and predicated upon Prophetic Tradition, then, medieval Muslim jurists frequently sought to distinguish between a:[6]

- greater jihad (*al-jihad al-akhbar*): the struggle with one's self; and a
- lesser jihad (*al-jihad al-asghar*): warring in the cause of God.

Consequently, cognizant that within Islam (1) because the Qur'an, Surat al-Baqarah 2:216 stipulates: "Prescribed to you is fighting" (using the verb *qital*, not *jihad*), "jihad of the sword" does not equate unequivocally to "holy war" and (2) the creed does not exclusively limit faith-based war to the concept of jihad, then, in a strict military context, jihad is perhaps best described as an early medieval Muslim mandate seeking what St. Thomas Aquinas would later call a "just peace," as is concurrently also evidenced in the following Qur'anic verse.

Precept 3: *War's mandate is an endless quest for peace.*
Verse:
And make not Allah, by your oaths, a hindrance to your being righteous and observing your duty unto Him and making peace among mankind. (Surat al-Baqarah 2:224)
Comment:
Accordingly, the Qur'an makes clear that "there is no compulsion in religion," and that jihad is to be used as an instrument to promote peace

and not as a rationale to incite war. Thus, Surat al-Baqarah 2:109 admonishes the faithful: "Pardon and forgive until Allah gives His command!"

It is this concept of jihad as a strictly defensive weapon, therefore, that brings it into conformity with modern rules for war, but it is a reality that concurrently carries the mandate that the antiquated partitioning of the world into two arrayed spheres of belief—the world of the Believers (*Dar al-Islam*) and the world of the Unbelievers (*Dar al-Harb*), a dichotomy that does not appear in Islamic juridical literature until the late eighth century and then only genuinely evolved during the Crusades—must forever be abandoned.

Indeed, if all but defensive war is explicitly prohibited, then recourse to it becomes sanctioned only if the Muslim community is, without provocation, attacked. For in addition to the admonition in Surat al-Baqarah 2:190—

> Fight in the way of Allah against those who fight against you, but begin not hostilities. Allah loves not aggressors

—the Qur'an prescribes:

Precept 4: *Unprovoked or preemptive war is not sanctioned by Islam.*
Verses:
Sanction is given to those who fight because they have been wronged; and Allah is indeed able to give them victory; those who have been driven from their homes unjustly only because they said: "Our Lord is Allah!" (Surat al-Hajj 22:39–40)
Comment:
The Islamic doctrine of war can thus be viewed as predicated on an ongoing quest for peaceful coexistence and is permissible only for defensive purposes. It is within the context of a defensive response to injustice and oppression, therefore, that the Islamic concept of "just war" must be understood—a war just equally in its cause (*jus ad bellum*) and in its conduct (*jus in bello*).

Precept 5: *Accordingly, the Qur'an forbids wanton killing—stipulating that life is not to be taken indiscriminately and without regard to divine command.*
Verse:
And that you slay not the life which Allah has made sacred except in the course of justice. Thus He commanded you in order that you may discern. (Surat al-An'am 6:151)

Comment:
The murder of a single innocent, the Qur'an (5:32) enjoins, is as if one had murdered all mankind. Hence, rogue operations and any other acts of violence that involve taking life, unless undertaken within the context of legitimate jihad pursuant to a formal *fatwa* (*nida' al-jihad*) issued by an acknowledged religious leader (*imam*) of the Islamic community (*ummah*), are effectively prohibited by this Qur'anic injunction—as jihad is, first and foremost, an exclusive state enterprise solely managed by the chief of state, the *imam*. (It was, in fact, the abolition of the Islamic caliphate by incoming secular Turkish president Kemal Attaturk in 1924 that was the coup de grace, thereby depriving Islam of its titular God-head, that unleashed the early modern radical jihadis in their free lance operations.)

Once declared, however, such jihad becomes an obligation absolute (*fard wajib*) upon all believers:

Precept 6: *A formally declared war imposes a collective obligation (fard kifayah) to wage jihad.*
Verse:
Warfare is ordained for you, though it is hateful to you. But it may happen that you hate a thing which is good for you and that you love a thing which is bad for you. Allah knoweth. You know not. (Surat al-Baqarah 2:216)
Comment:
Accordingly, a call to jihad issued by a duly enfranchised *imam* constitutes a formal act of conscription issued to, and binding upon, all able-bodied believers.

JIHAD IN PURSUIT OF JUST PEACE

Notwithstanding the so-called sword verses cited, however, the Qur'an also makes clear that jihad—a recourse that originated only late in the Prophet Muhammad's rule over al-Madinah—may not be used to compel conversion to Islam:

Precept 7: *Religion may not be imposed by force.*
Verse:
There is no compulsion in religion. The right direction is henceforth distinct from error. And he who rejects false deities and believes in Allah has grasped a firm handhold that will never break. (Surat al-Baqarah 2:256)
Comment:
Accordingly, the Qur'an makes clear that faith may not be imposed by co-ercion or the sword.

The voluntary nature of conversion to Islam affirmed in Surat al-Baqarah (2:256) is, in fact, echoed in a multitude of other verses, among them:

Precept 8: *Conversion to Islam is voluntary.*
Verses:
"It is the truth from the Lord of you all. Then, whosover wills, let him believe, and whosoever wills, let him disbelieve. . . . Would you (O Muhammad) compel men until they are believers." It is not for any soul to believe except by the permission of Allah. . . . I shall not worship what you worship. Nor will you worship that which I worship. To you, your religion, and to me, my religion. (Surat: al-Kahf 18:29; Yunus 10:99–100; al-Kafirun 109:4–6)
Comment:
Thus, conversion to Islam may not be coerced through jihad or via any other means. For the so-called sword verses cited notwithstanding, the Qur'an makes clear that jihad unequivocally may not be used to compel conversion to Islam, as the act of submission is undertaken of one's own volition.

In sum, jihad, in proper context, has both communal and individual dimensions. In its most general meaning, *collectively*, jihad refers to the obligation incumbent upon all Muslims, as a community at large (*ummah*), to follow and realize God's will. *Individually*, it involves not only "honor within battle" (*'ird*), but equally the personal struggle to live a moral, pious life as a true Muslim. In this context, then, devotion to prayer, spreading Islam through preaching and education, and serving as a moral exemplar to others are likewise legitimate forms of jihad.

Collectively, jihad requires defending the faith against the enemies of Islam, be they polytheists or apostates. But such military jihad must be waged strictly for causes that are just. It is not to occur in the form of overtly aggressive warfare—a proscription that would appear to rule out, for instance, the subversive activities of the *khawarij* in seventh-century Mesopotamia, those of Egypt's Muslim Brotherhood commencing in the mid-twentieth century, or those of al-Qaeda now at the onset of the twenty-first century.

Contrary to the contentions of some, however, the word jihad does, in fact, appear within the Qur'an, though almost invariably within the context of "striving in God's cause."[7] Surat al-Furqan 25:52 asserts, for instance:

Fa la tuti' al-kafirin wa jahiduhum bihi jihadan kabiran. (So obey not the disbelievers, but strive against them by preaching with utmost endeavor. — Qur'an, al-Madinah translation).

Surat al-Baqarah 2:190 similarly proclaims:

Fight in the path of Allah (*fi sabil Allah*) those who fight you but do not transgress limits (*wa la ta'tadu*) for Allah loveth not transgressors.[8]

The concept of jihad likewise has other connotations. Surat al-Hajj 22:78, for instance, exhorts Muslims to "strive hard in Allah's cause as ye ought to strive" (*wa jaahidu fi Allah haqqa jihadihi*); whereas Surat al-Tawbah (9:24) similarly refers to "striving in His cause" (*jihad fi sabilihi*) in conjunction with preserving commerce. Indeed, several Prophetic Traditions likewise define the precept in commercial terms such as:

If you make profit from what is permitted, it is jihad (holy war); and if you use it for your family, then it is like *sadaqah* ("alms")[9]

To seek lawful gain is jihad;[10]

The most excellent jihad is to speak up for truth in the face of tyranny.[11]

Thus, jihad is not limited to the military sphere. Given this doctrinal reality, then, it is not redundant to reiterate that the Arabic for war, *harb*, applicable when dealing with brigands and insurgents, and the connotation of jihad, which literally means earnest striving or struggle, are not synonymous—with a clear distinction equally made between "jihad of the sword" and "jihad of the heart." For, as shown, longstanding tradition holds that a variety of endeavors, including commerce, earning a livelihood for one's family, and speaking truth in the face of oppression are equal forms of jihad.[12]

It is likewise noteworthy that the less friendly Arabic word for killing, *qital*, seldom appears in conjunction with the phrase *fi sabil Allah* (in God's cause) within the Qur'an. Indeed, the Qur'an explicitly admonishes against using religion as a pretext to breach the peace. It is the amalgam of these contexts, then, that lends cogency to the sequential Qur'anic verses:

He it is who hath sent His Messenger with the guidance and the religion of truth, that he may make it conqueror of all religions however much idolaters may be averse.

Shall I show you a commerce that will save you from painful doom. You must believe in Allah and His Messenger and strive for the cause of Allah with your wealth and lives.

This is better for you if ye did but know. For He will forgive you your sins and bring you into Gardens under which rivers flow, and pleasant dwelling in the Garden of Eden. This is the supreme triumph. (Surat al-Saff 9–12)[13]

Other appearances of the term jihad within the Qur'an—all within the context of striving and all in conjunction with the phrase "in the cause of God" (*fi sabil Allah*), a phrase which itself appears within the Qur'an *seventy times*—include the following as presented in table B.2:

Table B.2.

On the Use of the Phrase "fi sabil *Allah*" within the Qur'an

Verse:	Passage:	Translation:
4:95	al-mujahidun fi sabil Allah bi-amwalihim wa anfusihim	those who strive in Allah's Cause with their wealth and their lives.
8:72, 8:74, 8:75, 9:20	inna allidhin aminu wa hajaru wa jahadu bi-amwalihim wa anfusihim fi sabil Allah	verily those who believed and emigrated and those who fought with their property and their lives in the Cause of Allah.
9:24	. . . ahabba ilaykum min Allah wa rusulihi wa jihad fi sabilihi	. . . are dearer to you than Allah or His Messenger or striving in His cause.
9:81	wa karihu an yujhidu bi-amwalihim wa anfusihim fi sabil Allah	and they hated to strive and fight with their properties and their lives in the cause of Allah.
29:69	wa allidhin jahadu fina, la nahhiinnahum subulana	as for those who strive hard in Us (Our Cause) We will surely guide them to Our Paths.
60:1	inna kuntum kharajtum jihadan fi sabili	if you come forth to strive in My cause.
61:11	wa yujahidu fi sabil Allah bi-amwalikum wa anfusikum	and that you strive hard and fight in the cause of *Allah* with your wealth and your lives.

RESTRICTIONS ON THE PURSUIT OF JUST WAR

Still other Islamic prescriptions for war—governing hostage taking, martyrdom, and suicide—are covered in the Qur'an. Killing hostages is forbidden equally because it is (1) murder, (2) a targeting of noncombatants, and (3) a misuse of responsibility:[14]

Precept 9: *The killing of hostages is forbidden.*
Verse:
For that cause, We decreed for the Children of Israel that whosoever kills a person for other than manslaughter or corruption in the earth, it shall be as if he had killed all of humankind. (Surat Al-Ma'idah 5:32)
Comment:
The slaying of noncombatants to further a military or political cause is thereby expressly forbidden as a mortal sin by the Qur'an.

That *martyrdom* is sanctioned in the Qur'an is evidenced by the following selections:

Precept 10: *Sacred martyrdom merits heavenly rewards.*
Verses:
Let those fight in the name of Allah who sell the life of this world for the other. He who fighteth in the name of Allah, be he slain or victorious, upon him We shall bestow a vast reward. (Surat al-Nisa' 4:74)
Allah has purchased of the Believers their persons and their goods. For theirs in return is the Garden of Paradise: they fight in His Cause and slay and are slain. (Surat al-Tawbah 9:111)
Comment:
The Islamic scriptures are thus unequivocal in affirming that martyrdom is sanctioned in Islam.

Therefore, God richly rewards martyrs, as the Qur'an unconditionally affirms:

Precept 11: *The heavenly rewards for martyrs are explicitly prescribed.*
Verse:
Think not of those who are slain in the way of Allah as dead. Nay, they are living. With their Lord, they have provision. They rejoice in what Allah has bestowed upon them of His bounty. (Surat Al-i 'Imran 3:169)
Comment:
Hence, though modern terrorist leaders have argued that suicide-bombing attacks are, in reality, not suicide, but instead martyrdom (*istishhad*), the Qur'an clearly distinguishes between the conflicting two acts, condemning the former while extrolling the latter, as subsequent analysis will show.

Such Qur'anic affirmations find further vivid expression in a saying attributed to companion of the Prophet and second caliph of Islam Umar b. al-Khattab:

Whoever has died in the Cause of Allah has died a martyr.[15]

It is equally evident in Prophetic Traditions documented by al-Bukhari, among them:

He who has been killed to uphold the Word of Allah has been martyred for His sake.

Allah provides assurance that he will admit the *mujahid* in His Cause into Paradise; or He will return him to his home in safety with rewards and booty.[16]

In the words of Islamic scholar John Esposito:

> These holy warriors (*mujahidin*) will be rewarded in this life with victories and the spoils of war. Those who fall in battle will be rewarded as martyrs (*shah'id* or "witness") for the faith.[17]

Indeed, the rewards of martyrdom are wide ranging, as related by al-Khatib al-Tabrizi:

> Allah's Messenger said: A martyr has six privileges with Allah. He is forgiven of his sins on the first shedding of his blood; he is shown to a proper place in Paradise; he is redeemed from torments of the grave; he is made secure from the fear of hell and a crown of glory is placed upon his head of which one ruby is worth more than the entire world; he will marry seventy-two black-eyed *huris*, and his intercession will be accepted for seventy kinsmen.[18]

It is equally critical to note, however, that while the Qur'an does encourage Muslim warriors to reap the rewards of martyrs, it does not compel them to do so. Indeed, in a chapter captioned as devoted to the virtues of formalized ranks (*saff/sufuf*), it appears to explicitly circumscribe how martyrdom may be earned in its prescribed rules for the conduct of war, instructing soldiers to fight not as unstructured units or self-anointed freedom fighters, but instead in closed ranks as a Community of Believers in its defense—and that in conventional battlefield formation:

Precept 12: *War must be fought not by underground insurgents but instead by formal military units arrayed in uniform ranks.*
Verse:
Allah loveth those who battle for His cause in ranks as if it were a solid structure.
(Surat al-Saff 61:4)
Comment:
The sanctioned Islamic prescription for the conduct of war is thus through conventional battlefield deployment and not through clandestine terrorist cells.

Hence, the Qur'an does not endorse, and appears to explicitly discourage, fighting in detached decentralized units or operating independently as self-appointed free agents—or terrorist organizations whose members move among, and dress as, civilians, or park their weapons within civilian neighborhoods, employing them as defensive shields, all deviant approaches that, in fact, would seem to contravene "fighting in the way of God," which is the prescribed path to martyrdom.

While *martyrdom* is Qur'anically sanctioned on the confines of the conventional battlefield, however, *suicide* in its quest definitely is not, as God is the Creator of Life, which may not be unilaterally abrogated by man. Indeed, neither suicide nor involuntary homicide is permissible in Islam as the following verses make clear:

Precept 13: *The Qur'an, in numerous verses, unequivocally prohibits suicide.*
Verse:
Oh ye who believe! Eat up not your property amongst yourselves in vanities; but let there be amongst you traffic and trade by mutual goodwill; nor kill (or destroy) your selves. For verily Allah hath been to you most Merciful. (Surat al-Nisa' 4:29, 'Ali translation)
Comment:
Qur'anic prescriptions must be viewed within the context of their times. This was a tumultuous trade era, history reveals, wherein the merchants of Makkah would engage in intense commercial competition (*munafarah*) and in its quest, frequently contemplate ritualistic suicide (*i'tifad*) in the event of financial failure. Hence, a ban on killing oneself in conjunction with trade transactions appears explicitly tailored to the age.

This prohibition of suicide is further strengthened by the prescriptions of Surat al-Baqarah 2:195:[19]

Precept 14: *Creating financial circumstances that lead to suicide is to be equally avoided.*
Verse:
Spend your wealth for the Cause of Allah, and do not be caused by your own hand into ruin; and do good. Lo! Allah loves those who do good. (Surat al-Baqarah 2:195)
Comment:
The modern notion of suicide bombing thus would appear to be effectively prohibited by the combination of these verses.

These Qur'anic verses, in turn, are buttressed by a wealth of Prophetic Traditions that similarly admonish believers against suicide, threatening them with a series of dire reciprocal netherworld retributions, among them:

- Whosoever kills himself will be excluded from Heaven forever;
- Whoever kills himself in any way will be tormented that way in Hell;
- He who kills himself with a blade will be tortured with it in Hell's fires;
- He who strangles himself on earth will be strangled in Hell;
- He who stabs himself on earth will be stabbed in Hell;

- He who kills himself by throwing himself off a mountain will be forever cast in Hell;
- He who kills himself with poison will drink poison in Hell; and
- Whoever kills himself in any way in this world will be tormented that way on the Day of Resurrection.[20]

Thus, the multiple Qur'anic admonitions, taken in aggregate, in their approach to war are neither unfathomable nor arcane. Indeed, they enjoy both classic and modern parallel. Medieval Christian "peace of God doctrine" banned attacking women, children, the aged, infirm, pilgrims, and clerics in war's pursuit. The Qur'an, as shown, in equal measure, forbade inflicting violence, terror, and other forms of collateral damage intentionally upon civilian noncombatants in battle.[21]

Compare the counsel of Abu Bakr (632–634), the first caliph of Islam after Prophet Muhammad's death in 632, in dispatching an Islamic army to invade Byzantine-occupied southern Syria, with God's general instructions for warfare to the Israelis as reflected in the biblical book of Deuteronomy:[22]

Caliph Abu Bakr on War

Stop, O people, that I may now give you ten rules for guidance on the battle field. Do not commit treachery or deviate from the right path. You must not mutilate dead bodies. Neither kill a child, nor a woman, nor an aged man. Bring no harm to trees nor burn them with fire, especially those that are fruitful. Slay not any of the enemy's flock save for your food. (As described in al-Tabari 1879–1901, vol. 5, p. 1850)

King James Bible on War

And when the Lord thy God hath delivered it into thy hands, thou shall smite every male thereof with the sword. But the women and children and cattle, and all that is in the city, all the spoils thereof, shalt thou take unto thyself; and thou shall eat of the spoils of those enemies which the Lord thy God hath given thee. This thou shall do unto all of the cities that are far off from thee. . . . When thou shalt besiege a city for a prolonged time, in making war against it to take it, thou shall not destroy the trees thereof; for thou may eat of them, and thou shalt not cut them down to employ them in siege. (As prescribed in Deuteronomy 20:12–15, 19)

Likewise compare them again with the modern principles for war as reflected in The Hague and Geneva Conventions delineated in chapter 2. There are no substantive differences. For in aggregate, there is nothing within the Islamic Code of Conduct for War that varies in substance either from classic or more modern prescriptions for humane warfare—or countenances or condones the atrocities of terror that too often are today perpetrated in its name.

This, then, was the "Manual for War" that governed the early Islamic conquests. It becomes critical at this point, therefore, to explore how early Muslims pursued, with equal zeal, a corresponding fervent quest for peaceful coexistence.

Appendix C
Islam's Code of Conduct for
Pursuing "Just Peace"

If they incline to peace, incline thou to it and trust in Allah.

—Surat al-Anfal 8:61

ON ISLAM AND THE PEOPLES OF THE BOOK

As chapter 2 and appendix B make clear, the prime purpose of just war, as prescribed by classic Islamic doctrine, was to achieve enduring peace. Amicable coexistence with monotheistic coreligionists was integral to, and consistent with, that doctrine. The Qur'an, in fact, explicitly upbraids the Jews and Christians for having abandoned tenets of their faiths that it deemed to be concurrent cornerstones of Islamic doctrine.

In this context, Prophet Muhammad can be found excoriating the Jews for having betrayed the teachings of Abraham when, having been entrusted with the laws of the Torah, they ignored them:

And who forsakes the religion of Abraham except he who befools himself. We chose (Abraham) in the world and lo: in the Hereafter, he is among the righteous. . . . We shall worship your God, God of your fathers, Abraham and Ishmael and Isaac, One God, and to Him have we surrendered (as Muslims). (Surat al-Baqarah 2 130–133)

The similitude of those whom are entrusted with the Law of Moses, yet apply it not, are as donkeys carrying books. Wretched are the folk who deny the revelations of God. (Surat al-Jumu'ah 62:5)

As such, the Qur'an (Surat al-Ma'idah 5:13) admonishes, the Jews have breached their covenant with God. In like manner, Muhammad reproaches the contemporary Christians:

> If they had observed the Torah and the Gospels and that which was revealed to them from their Lord, they would have been nourished from above. (Surat al-Ma'idah 5:66)

In this, then, he is not unlike the prophet Isaiah condemning his fellow Jews as "a sinful nation, a people laden with iniquity" (Isaiah 1:4) or John the Baptist labeling contemporary fellow Jews as "a nation of vipers" (Luke 3:7)—all the while castigating them as coreligionists with whom modicums of peaceful coexistence must nonetheless to be sought.

Indeed, the Qur'an not only prosecutes a compelling case for peaceful coexistence, it also reveals itself as the culmination of a continuum of religions, a confirmation of all of the scriptures that have preceded it. For, as it demonstrates, as detailed in fifteen integrated, sequential precepts that the religious rights of all Muslims and Peoples of the Book: Jews, Christians, and Sabaeans alike, must be respected and that all true scriptures are part of a heavenly concealed "Mother of Books" (*Umm al-Kitab*):[1]

Precept 1: *God's truth is revealed as a Scriptural Continuum.*
Verses:
In their story, there is a lesson for men of understanding. It is no invented story but a confirmation of existing (scripture) and a detailed explanation of everything and a guidance and mercy for folks who believe . . . (Surat Yusuf 12:111)
And with Him, all is measured. He is the Knower of the invisible and the visible, the Great, the High Exalted. (Surat al-Ra'd 13:9)
Comment:
The Qur'an thus does not abrogate or nullify previous scriptures, but instead expressly reaffirms them.

This confirmation thus means that the Torah, the Gospels, and the Qur'an are to be read and interpreted as part and parcel of a single, sequential divine text, of which the Qur'an is the final revelation. Accordingly, it advises Muslims to interact with Jews and Christians as cobelievers:

Precept 2: *Muslims, Jews, and Christians share a common belief in the God of Abraham.*

Verse:

Say (O Muhammad): "We believe in Allah and that which is revealed to us and that which was revealed to Abraham and Ishmael and Isaac and Jacob and the Tribes, and that which was given to Moses and Jesus and the Prophets from their Lord. We make no distinction between any of them (by believing in some and denying others), and to Him (alone) have we surrendered (in Islam)." (Surat Al-i-'Imran 3:84)

Comment:

Hence, the Qur'an professes no preferential distinction amongst the scriptures or doctrines of any of the three heavenly religions.

Indeed, the Qur'an leaves no doubt that Jews, Christians, and Muslims are of a common heritage and common legacy as Peoples of the Book who share the same values, read the same scriptures, and worship the same God. It thus promises "to all who believe" that on the "Day of Judgment":

Precept 3: *Those who are true believers will share a common destiny.*

Verse:

Lo! Those who believe, and those who are Jews, Sabaeans, and Christians—whosoever believes in Allah and the Last Day and does right—no fear shall come upon them neither shall they grieve. (Surat al-Ma'idah 5:69)

Comment:

Accordingly, the Peoples of the Book—Jews and Christians alike—are promised by the Qur'an equity and equality of justice with Muslims in the dispensation of divine treatment.

To that end, the Qur'an admonishes Jews and Christians as Peoples of the Book to take counsel in their own scriptures:

Precept 4: *Each People of the Book must heed its own scripture.*

Verse:

Lo! Allah guides not disbelieving folk. Say: "O People of the Scripture! You have nothing of guidance until you have observed the Torah and the Gospel and that which was revealed to you from your Lord." (Surat al-Ma'idah 5:68)

Comment:

In this manner, the Qur'an not only counsels tolerance for Jews and Christians who live within Islamic society, it concurrently directs Prophet Muhammad to instruct them to follow the teachings of their own scriptures.

Based upon their common legacy of revelation, then, Muslims are admonished to seek comity with their coreligionists, the Christians and Jews:

Precept 5: *For Peoples of the Book share a common spiritual bond.*
Verse:
And argue not with People of the Scripture unless it be (in a way) that is better, except with such of them as do wrong; and say: "We believe in that which was revealed to us and revealed to you; our God is your God; and to Him, we surrender (as Muslims)." And argue not with People of the Scripture unless it be (in a way) that is better, except with such of them as do wrong; and say: "We believe in that which was revealed to us and revealed to you; our God is your God; and to Him we surrender (as Muslims)." (Surat al-'Ankabut 29:46)
Comment:
The Qur'an is here revealed recognizing Jews, Christians, and Muslims as sharing the legacy of a common God as well as the ongoing need for social interaction and amity and understanding among peoples.

Therefore, all Peoples of the Book are scripturally enjoined to collaborate in pursuit of mutual goals:

Precept 6: *Peoples of the Book must thus adopt collegiality in the pursuit of common cause.*
Verse:
Had it not been for Allah's repelling some men by means of others, then cloisters and churches and oratories and mosques wherein the name of Allah is often mentioned, would assuredly have been pulled down. Verily Allah helps one who helps Him. (Surat al-Hajj 22:40)
Comment:
Defending the common faith is defined, then, as not only in the interest of Islam but in that of all religions joined in mutual cause as Peoples of the Book.

But while the Qur'an recognizes the "commonality of God" among believers of the three heavenly religions, it concurrently recognizes theological differences amongst the Peoples of the Book which are portrayed as integral to a divine plan wherein each Community of Believers (*ummah*) was to have its own messenger:

Precept 8: *Each Community of Believers has been sent its separate messenger.*

Verse:
And for every nation there is a Messenger. And when their Messenger comes (on the Day of Judgment), it will be judged between them fairly, and they will not be wronged. (Surat Yunus 10:47)
Comment:
Hence, the Qur'an recognizes all scriptural prophets—including Abraham, Jesus, and Muhammad—to be coequals before God, with Muhammad the last and final—the "Seal"—of the Prophets.

Accordingly, God sent to the Jews Moses with the Torah to provide His guidance to mankind; Jesus with the Gospels to the Christians to confirm the Torah; and Prophet Muhammad with the Qur'an to Muslims to confirm each of these earlier revelations.

This Qur'anic advice is nonetheless accompanied by a stern warning not to dismiss any iteration of "His Divine Revelation" irrespective of the manner, or through whose messenger, it was revealed:

Precept 9: *Each messenger is afforded equal status before God.*
Verse:
Lo! We did reveal the Torah wherein is guidance and a light by which the Prophets who surrendered to Allah judged the Jews and the Rabbis; and the priests (judged) by such of Allah's Scriptures as they were bidden to observe, and there too were they witness. So fear not people but fear Me. And barter not My Revelations for little gain. For whoever judges not by that which Allah has revealed: such are disbelievers. (Surat al-Ma'idah 5:44)
Comment:
This revelation, therefore, stands in affirmation that all prophets—from Moses through Abraham, through Jesus, through Muhammad—enjoy equal status before God and thereby are to be afforded equal deference by all believers.

Precept 10: *Accordingly, each set of believers has been sent its own revelation.*
Verses:
How do they come to you for judgment when they have the Torah wherein Allah has delivered judgment for them. . . . And We caused Jesus, son of Mary, to follow in their footsteps, confirming that which was (revealed) before him; and We bestowed on him the Gospel wherein is guidance and a light confirming that which was revealed before it in the Torah, a guidance and an admonition to those who are pious. (Surat al-Ma'idah 5:43, 46)

Comment:
With this proclamation, then, both the Torah and the Gospels are confirmed as the legitimate precursors of the Qur'an, which is itself the ultimate "Seal" of the scriptures.

These verses, in turn, are immediately followed by the affirmation:

Precept 11: *Each revelation to each set of believers has been sent down in its own book.*
Verse:
Let the people of the Gospel judge by that which Allah has revealed therein. . . . And to you have We revealed the Scripture with the truth, confirming whatever Scripture was before it as a watch over it. (Surat al-Ma'idah 5:47–48)
Comment:
The Qur'an is thereby established as the continuation and final installment of divine revelation, not as its progenitor.

In this manner, the Qur'an explains, Allah sought to give to each set of heavenly believers "its own law and path and way of life." Accordingly, it prescribes that each set of believers be judged in accordance with its unique set of rules:

Precept 12: *Each set of believers will likewise be judged by its own rules.*
Verse:
So judge between them by that which Allah has revealed, and follow not their desires away from the truth that has come to you. For each, We have appointed a divine law and a traced-out way. Had Allah willed, He could have made you one community. But that He may try you by that which He has given you (He has made you as you are). So vie with one another in good works. To Allah, you will all return, and he will then inform you of that wherein you differ. (Surat al-Ma'idah 5:49)
Comment:
The Qur'an thereby echoes the Judeo-Christian biblical admonition: "Judge not that ye be not judged!"—while counseling people of all faiths to vie with each other in the quest for ultimate virtue.

ON THE MANDATE OF THE "UNITY OF GOD"

The ultimate issue of who is doctrinally right or wrong is thus left for God to judge, and not to mortal man. Predicated upon this divine tenet, then, while lamenting that—

The Christians say the Jews follow nothing and the Jews say the Christians follow nothing, yet both are readers of the Scripture.

—the Qur'an prescribes a monotheistic compromise for peaceful coexistence among Peoples of the Book:

Precept 13: *Peace-loving peoples of all faiths must seek a common ground.*
Verse:
Say: "O People of the Scripture. Come to an agreement between you and us that we shall worship none but God (Allah); and that we shall ascribe no partners to Him; and that none of us shall take others for our lord beside God (Allah)." (Surat Al-i-'Imran 3:64)
Comment:
In this admonition, therefore, true believers are counseled to persevere with faith in a common and indivisible God—in accordance with the Islamic doctrine of His unity (*tawhid*).

Accordingly, the formula that the Qur'an proposes as its modus vivendi among believers is one that poses profoundly compromising doctrinal questions at least for Christians. For it is indeed at direct variance with Christian doctrine, though not with that of the Jews, on a variety of issues, including those of the divinity of Christ and his license to stand in judgment of mankind on the Day of Reckoning—all of which are embedded in the deep-seated conflict between the Muslims' belief in the unity (*tawhid*) of God and the Christian corresponding adherence to the concept of the Trinity (*tathlith*): "God the Father, God the Son, and God the Holy Spirit." As Muslims steadfastly believe that God is "one," incapable of physical death, hence, eternal[2]:

Precept 14: *Foremost among scriptural teachings is that God is the One, the Eternal.*
Verses:
Say: "He is Allah, the One! Allah, the eternally besought of all! He begets not, nor was He begotten. And there is none comparable to Him." (Surat al-Ikhlas: 112: 1–4)
Comment:
Thereby, an eternal, perfect, indivisible "unity" of God is revealed by the Qur'an.

Accordingly, the Qur'an admonishes Christians that:

Precept 15: *God's unity must be steadfastly observed.*
Verse:
O People of the Scripture! Do not exaggerate in your religion nor utter anything concerning Allah except truth. The Messiah, Jesus, son of Mary, was only a

Messenger of Allah and His Word which He conveyed to Mary and a spirit from Him. So believe in Allah and His Messengers, and say not "Three"—Cease! It is better for you. (Surat al-Nisa' 4:171)
Comment:
Accordingly, from the Muslim perspective any possible equivocation in the interpretation of Islam's outright rejection of the concept of the Trinity is effectively dispelled by this Qur'anic verse.

Indeed, the early medieval Arab chroniclers assert that this *tawhid* versus *tathlith* debate early on played a catalytic role in shaping the very fabric of contemporary Islamic society, including even tangible aspects of its physical fabric—in so doing, ultimately precipitating the "Arabization" of its chanceries and its coinage.

There is compelling source evidence, for instance, that a late seventh-century interruption in the shipment of papyrus to Merovingian Gaul may well have resulted from a dispute between the Byzantine emperor Justinian II and the Umayyad caliph 'Abd al-Malik b. Marwan, wherein that caliph had substituted Islamic formulae attesting to the *tawhid* for a previous invocation of the Christian Trinity on *tiraz* and papyri destined for export. The ninth-century Arab historian al-Baladhuri explicitly claims, in fact, that the caliph 'Abd al-Malik embargoed the export of papyri rolls to Byzantium precisely because of this dispute:

> Khalid b. Yazid advised 'Abd al-Malik to declare the use of Greek dinars to be illegal to prevent their circulation; and to stop exporting papyrus (*qaratis*) to Byzantium. Accordingly, no papyri were exported there for a time.[3]

As a consequence, the sources relate, 'Abd al-Malik b. Marwan proceeded to develop his own epigraphically pure tri-metallic—gold, silver, copper—Islamic currency and to convert the lingua franca of the Royal Court and its bureaucracy exclusively to Arabic.

Yet, however decisive this dramatic development, it was, from an ideological standpoint, a somewhat improbable doctrinal confrontation inasmuch as the Christian concept of God's Trinity is sustained by far less scriptural foundation in the Bible than is the Islamic concept of God's Unity in the Qur'an—with the former emanating seemingly more as a byproduct of ex post facto patriarchal exegesis in the first four Gregorian centuries.

Certainly, the issue is not unequivocal. For in the Bible, there is no single reference wherein the Three Divine Personages are denoted collectively. Indeed, the term *trias* (of which the Latin *trinitas* is a translation) can first be found in a slightly different connotation in Theophilus of Antioch circa 180 wherein he speaks of "the Trinity of God, His Word, His

Wisdom." It reappears as *trinitas* on a similar passim basis in both Tertullian and Origen over the next two centuries.[4]

The spiritual basis for the concept, in turn, derives from Matthew 28:19, wherein Jesus, after his Resurrection, exhorts his disciples to—

> Go ye therefore, and teach all nations, baptizing them in the name of the Father, and the Son, and the Holy Ghost.

—and from I John 5:7, wherein the "Word," but not the "Lord," is curiously specified:

> For there are three who bear record in heaven, the Father, the Word, and the Holy Ghost, and these three are one.

The Trinity's adherence, however, was not universally subscribed, as intense debate raged throughout the early Christian centuries as to the "true nature" of Jesus, leading to several major church councils that attempted to establish a firm theological view on the essence of God's Trinity. Indeed, the Islamic view of the nondivinity of Christ strongly paralleled an Eastern Orthodox one which Rome had earlier denounced as the "monophysite heresy"—a prevailing "unity of god" global view that persisted throughout much of the Near East up to the birth of Islam. The great popularity of the view, in fact, may significantly help to explain the theological readiness of much of the region to accept Islam's portrayal of Jesus when it emerged as a formal testament of faith in the seventh century.[5]

Over time, however, the Trinitarian view came to be affirmed as an article of faith in a number of Christian rescripts—the most noteworthy of which came in the proclamation issued at the Council of Nicaea convened by Byzantine Emperor Constantine in Nicaea, in what is now Turkey, on May 20, 325, which ruled—

The Proclamation at Nicaea

We believe in one God, the Father Almighty, maker of all things visible and invisible; and in one Lord, Jesus Christ, the Son of God, the only begotten of the Father—that is, of the substance (Gr. = *ousia*) of the Father—God from God, light from light, true God from true God, begotten not made, of one substance (Gr. = *homousion*) with the Father, through whom all things were made—those things that are in heaven and those things that are on earth—Who for us men and our salvation came down and was made man, suffered, rose again on the third day, ascended into the heavens, and will come to judge the living and the dead. And we believe in the Holy Spirit.

—and the Athanasian Creed (350 A.D.), produced shortly thereafter, which attempted to necessarily reassure and standardize belief in the face of disagreement, particularly in light of somewhat unsettling Old Testament admonitions that tend to comport more with the Qur'an, such as:

Hear, O Israel: the Lord our God is One Lord. (Deuteronomy 6:4)

Thou shalt have no other gods before Me. (Deuteronomy 5:7)

Thus saith the Lord, King of Israel, and his Redeemer and Lord of Hosts: "I am the first and I am the last; and beside Me, there is no god." (Isaiah 44:6)[6]

Indeed, even the New Testament is not without equivocation, with Christ himself referring to himself as the "Son of Man." Accordingly, the Apostle Paul tells the Corinthians:

We know that an idol is nothing in the world and that there is no other God but one. (I Corinthians 8:4)

He makes the same assertion to Timothy that:

For there is one God, and one mediator between God and men, the man Christ Jesus. (I Timothy 2:5)

And therein lies the great debate—with the formal Church, at times, simply writing it off as just another one of those "unfathomable mysteries."

But irrespective of whether, on the Christian side, "God found out about the Trinity in 325 A.D.," as noted Aramaic biblical scholar Rocco Errico has asserted, on the Muslim side, the *tawhidi* conviction has been central to the faith since its inception and remains integral to arguments of would-be modern reformers that Islam must return to the seminal tenets of its doctrine—to wit: a genuine *salafiyah* movement.

ON ISLAM'S LEGACY AS A RELIGION OF TOLERANCE

For as the Qur'anic verses cited illustrate, Islam, throughout its long legacy, has advocated a political doctrine that fosters tolerance and peaceful coexistence. Indeed, the scripture teaches that "if even one person is killed unjustly, the act is tantamount to killing of all mankind," and the faith's principal daily greeting is: "*as-salamu 'alaykum*" meaning: "may peace be with you!"

Its theological differences with Christianity and Judaism are likewise surprisingly limited. In principle, in fact, it has less of a problem with either of those two faiths than they have with each other or with Islam. For Islam views itself as no more than their continuation and completion—God's final synthesized manifesto, the ultimate seal upon the historical process of revelation.[7]

Admittedly there are some—not the least among them Robert Spencer, Bat Ye'or, David Littman, Daniel Pipes, and Ibn Warraq—who deny this reality to be fact, decrying present perceived religious suppression, presumed political discrimination, and alleged civil rights violations in certain Middle East states wherein Islam today is practiced.[8]

But is it just to blame an entire religion because select actions carried out by certain professed adherents may be deemed by some to be uncivil or unjust? Such practices, if they do indeed exist, are not founded in Islamic doctrine, as this inquiry has shown. To the contrary, to attribute to the Qur'an the inhumanities specified by the critics cited is tantamount to indicting Christianity and the Gospels for atrocities perpetrated by the Serbs in Bosnia and Kosovo.

Islam has, in fact, historically been a religion of tolerance from its inception, with the incipient genius of early Arab-Muslim civilization firmly founded equally upon its outreach and upon its multicultural, multireligious, and multiethnic diversities. Building upon these inherent social strengths, as demonstrated, multitudes of verses exhorting peaceful coexistence pervade the Qur'an. The pursuit of such precepts was prevalent in early Islamic practice as well and is evident in a multiplicity of Prophetic Traditions.

Among them, Prophet Muhammad, in his early preaching, looked to the Jews and Christians of Arabia as natural allies whose faiths had much in common with Islam. Indeed, he anticipated their acceptance and cooperation, and his de facto embryonic constitution to provide for administering al-Madinah granted them full autonomy in internal religious affairs. When the Islamic community was first established there, in fact, Muslims, like Jews, were obliged to face Jerusalem to pray.[9]

This fabric of deeply-woven tolerance would continue to be spun under Muhammad's caliphal successors. The renowned Crusader historian Steven Runciman relates a legend—and it is equally a Christian and a Muslim one—that holds that when the caliph Omar entered the holy city Jerusalem upon its capture by Muslim forces in 638, he was received by the presiding Christian patriarch Sophronius who invited him to visit the Church of the Holy Sepulchre.[10]

As the Islamic hour for prayer arrived while Omar was at the church, the caliph asked where he might pray. But though the patriarch invited

him to spread his prayer rug inside the sanctuary, he deferred lest his followers claim the prayer site for Islam, offering his prayers instead outside
on the Porch of the Martyrium.[11]

Indeed, for centuries thereafter, Islamic rulers—Umayyad, 'Abbasid,
and Fatimid—extended similar religious tolerance to the Christians and
the Jews. As Peoples of the Book, they were required to pay taxes and prohibited from bearing arms, but their religious observances and places of
worship were nonetheless protected. This was no transitory trend—as
from the eighth to twelfth centuries, the 'Abbasid caliphate ruling from
Baghdad, and its Umayyad counterpart in Cordoba, intently patronized
man's ongoing quest for knowledge irrespective of its provenance, producing a rich flowering of science, arts, philosophy, and culture throughout the entire learned world.[12]

It was now that peoples of many ethnic backgrounds within the Dar al-
Islam were inventing algebra, astronomy, and much more. It was now
that classic Graeco-Roman science and philosophy were translated into
Arabic and preserved. Countless Christian and Jewish intellectuals, in
fact, migrated to these intellectually enlightened Islamic capitals at this
time to escape the ideological repressiveness that attended Europe's Dark
Ages. It was now that great Jewish philosophers were liberated to create
their historic works within the openly pluralistic culture of Islam.[13]

This veneer of tolerance and amity would carry over into the conduct
of the Crusades—a phenomenon deeply etched into Muslim collective
memory—as well, though it was clearly not reciprocal. Indeed, when in
1099, warriors of the First Crusade captured and established sovereignty
over Jerusalem, the historic capital of the biblical holy land, in the blood-
drenched aftermath, there were left no Muslim survivors. The Dome of
the Rock was instead converted into a church and al-Aqsa mosque, then
renamed the Temple of Solomon, became the residence for the crusader
king.[14]

By contrast, when in 1187, Salah al-Din al-Ayyubi (Saladin) recon-
quered the holy city of Jerusalem in Islam's name, his military was as
magnanimous in victory as it had been tenacious in battle. Civilians were
spared and churches and shrines were generally left untouched. Whereas
Richard the Lionhearted had massacred the populace of Acre upon its
conquest despite promises to the contrary, Saladin was faithful to his
word and compassionate to noncombatants.[15]

Indeed, today, though they deny the divinity of Christ, devout Muslims
venerate the Jewish patriarchs and revere Jesus as God's prophet and
apostle. Are the other heavenly religions competent to claim the same?

In short, throughout its history, both in doctrine and in practice, Islam
has proven to be a religion of consummate tolerance. This is precisely why

for every Irshad Manji writing dirges lamenting: "The Trouble with Islam!" there is a corresponding Imam Faysal 'Abd al-Ra'uf writing countervailing books rejoicing in: "What is Right with Islam!"[16]

Given this noble legacy, then, it is disconcerting, at the least, to contemplate the disparaging prisms through which the classic Islamic religion, throughout much of the planet, is currently portrayed.

Appendix D
The Use of Qur'anic Verses as Militant Propaganda

Truth has arrived, and falsehood has perished; for falsehood by its nature is bound to perish.

—Surat al-Isra' 17:81, 82

QUR'ANIC EXEGESIS AS A VISTA
TO EARLY ISLAMIC POLITICAL HISTORY

As noted in preceding appendices, given the medieval Muslims' commitment to both just war and equitable peace, the key analytic question in defining them becomes one of determining an appropriate and exacting methodology for engaging in precise Qur'anic exegesis. For in Islamic affairs, both political and diplomatic, the Qur'an is the quintessential guide, the "final revelation" of the "final prophet," Muhammad. Not only is it integral to Muslims' daily lives, it is the living constitution of the Islamic state. Reflecting this reality, eminent orientalist Bernard Lewis asserts that in contrast to the other major world religions:[1]

Islam from the lifetime of its founder was the state, and the identity of religion and the government is indelibly stamped on the awareness and memories of the faithful from their sacred writings, history, and experience.

It is not surprising, therefore, to find that most of the significant political and social movements in modern Muslim history have drawn

205

heavily upon classic Islam as a unifying and motivating force. Because recourse to religious symbolism is inherent to modern terrorist practice, therefore, its historic employment over time merits special contemplation.

For the use of Qur'anic verses as political battle cries struck onto its coinage is intrinsic to the history of Islam from its inception. Such employment certainly is not surprising as money has traditionally played a wide variety of utilitarian roles in all societies, including those thriving in the medieval Islamic Near East. It served as a measure of the value of goods and services; as a currency facilitating transactions involving their exchange; as a denominator of wealth; as a tool of international commerce and diplomacy; and finally, but not least, as an instrument of political and religious propaganda.

The widespread prevalence of those surviving medieval Islamic currency specimens, reposing in both public and private collections, or continually surfacing in newly discovered archaeological treasure troves, thus is a great asset for the economic and political historian alike. For the economic historian, their great utility in discovery is readily evident—as surviving coins are residual evidence of past monetary systems explicitly created to support then contemporary commercial transaction flows.

But for the political historian, they offer equal value, enabling a determination of the extent of territorial jurisdiction, the reconstruction of key political events and their chronologies, and the nature and extent of international diplomatic relations and ideological and religious affiliations. This phenomenon is particularly applicable to medieval Islamic currency, which often concurrently displays a wide variety of features and characteristics relating to the specific political, economic, and religious objectives of the rulers producing them—thus allowing for retrospective re-creations of their specific policy intents. In addition, epigraphically, the names of rulers or honorific pseudonyms (*laqab/alqab*), and often those of local provincial governors, appear upon the coins as well.

Together with the Friday sermon (*khutbah*), then, the use of religious symbolism on coins as propaganda instruments, though not an innovation, was unquestionably more effective and widespread among medieval Muslim dynasties than with most other contemporary regimes. All dynasties employed them. Upon examination, in fact, it becomes readily apparent that as a foremost symbol of territorial sovereignty and extraterritorial influence, coins distinguished by their fineness both epigraphically and qualitatively characterized the early currency issues of the Dar al-Islam.[2]

EXAMPLES OF QUR'ANIC EPIGRAPHY
ON EARLY ISLAMIC COINAGE

Indeed, early Islamic currency is replete with such powerful Qur'anic expressions as: "May God provide him strength for his victory" (*A'izz Allah nasrahu*); "May God support him" (*Ayyidahu Allah*); "May God support him in his victory" (*Ayyid Allah nasrahu*); "All honor is with God" (*'Izzat Allah Jami 'an*); and "All Power is with God" (*'Quwat Allah Jami'an*).[3]

The subsequent medieval history of Islam, moreover, abounds with just such usage. Even before they overthrew the Umayyad dynasty in 749, for instance, the 'Abbasids signaled their intent to do so commencing in 745 by striking a new *Hashimiyah* silver coinage—proclaiming their direct Islamic "blue blood" linkage to the historic tribe of Prophet Muhammad— that was then circulated in the easternmost provinces of the Dar al-Islam under their direct control.

These issues, struck in such eastern cities of the caliphate as Istakhr (745), Jayy (745, 747), Ramhurmuz (746), al-Taymarah (746–747), and Balkh (748–750), as well as at al-Kufah, al-Marw, and elsewhere, concurrently proclaimed a Qur'anic message explicitly selected to attract supporters:

> Say: "No reward do I ask of you for this except for the love of those near of kin." (Surat al-Shu'ra 26:23)[4]

Such obviously likewise was the intent of the military commander Kafur, the next to last formal ruler to preside over the Ikshidid dynasty in Egypt prior to its invasion by the Fatimid armies in 969. For though not a formal member of the Ikshidid lineage, he struck gold dinars in 968 in his own name bearing the Qur'anic verse—

> Truth has arrived, and falsehood has perished; for falsehood by its nature is bound to perish. (Surat al-Isra'17:81, 82)

—while concurrently indicating Makkah as their place of minting in a transparent effort to establish the reality of his own legitimacy by currying political favor with the notables of that holy city.[5]

If such earlier Muslims pioneered in the propagandistic use of Qur'anic verses on currency, however, it was the 'Abbasids who honed this technique to fine perfection—transforming the ready employment of coins from mere economic employment to a platform for ideological debate. Indeed, nowhere was their use for political purposes more clearly manifest than in the intense battles for succession waged first by

Caliph al-Hadi, the brother of another future caliph and immediate successor, Harun al-Rashid, and then by the latter's two sons, al-Amin and al-Ma'mun, each of which was attended by an equally intense "war of coins."

In the case of al-Hadi, in the year 786, just prior to his death, upon rebestowing the title of crown prince from Harun to his son Ja'far, whose age was merely five—he then had the latter's name struck on a currency issued that year announcing him as future caliph in the first-ever striking of a name of a crown prince designate on Islamic money. After al-Hadi's subsequent violent death at the tender age of twenty-four under somewhat murky circumstances on October 15, 786, however, his immediate successor, Harun al-Rashid, ascended to the 'Abbasid caliphate and proceeded to strike coins bearing his own name while concurrently carrying the phrase:

> As was ordered by Servant of God (*'Abd Allah*) Harun, Commander of the Faithful.[6]

In the case of al-Amin and al-Ma'mun, however, the transition was equally messy, yet not so expeditiously effected—albeit with as much panache and violence, as the ensuing battle for succession precipitated a bitter civil war that raged on between them for five years from 809 to 813 having far-reaching effects not only for sovereignty but also for the course of contemporary numismatics—as the quest for the former was borne out on the latter.

The evolution of this process was fascinating. Initially, while Caliph Harun was still alive and Amin vested with control over Islam's western provinces and al-Ma'mun over those in the east, al-Ma'mun, the eldest son, had been designated crown prince and heir apparent. Somewhat later, however, in the year 791, it appears that Caliph Harun, at the urging of his wife Zubaydah, formally designated his younger son al-Amin to be his crown prince and successor and struck new gold dinars bearing his name signaling this change that, on their obverses, also was engraved the Qur'anic verse:

> If they turn away, say: "Allah suffices me. There is no god save He. In Him is my trust." (Surat Al Tawbah 9:129)[7]

Concurrently, coins likewise were struck in the name of al-Ma'mun that carried the *laqab*: Successor to the Crown Prince of the Muslims (*Wali Wali 'Ahd al-Muslimin*).

Al-Ma'mun, still in control of the eastern provinces of the Dar al-Islam, however, reciprocated by proclaiming the legitimacy of his continuing claim to succession by striking at his Nisabur and Marw mints currency in his name that bore the expression:

Imam al-Ma'mun, Crown Prince of the Muslims, The Servant of God, Son of the Commander of the Faithful.[8]

Another coin series concurrently was struck throughout the eastern portion of the 'Abbasids' realm that likewise designated al-Ma'mun as the Crown Prince of the Muslims. The obverse faces of this issue read:

In the name of God, this dirham was struck in Nisabur in the year four and ninety and one hundred. There is no god save Allah alone. He has no partner.[9]

Their reverses, in turn, read:

Muhammad, Messenger of Allah, was sent with guidance and the true religion to proclaim it over all religion, though unbelievers may despise it. (Surat al-Tawbah 9:33)

Praise be to God. Muhammad is the Prophet of God. By the order of Prince Ma'mun, Crown Prince of the Muslims—Servant of God, Son of the Commander of the Faithful.[10]

In due course, however, with al-Amin having been formally installed as ruling caliph upon his father's death in 809—and al-Ma'mun still titular governor of Islam's easternmost provinces—al-Amin deposed his brother al-Ma'mun as crown prince and heir apparent and substituted his own son Musa, known by the *laqab*—

Al-Natiq b'il-Haqq, al-Muzaffar bi-Allah (The Conveyor of Truth, Made Victorious by God)

—in his stead, and then struck coins, larger than standard both in size and weight, bearing that laqab, as well as the expression—

As was ordered by Prince Musa, the son of the Commander of the Faithful

—in an obvious, and patently transparent, effort to formally signal a change in lineal succession.[11]

In the year 810, moreover—in an apparent attempt at total divestiture of al-Ma'mun—Caliph al-Amin ordered the deletion of any mention of his brother's name from Friday prayer services and ordered that of his son and successor-designate, Musa, be recited in its stead. In direct response, al-Ma'mun then dropped any pretense to being crown prince, a post with which he had originally been invested by his father, Caliph Harun, in 802, in favor of his own caliphal claim and struck on his new dinar issues the phrase:

By the order of Imam al-Ma'mun.

A representation of the Holy Ka'bah was likewise engraved upon this coinage issue.

Simultaneously, al-Ma'mun ordered the release of another currency issue in his name carrying the logo:

By the order of the Servant of God 'Abd Allah al-Ma'mun, Imam of the Faithful.

Then, after an initial victory of al-Ma'mun's military, commanded by Tahir b. al-Husayn, over that of al-Amin, when the people of Khurasan pledged their fealty to al-Ma'mun as true caliph, he, on this occasion, ordered struck another issue engraved with the expression—

By the order of Imam al-Ma'mun, Commander of the Faithful

—and indeed, yet another bearing the phrase:

By the order of Servant of God, al-Ma'mun, Commander of the Faithful.[12]

Thus, the 'Abbasid struggle for succession, and attendant clash of coins, would continue and would end only with the killing of al-Amin in Baghdad in 813 by al-Ma'mun's army and the latter's subsequent formal full assumption of the caliphate over the entire Islamic domain. On this occasion, as al-Ma'mun ascended to the caliphal throne of all of Sunni Islam, now victorious over both his brother al-Amin and sundry Byzantine outposts in Greater Syria, he ordered struck in his name in the year 814 coins that read—

With Allah is the decision, in the past and in the future. On that day will the Believers rejoice in the victory of Allah. (Surat al-Rum 30:3–4)

—as well as

Al-Imam—Muhammad is the Prophet of God—Al-Ma'mun.

This Qur'anic verse would then be perpetuated on subsequent 'Abbasid coinage until the dynasty's fall in 1258—whose issues also often bore testimony to the role of its capital, Baghdad, as the Islamic City of Peace (*Madinat al-Salam*) for public relations purposes as well.[13]

ON THE USE OF QUR'ANIC VERSES AS
RALLYING CRIES FOR MUSLIM REVOLUTIONARIES

Even would-be Muslim revolutionaries and secessionists would frequently proclaim their causes by issuing coins bearing Qur'anic verses, together with their own names that transmitted political slogans as symbols of their authority and power. When 'Abd al-Rahman al-Ash'ath rebelled against the caliphate of 'Abd al-Malik b. Marwan because of the perceived heavy-handed governance of al-Hajjaj b. Yusuf al-Thaqafi over Iraq, for instance, his currency carried the extract from the Qur'anic verse:

All honor is with Allah. (Surat al-Nisa' 4:139)[14]

Currency issued by the rebel Ibrahim b.'Abd Allah in al-Basrah also had engraved upon it the Qur'anic verse identical to that which would be struck upon the coinage of Kafur al-Ikhshidi in Egypt a century later:

Truth has arrived, and falsehood has perished; for any falsehood (by its nature) is bound to perish. (Surat al-Isra' 17:81, 82)[15]

The coinage ordered struck in 815 by anti-'Abbasid insurgent Abu al-Saraya' al-Surri b. Mansur al-Shaybani in al-Kufah, in turn, bore the Qur'anic verse as slogan of his revolutionary cause:

Truly Allah loves those who steadfastly fight arrayed in battle in His cause as if they were a bonded structure. (Surat Saff 61:4)[16]

Somewhat later, in the 'Alawis' anti-'Abbasid revolt and self-proclaimed caliphate in Tabaristan, their leader, al-Hassab b. Zayyid, likewise struck gold dinars in 876 that read:

God only wishes to remove all abomination from you. (Surat al-Ahzab 33:33)[17]

When the "black slaves" (*al-Zanj*), likewise opposed to 'Abbasid rule, rebelled in the 870–883 period, they too struck on certain coins, commencing in 873, extracts from various Qur'anic verses, such as:

God has purchased from the Believers their persons and their goods for Paradise—for those who fight in His Cause. (Surat al-Tawbah 9: 111)

If any fail to judge what God hath revealed, they are Unbelievers. (Surat al-Ma'idah 5:44)[18]

Thus, the employment of religious symbolism, and in particular, Qur'anic verses, as both political slogans and battle cries has been richly documented in Islamic history almost from its inception—making the careful study of their current employment as political propaganda instruments not only useful from a strategic analytic standpoint but also of historic consequence.

Notes

Introduction

1. By doctrine, the House of Islam was to be engaged in constant struggle with the House of War. Treaties were meant to be temporary expedients designed to sort through polarities lasting no more than a decade—contracted as mere stop-gap measures that served perceived honorable purposes such as to reduce ongoing religious persecution or to enhance the possibility of preserving peace. A third condition, House of Peace, gave qualified recognition to a territory that surrendered to the Islamic state either in exchange for a portion of its territory or for payment of an annual poll tax to be levied on each of its inhabitants. Famed tenth-century Arab historian al-Tabari termed this condition the "final ultimatum." (On this trichotomy, see M. Khadduri 1955, p. 17; J. Kelsey and J. Johnson 1991, p. 98ff.) (The translation is from the al-Madinah version.)

2. Terrorism, used in this analysis, is defined as an "intentional use of massive clandestine violence against noncombatants for revenge or intimidation purposes designed to attract an audience to advance political ends."

3. Some analysts have even identified what they label a sum of 109 Qur'anic "sword verses" from a total of 6,219 within the scripture.

4. Cited in W. Laquer 1977, p. 4. It is noteworthy that when American troops have taken up arms in the Mid-East recently, it has been, at times—as in the case of Bosnia—to protect Muslims from the atrocities of self-professing Christians.

5. Cited in C. Brinton 1960, p. 115; S. Glain 2005, p. 187ff. Terror and progress are thus not utterly incompatible. As Orson Wells (*The Third Man*) famously observed: "In Italy, for 30 years under the Borgias, they had terror, murder, and bloodshed, but they produced Michelangelo and Leonardo da Vinci and the Renaissance. In Switzerland, immediately to the north, they had brotherly love. They had five hundred years of democracy and peace. And what did they produce? The cuckoo clock!"

6. Or alternately stated: "War changes men" and the law of Lord Acton: "Power corrupts, and absolute power corrupts absolutely" has not been repealed. (To quote an African proverb: "Until lions have their own historians, tales of the hunt will invariably glorify the hunter!")

7. In this context, then, other verses from Surat al-Tawbah that follow are also far better understood. Among them:

> O Prophet. Fight hard against the disbelievers and the hypocrites. Be harsh with them. Their ultimate abode is Hell, an evil journey's end. (Surat al-Tawbah 9:73)

> O ye who believe. The polytheists only are unclean. . . . Fight against such of those who have not been given the Scripture and believe not in Allah nor in the Last Day. (Surat al-Tawbah 9:28–29)

8. R. Aslan 2005, pp. xv, 1, 78–79; B. Lewis 2002, passim, 2003; S. Huntington 1996, passim; I. Manji 2003, passim. Iranian-born religious scholar Reza Aslan presses the compelling point:

> Almost immediately following the attacks upon New York and Washington, D.C., many pundits throughout the United States and Europe declared that September 11, 2001, had triggered a dormant "clash of civilizations," to use Samuel Huntington's now ubiquitous term. . . . A few respected academics carried this argument further still by suggesting that the prime failure of democracy to emerge in the Islamic world was due to Muslim culture which they claimed was intrinsically incompatible with such great values as liberalism, pluralism human rights, and individualism. . . . It was therefore just a matter of time before these two great civilizations clashed each with the other in a catastrophic way. And what better example do we need of this inevitability than September 11?

9. On these developments, see S. Runciman 1966, passim.

10. Ibid.

11. Yet in actual context, an *imam*'s call to jihad as an instrument of religious outreach, in its proper context, is analogous to, and can be no more invidious or dangerous than, an evangelical preacher's altar call.

12. O. Roy 1994, p. 1; L. Wright 2006, pp. 63ff. Too often also, the name Saudi is lumped among those terms as well. Yet most religious Saudis prefer not to be called Wahhabis at all but instead *muwahhidun* (unitarians) reflecting their belief in the oneness of God; or as *salafiis*, descendants of the Founding Fathers of Islam, the Companions of Prophet Muhammad, products of a doctrinally nonviolent tradition and evolution. The modern distinction being that while Islam is a religion, not a political ideology, Islamism has become an amalgam of both—a religio-cultural-political framework for challenging issues of modernism. (On this see G. Fuller 2003, pp. 14, 193.) The posited linkages are implausible at best. Wahhabism and the modern Saudi state have been affiliated since its inception over a century ago. Yet the incipient rise of terrorism in the kingdom is a product of just the past two decades. (On this see G. Fuller 2003, pp. 14, 193; A. Garfinkle 2004, p. 91.)

13. Notwithstanding that the seventh-century al-khawarij, among other early Islamic schisms, also viewed themselves as revivalist movements.

14. Cited by M. Zuckerman, October 24, 2005, p. 76.

15. To these ends, while recognizing that Muslims may disagree among themselves about the significance of certain aspects of Prophetic Tradition, the Qur'an itself is bedrock and absolute, a methodological note becomes in order. For comparative purposes, then, this analysis relies upon three translations of the Qur'an:

- Pickthall, M. *The Meaning of the Glorious Koran* (New York: Mentor, 1955; revised, International Committee for the Support of the Final Prophet, *The Qur'an Translated: Message for Humanity*, Washington, D.C.: Darussalam, 2005). Pickthall was a British Western convert to Islam.
- 'Ali, 'Abd Allah Yusuf, *The Meaning of the Holy Qur'an* (Brentwood 1993), a translation completed by a self-nominated moderate Muslim.
- Al-Hilili, M. and Khan, M. *The Noble Qur'an* (Al-Madinah, Kingdom of Saudi Arabia: Kink Fahd Complez, 1996), a translation called by some the Wahhabi version—formally approved by the then Shaykh al-Islam resident in Makkah, 'Abd al-'Aziz bin 'Abd Allah bin Baz.

Unless otherwise indicated, the Pickthall version is employed in the exegetical analyses of chapter 2 and appendices B and C.

16. See P. Bergen 2006, pp. 114, 143–49, 194–208, 255, 287–89; D. Gold 2003, p. 97.

Chapter 1: The Concept of "Jihad" in Historic Context

1. Analysis builds upon the longstanding, classically defined Islamic approach to international relations articulated at appendix A.

2. Yet the point often missed is that the fifteen of nineteen terrorists notwithstanding, 23.69 million of the kingdom's 23.7 million citizens harbor no such hostile feelings, most of whom favor amicable relations with the West.

3. Among them, within the Islamic world, Islamic terrorists may, at times, sound chords that hold some resonance for other, more moderate Muslims for which they may express some affinity. But that reality in itself does not imply that the latter advocate violence in their pursuit, but instead renders perceiving Middle East culture not unlike the proverbial onion wherein one must peel back layer after layer to fully ascertain the truth that lies at its core.

4. Middle East Media Research Institute, March 5, 2003, passim.

5. Ayman al-Zawahiri, "Knights Under the Prophet's Banner," 2 December 2001, part 11, available online at www.fas.org

6. Lest there be any doubt of this reality, see A. Naji 2006, passim.

7. See U.S. National Security Council NIE April 2006, passim.

8. See U.S. National Security Council NIE April 2006, passim.

9. U.S. National Security Council NIE. January 2007, p. 4.

10. Y. Fouda and N. Fielding 203, p. 196; G. Michael 2006, p. 304; A. Rasanayagm 2005, p. 214.

11. B. Lawrence 1998, pp. 4, 34–35; In comparison, at year-end 2006, 0.74 percent of the U.S. populace is now incarcerated for criminal activity, the highest percentage in the industrial world.

12. J. Kelsey and J. Johnson 1991, pp. 34–43; B. Lewis 2003, pp. xvii–xix; W. Phares 2005, pp. 48–50. Radical jihadists perceive history as a linear course characterized by application of the mandates of the Qur'an and the *shari'ah*—rejecting secular international law and structures. Islamic fundamentalists, on the other hand, can be less doctrinaire—viewing history as a continuum intertwining past and present that can serve as a guide to the future.

13. B. Lewis 2002, p. 127; W. Phares 2005, pp. 20–21, 162.

14. P. Fregosi 1998, pp. 19–20. Thus making the jihad already five and one-half centuries old when the Crusaders set out on the campaign to take the Holy Land. Yet while the Crusader holy wars were not a part of Christian teachings and as such, were unregulated, jihad is Islamic at its roots and has a precise code of conduct that defines its execution.

15. B. Lewis 2002, p. 6.

16. Al-Basri 1853–1854, pp. 8–11, 40–42.

17. Al-Waqidi 1855–1856, p. 402; Ibn 'Asakir 1914–1932, vol. 5, pp. 92, 102.

18. Al-Baladhuri 1866, pp. 121ff.; ibidem. 1978, pp. 127ff.

19. Al-Baladhuri 1866, p. 137; al-Tabari 1879–1904, vol. 1, pp. 2395–96.

20. Al-Tabari 1879–1904, vol. 1, p. 2346; Ibn al-Athir 1867, vol. 2, p. 400; al-Baladhuri 1978, pp. 299ff.

21. Al-Tabari 1879–1904, vol. 1, p. 2592; Ibn 'Abd al-Hakam 1922, pp. 53, 58; al-Baladhuri 1978, pp. 214ff.

22. Ibn 'Abd al-Hakam 1922, p. 82; al-Baladhuri 1978, pp. 221–25.

23. Al-Ya'qubi 1883, vol. 2, p. 179; Ibn 'Abd al-Hakam 1922, p. 183; al-Baladhuri 1978, pp. 225ff.

24. Al-Maqqari 1855, vol. 1, p. 189.

25. Al-Idrisi 1899, p. 36; al-Baladhuri 1866, p. 230; ibid. 1978, pp. 232ff.; Ibn 'Abd al-Hakam 1922, p. 206; Ibn al-Athir 1867, vol. 4, p. 444.

26. Al-Dabbi 1884–1885, p. 303.

27. Ibid., p. 353

28. Fregosi 1898, pp. 3ff.

29. B. Lewis 2002, pp. 4ff.; P. Fregosi 1998, p. 22, 24–25.

30. T. P. Schwartz-Barcott 2004, pp. 171–72; M. Evans 2003, p. 48.

31. T. P. Schwartz-Barcott 2004, pp. 165–66; B. Lewis 2002, pp. 4ff.; particularly since the Mongols were a more devastating force within the Islamic world in that era than were the Crusaders.

32. B. Lewis 2002, pp. 6–7.

33. P. Hitti 1970, p. 315.

34. Ibid., pp. 577ff.

35. Ibid., pp. 578ff.

36. Ibidem.

37. Ibid., pp. 373ff.

38. Ibid., pp. 379–80.

39. Ibid., pp. 376ff., 573.

40. See B. Lewis 1981, pp. 12ff.

41. P. Marsden 1998, p. 68; T. P. Schwartz-Barcott 2004, p. 3.

42. For detailed discourse on this phenomenon, see appendix D.

43. 'A. al-Na'im, 1996, p. 20.

Chapter 2: On the Islamic Doctrine of War

1. On these practices, see M. Haykal 1976, pp 15–16, 115–30; F. Donner 1981, pp. 20–25; 'A. al-Na'im 1996, p. 142.

2. M. Hamidullah 1966, pp. 51ff.; F. Donner 1981, pp. 37ff.; 'A. al-Na'im 1996, loc. cit.

3. M. Khadduri 1966, pp. 15ff.; 'A. al-Na'im 1996, loc. cit.

4. J. Kelsay 1993, p. 34.

5. On these four preconditions, see J. Kelsay 1993, pp. 35ff., 39ff., 47ff.

6. J. Kelsay and J. T. Johnson, eds., 1990, pp. xiv, 73.

7. J. Kelsay and J. Johnson, eds., 1990, pp. 58ff.; D. Hollenbach 1983, pp. 37–46; D. Lackey 1988, pp. 28–97. Regulations annexed to The Hague Convention IV (1907) makes it forbidden to "kill or wound treacherously individuals belonging to the hostile nation or army."

8. 'Umar b. Ibrahim al-Awasi al-Ansari 1961, pp. 7ff.; see M. Khadduri 1966, passim; Y. Aboul-Enein and S. Zuhur 2004, p. 2; J. Kelsay 1993, p. 36.

9. Center for Law and Military Operations 2002, pp. 36–37; M. Haleem 1999, pp. 61ff.; T. P. Schwartz-Barcott 2004, pp. 41–42; Y. Aboul-Enein and S. Zuhur 2004, p. vii.

10. Al-Mawardi 1853, pp. 58, 79.

11. M. Haleem 1999, p. 63.

12. In comparison, see the Bible, Leviticus: 24:20: "Breach for breach; eye for eye, and tooth for tooth," its equivalent expressed in Surat al-Ma'idah 5:45. Hence, it may be the martial precept of reciprocity (Latin *lex talionis* = war of retribution = Arabic *mu'amilah bil-mithl*) is common to the conduct of war in both the East and West. (On this, see S. Bar 2006, pp. 67, 71–72.)

13. Muslim 19:4313.

14. Ibn Khaldun 1965, vol. 2, p. 823; R. Peters 1996, pp. 116ff., 167.

15. The sanction for war for apostasy issues from the Qur'an:

> But when they break their oaths after their covenant, and thrust at your religion, then fight the leaders of unbelief. (Surah al-Tawbah 9:12)

The rationale for capital punishment for apostasy is straightforward. Unlike a pluralistic jurisdiction wherein Church and State are separate, in a theocratic state, the vow of faith is a pledge of allegiance, making apostasy tantamount to treason.

It was this sanction of war for apostasy that led to the so-called *hurub al-riddah* against backsliders on the Arabian Peninsula following Prophet Muhammad's death in 632.

16. M. Habeck 2006, p. 108

17. Muslim cited in R. Peters 2005, p. 4.

18. Taking a lead from Surat al-Nahl 16:106, which stipulates that "Anyone who, after accepting faith in Allah, expresses unbelief—except under compulsion, his heart remaining firm in faith . . . on them is the wrath of Allah," some Muslim scholars, primarily Shi'i—hold that the practice known as dissimulation, a denial of faith when confronting an imminent danger or other duress, is sanctioned by Islam. Historically, it was employed to plant spies behind an enemy's lines, there to engage in acts of counterinsurgency. In a modern context, it is the employment of this precept that enables the jihadists to operate freely—remaining anonymous

and inactive for protracted periods by melding into a civilian populace waiting for propitious moments to strike. (Another doctrinal difference between the Sunni and Shi'i jurists is that while the former contend that jihad may be waged by any Muslim authority against the Dar al-Harb, the latter claim that only a divinely appointed *imam* may declare a jihad that is not defensive. On this, see J. Kelsay and J. T. Johnson 1990, pp. xvi, 39, 44, 200; G. Kepel 2002, p. 139; R. Peters 1996, pp. 50ff., 164; L. Wright 2006, p. 124; S. Bar 2006, p. 31.

19. And He shall judge among the nations and shall rebuke many people; and they shall turn their swords into plowshares and their spears into pruning hooks; no nation shall lift up a sword against nation, neither shall they learn war anymore. (Isaiah 2:4)

20. B. Lewis 2003, pp. 31, 143; these injunctions, nonetheless, did not prevent the Crusades. The first individual option professional practitioners of jihad may well have been the eleventh-thirteenth–century Greater Syrian "Assassins" who, self-intoxicating on hashish, transformed the act named after them into a both system and an ideology—assassinating many major Crusader and rival Islamic leaders through "religious execution" with equal equanimity and impunity.

Chapter 3: Getting From "There" to "Here"

1. R. Aslan 2005, pp. 143–44.

2. B. Lewis 2002, pp. 99ff.; J. Kelsay 1993, pp. 33ff.; O. Roy 1994, pp. 28ff.

3. Ibn Qayyim n.d., 1:10; K. Abu al-Fadl 2003, pp. 15ff.

4. 'A. al-Na'im 1996, pp. 21ff.; R. Aslan 2005, pp. 164–65; N. DeLong-Bas, pp. 96–97.

5. See 'A. al-Na'im 1996, pp. 17, 21, 23ff. and sources cited in preceding footnote. The predicate derives from a saying attributed to Prophet Muhammad that "My people (*ummati*) will never be unanimous in error." See also Qur'an 4:115.

6. B. Lewis 2003, p. 140.

7. 'A. al-Na'im 1996, pp. 25, 27ff.; N. DeLong-Bas, pp. 97ff.

8. R. Aslan 2005, pp. 157–58. Viewed in this context, the Qur'an is not only divinely inspired as God's Word, it is divine in its own right and therefore immutable and eternal. Christianity actually adheres to the same precept as reflected in the Bible:

> In the beginning was the Word and the Word was with God and the Word was God. (*En arche en ho logos, kai ho logos en pros ton theon, kai theos en ho logos.*) (John 1:1).

9. R. Aslan 2005, p. 144.

10. Ibidem.

11. On these developments, see A. Al Fahd 2004, pp. 487ff.

12. R. Aslan 2005, pp. 240–41; Ramadan 2004, p. 25; D. Commins 2006, p. 11. *Salaf* is a title generally given to Companions of Prophet Muhammad and to pious Muslims who were born within the first three generations of Islam. For a salafi, only the Qur'an and *ahadith* are deemed to have juridical legitimacy.

13. J. Esposito 2005, p. 118; M. Rasheed 2002, p. 17; ICG 2004, p. 1; N. DeLong-Bas 2004, pp. 8ff.; M. Sageman 2004, p. 8.

14. See A. 'al-Na'im 1996, pp. 35–37; M. Sageman 2004, loc cit.; the early Wahhabi movement closely adhered to the puritanical teaching of Ibn Taymiyah of *takfir*—declaring to be apostates those with whom they ideologically disagreed.

15. ICG 2004, p. 1; R. Baer 2003, pp. 85ff.

16. T. al-Hamad 1986, passim; A. Al Fahd 2004, pp. 511–14; R. Aslan 2005, loc. cit.; M. Rasheed 2002, pp. 15–16; R. Dreyfus 2005, pp. 38–44.

17. M. Rasheed 2002, pp. 51–52; G. Posner 2005, pp. 21, 28.

18. G. Kepel 2004, p. 160; M. Rasheed 2002, pp. 57–58.; A. Abu Khalil 2004, pp. 81–83; though in the early nineteenth century, they faced a modicum of opposition from certain other *'ulama'* residents within the Najd. (On this, see D. Commins 2006, pp. 52–57; R. Dreyfus 2005, pp. 45–46.)

19. M. Rasheed 2002, pp. 59–71; (or *jund tawhid Allah*: = soldiers enforcing the unity of God). Subsequent to a successfully suppressed *Ikhwani* revolt against him in 1929 on charges of impiety, and with his need for further conquest then over, Ibn Sa'ud proceeded to dismantle the fractious military force, claiming that only the *'ulama'* were empowered to rule on issues of state. (On this, see R. Baer 2003, p. 86; D. Commins 2006, pp. 81–82, 89–93; R. Dreyfus 2005, p. 45; D. Gold 2003, pp. 44–45, 50.)

19. For an excellent discussion of these latter developments, see A. Al Fahd 2004, pp. 51ff.

20. R. Mitchell 1969, p. 5; J. Esposito 2005, p. 129; R. Aslan 2005, pp. 229–33; O. Roy 1994, pp. 32ff.

21. R. Mitchell 1969, pp. 207, 322; F. Gerges 2006, p. 23; R. Dreyfus 2005, pp. 21ff.; S. Bar 2006, p. 27; D. Gold 2003, pp. 54–55, 92.

22. R. Aslan 2005, pp. 235–36; A. Abu Khalil 2004, p. 81; J. Kelsay and N. Johnson 1990, p. 139; D. Commins 2006, pp. 140ff.; L. Wright 2006, p. 108 (quoted).

23. M. Huband 1999, p. 82; R. Aslan 2005, p. 237; J. Esposito 2005, p. 152; L. Wright 2006, p. 25; R. Dreyfus 2005, p. 63; D. Gold 2003, p. 89.

24. N. Delong-Bas 2004, p. 257; R. Aslan 2005, p. 238; D. Commins 2006, pp. 147–48; L. Wright 2006, pp. 7–8; R. Dreyfuss 2005, pp. 103–4.

25. Sayyid Qutb 1967, p. 87; M. Juergensmeyer 2001, p. 82; M. Sageman 2004, p. 55. Indeed, it was in Egyptian prisons and universities that, in the eyes of many, the modern precept of *salafi* jihadism was born. In Sayyid Qutb's words: "Islam is, in effect, a revolt against any situation wherein sovereignty, or indeed God-head, is given to human beings."

26. Sayyid Qutb, *Ma'alim fi al-Tariq*, cited in B. Lawrence 1998, p. 68; M. Sageman 2004, pp. 8–9; S. Schwartz 2002, p. 134; S. Coll 2004, pp. 112–13; D. Commins 2006, p. 148; F. Gerges 2006, p. 37; G. Fuller 2003, p. 52.

27. M. Huband 1999, pp. 86ff.; R. Aslan 2005, pp. 238ff.; G. Kepel 2002, pp. 23 ff.; A. Rasanaygam 2005, pp. 52, 224–25, 228; R. Dreyfuss 2005, pp. 157ff.; D. Gold 2003, pp. 92–93.

28. J. Stern 2003, pp. 46, 263–66; L. Wright 2002, p. 77; M. Sageman 2004, p. 26; R. Peters 1996, p. 155; F. Gerges 2006, pp. 21ff.; P. Bergen 2006, p. 66.

29. R. Aslan 2005, pp. 241ff.; A. Abu Khalil 2004, p. 32; G. Posner 2005, p. 35; G. Kepel 2002, pp. 51–52.

30. M. Rasheed 2002, pp. 112, 115, 117; M. Fandy 1999, p. 46; D. Commins 2006, pp. 551–52. R. Dreyfuss 2005, pp. 238ff.; D. Gold 2003, p. 75.

31. M. Rasheed 2002, pp. 117, 128–29; 1969, the very year that King Idris of Libya was overthrown in a military coup d'état led by Colonel Muammar al-Qaddafi. The Saudis had briefly embraced Nasser during 1954–1956, until his regional imperial ambitions became more evident after his nationalization of the Suez Canal in 1956. Though mutual commitments to withdraw from Yemen were exchanged in August 1966, the Egyptian and Saudi invasions of Yemen did not officially come to an end until after the Arab-Israeli war of June 1967.

32. M. Rasheed 2002, pp. 130–34; J. Kechichian 2001, p. 99. An earlier coup attempt had been suppressed in 1962 and yet another was reportedly attempted at Tabuk in 1977.

33. M. Fandy 1999, pp. 44–45; M. Rasheed 2002, pp. 109–10, 112, 123, 124. This movement, heavily steeped in merged lofty visions of Arab nationalism and Nasserite socialism, would ultimately collapse only upon its failure to generate grassroots support among other senior princes and a neutralization of underlying issues with the accession of King Faisal in 1964. A key factor in this development was his promulgation in 1962, while still crown prince, of a ten-point program that promised implementation of a constitution, consultative council, local government, and economic development reform. (On this, see D. Commins 2006, p. 106; R. Dreyfuss 2005, pp. 96–97; D. Gold 2003, p. 75.)

34. On these developments, and attendant evolution of the U.S. Military Training Mission (USMTM), see D. Long 1997, pp. 116ff.; T. Lippman 2004, pp. 278–79; S. Coll 2004, p. 26; D. Commins 2006, p. 193; R. Dreyfuss 2005, pp. 131–32. In this process, the Jiddah-based Muslim World League printed millions of Qur'ans for global export and a global mosque construction program was implemented. A 1972 affiliate, the World Assembly of Muslim Youth proselytized amongst the youth. Concurrently, over 1,500 mosques, 210 Islamic centers, 202 Islamic colleges, and 2,000 schools were built in the quest to recruit and educate Muslims in non-Muslim countries. The Muslim World League spearheaded these operations.

35. R. Dreyfuss 2005, pp. 126–27, 131ff., 143; M. Rasheed 2002, pp. 133–34, 221; D. Gold 2003, pp. 99–100.

36. R. Aslan 2005, p. 240. It is not surprising, then, that al-Qaeda doctrinal leader Ayman al-Zawahiri is an Egyptian cleric or that his pupil Osama bin Laden was raised in the heartland of southwest Arabia. (On this, see D. Commins 2006, p. 172; D. Gold 2003, pp. 216–17.)

37. ICG 2004, pp. 1ff.; J. Esposito 2005, pp. 260ff. In many ways, not unlike the Levantine Arab awakening that had set in two centuries before, except that this one at its core was theocratic rather than nationalistic, in nature. On this also, see G. Kepel 2002, p. 32. In recent decades, Egypt's Muslim Brotherhood has sought to somewhat distance itself from the shrill stridency of Sayyid Qutb's teachings.

38. J. Esposito 2005, loc. cit.; G. Kepel 2004, p. 156; S. Coll 2004, p. 85; L. Wright 2006, p. 78; R. Dreyfuss 2005, p. 128; D. Gold 2003, pp. 93–95, 217.

39. R. Aslan 2005, pp. 86–87; M. Huband 1999, p. 2; B. Lawrence 1998, p. 88; R. Baer 2003, p. 127; J. Bradley 2005, p. 69; C. Unger 2004, p. 93; G. Kepel 2002, p. 314; D. Commins 2006, p. 186; A. Rasanayagam 2005, pp. 218–19; F. Gerges 2006, p. 120;

L. Wright 2006, pp. 78–80, 95ff.; D. Gold 2003, notwithstanding that the Muslim Brotherhood formally renounced terror as a political and diplomatic tool, albeit under duress, in 1971.

40. On these developments, see G. Keppel 2004, pp. 85ff., 171ff.; R. Baer 2003, loc. cit.; S. Coll 2004, p. 155; D. Commins 2006, pp. 174–75, 186.

41. G. Keppel 2004, pp. 171–73.

42. G. Kepler 2004, p. 83; M. Sageman 2004, p. 26; O. Roy 1994, pp. 116ff.; S. Coll 2004, pp. 154, 381–83; A. Rasanayagam 2005, p. 228; F. Gerges 2006, p. 22; L Wright 2006, pp. 60–61; R. Dreyfuss 2005, pp. 131ff.

43. A. Abu Khalil 2004, p. 190; D. Gold 2003, pp. 78, 89–92. The University of al-Madinah was, as noted, a particular locus of Muslim Brotherhood activity.

44. G. Keppel 2004, pp. 84–85.

45. B. Lewis 2003, p. 82; C. Unger 2004, p. 95; S. Coll 2004, p. 28; D. Commins 2006, pp. 164ff. This scheme was actually hatched within a Muslim Brotherhood-inspired study group led by al-'Utaybi at the University of al-Madinah in the early 1970s.

46. M. Rasheed 2002, pp. 143–45; T. Lippman 2004, p. 209; D. Commins 2006, p. 168; L. Wright 2006, pp. 88ff, 94.

47. This is a claim made, for instance, by European Middle East political historian Gilles Kepel (2004, pp. 167, 180); see also Jamestown Foundation 2004, p. 284.

48. J. Kechichian 2001, p. 101.

49. M. Rasheed 2002, p. 147; J. Kechichian 2001, p. 99; D. Commins 2006, pp. 169–70; D. Gold 2003, pp. 106–9.

50. M. Rasheed 2002, loc. cit.; see also W. Phares 2005, pp. 53ff.

51. R. Aslan 2005, pp. 132–33; G. Posner 2005, p. 19; G. Kepel 2002, pp. 30, 331ff.; D. Commins 2006, p. 23.

52. B. Lawrence 1998, pp. 58–59.

53. Al-Ghazali cited in R. Peters 1976, p. 181; L. Wright 2006, p. 122.

54. R. Peters 1996, p. 7.

55. G. Kepel 2002, p. 316; D. Commins 2006, pp. 178ff., 197ff.; F. Gerges 2006, p. 127; P. Bergen 2006, pp. 1ff., 134, 149–50; D. Gold 2003, pp. 161ff.

56. ICG 2004, pp. 5, 11; M. Fandy 1999, pp. 51–52. Similar petitions of protest would be filed a decade later by members of the Islamic Awakening movement in January and again in December 2003. See also S. Coll 2004, p. 475; D. Commins 2006, pp. 181ff.

57. M. Fandy 1999, p. 25.

58. A. Abu Khalil 2004, p. 62.

59. M. Fandy 1999, pp. 36–37; T. Lippman 2004, p. 303; A. Rashid 2002, p. 477.

60. N. Obaid 1999, passim; T. Lippman 2004, loc. cit.

61. M. Fandy 1999, p. 56; D. Commins 2006, p. 180.

62. A. Abu Khalil 2004, pp. 124–27; T. Lippman 2004, p. 317; D. Commins 2006, p. 180.

63. D. Long 1997, p. 121; A. Abu Khalil 2004, p. 211; D. Commins 2006, pp. 194ff.

64. R. Aslan 2005, pp. 246ff. The so-called Assassins, or Isma'ili Nizaris, for over two centuries, from 1090 to 1275, operated from their base in Jabal Alamut in Greater Syria, engaging in for-hire targeted assassinations, not unlike the terrorists

of today, ostensibly to advance the cause of a more pure version of Islam. (On them, likewise see H. Kushner 2003, p. 38.)

Chapter 4: Jihad: Do Wahhabis Get a Bad Rap?

1. N. Delong-Bas 2004, p. 193; W. Phares 2005, p. 56.
2. See S. Huntington 1996, pp. 275ff.
3. S. Huntington 1996, pp. 247ff.
4. J. Stern 2003, p. 92.
5. J. Stern 2003, pp. 93ff.
6. G. Fuller 2003, pp. 152–53.
7. Within Islamic thought, fundamentalists have taken the Qur'an and Prophetic Tradition literally; traditionalists accept the status quo so long as it is not openly anti-Islamic; and modernists accept contemporary interpretations of the Qur'an and Prophetic Tradition.
8. H. Kushner 2002, pp. 40–41.
9. N. Delong-Bas 2004, p. 4.
10. N. Delong-Bas 2004, p. 282; depicted here as presented in *Mu'allafat al-Shaykh al-Imam Muhammad bin 'Abd al-Wahhab: al-Fiqh* (Riyadh: 1881), vols. 1–3.
11. N. Delong-Bas 2004, p. 287.
12. N. Delong-Bas 2004, p. 69.
13. Ibid., pp. 194, 203.
14. Ibid., p. 288.
16. Ibid., pp. 288–89.
17. *Muhammad ibn 'Abd al-Wahhab*, 1881, vol. 2, pp. 359–62; R. Peters 1996, p. 29.
18. *Muhammad ibn 'Abd al-Wahhab*, 1881, vol. 2, pp. 364–67.
19. R. Peters 1996, p. 120; N. Delong-Bas 2004, p. 240.
20. *Muhammad ibn 'Abd al-Wahhab*, 1881, vol. 2, pp. 359ff. In each instance, it is worthy of note, he employs the third measure verb *qaatala*, "to fight," rather than the first measure verb *qatala*, "to kill."
21. *Muhammad ibn 'Abd al-Wahhab*, 1881, vol. 2, pp. 360, 372–73, 394–96, 400.
21. Ibid., p. 390.
22. Ibid., pp. 363–64, 380, 387–88.
23. Ibid., p. 398.
24. Ibid., p. 400.
25. Ibid., pp. 398–99.
26. Ibid., p. 402.
27. Ibid., p. 398.
28. *Muhammad ibn 'Abd al-Wahhab*, 1881, vol. 1, p. 23, vol. 3, pp. 9–11.
29. R. Peters 1996, p. 120.
30. N. Delong-Bas 2004, p. 242.
31. Ibid., p. 243.
32. On this, see G. Rentz 1958, p. 41; H. Laoust 1971, vol. 3, passim; C. Helms 1981, p. 82. The *khawarij* global view divided the world into two distinct domains, Dar al-Islam and Dar al-Harb. Therein, there were only two types of human endeavor—permissible (good) and forbidden (evil)—and hence only two possible statuses for mankind: Muslim and *kafir* (pagan). In this, there was no in between.

Viewing themselves as the soldiers of God arrayed in cosmic battle against the forces of evil, they deemed anyone committing any act considered to be forbidden to be a *kafir*—an infidel guilty of treason before Islam and hence to be punished through jihad. As God's righteous instruments of justice, therefore, they were obliged to engage all methods of warfare—including revolution, violence, and guerrilla warfare—which they viewed to be at once legitimate and obligatory. On this, see N. Delong-Bas 2004, p. 249.

33. H. Brydges 1834, vol. 2, p. 9.

34. N. Delong-Bas 2004, p. 249.

35. Ibn Taymiyah quoted in R. Peters 1999, p. 49; J. Kelsay and N. T. Johnson 1990, p. 134.

36. N. Delong-Bas 2004, p. 50.

37. Sayyid Qutb 1968, pp. 111, 116–19, 122, 142.

38. Ibid., p. 113.

39. Sayyid Qutb 1968, pp. 86, 114–16, 122–23, 172; D. Commins 2006, pp. 148–49. The late Saudi Shaykh al-Islam 'Abd al-'Aziz bin Baz in the early 1990s would, in fact, frequently criticize the teachings of Sayyid Qutb as inconsistent with tenets of the Qur'an.

40. Sayyid Qutb 1968, pp. 141 (quoted), 136–40.

41. N. Delong-Bas 2004, pp. 261–62, 267.

42. A. Rashid 2002, p. 318; N. Delong-Bas 2004, p. 266.

43. Interview with bin Laden cited in A. Rashid 2000, p. 132.

44. M. Fandy 1999, pp. 177ff., pp. 181–82 in particular; N. Delong-Bas 2004, p. 269.

45. G. Kepel 2002, p. 317.

46. Osama bin Laden cited in M. Fandy 1999, p. 189; Delong-Bas 2004, pp. 270ff.

47. M. Fandy 1999, p. 191. In so doing, however, he takes Ibn Taymiyah out of context in a manner reminiscent of how eighteenth-century Massachusetts pilgrims, calling for more modest female hairstyles, cited the scriptural verse, "Let those who dwell on the housetop not come down," as teaching, "Top knot, come down!"

48. M. Fandy 1999, p. 177; N. Delong-Bas 2004, p. 274.

49. M. Fandy 1999, pp. 188, 193.

50. N. Delong-Bas 2004, pp. 270, 274; M. Fandy 1999, p. 182; G. Kepel 2004, p. 174; T. Tsu 2005, p. 40.

51. Expressed in a bin Laden fax to Al-Jazirah television Qatar, on September, 21, 2001, and reprinted in the *Boston Globe* on September 24, 2001; see also M. Fandy 1999, p. 192; N. Delong-Bas 2004, pp. 274–75.

52. On this, see P. Bergen 2006, pp. 114, 143, 148–49, 194–208, 255, 287–89; D. Gold 2003, p. 97.

53. D. Commins 2006, pp. 172ff. Such realities, of course, thus make al-Qaeda a creation of the handiwork of Sayyid Qutb, not of Muhammad ibn 'Abd al-Wahhab.

54. D. Commins 2006, p. 185; Q. Wiktorowicz 2001, p. 19.

55. C. Unger 2005, pp. 184–95; N. Delong-Bas 2004, pp. 278–79; D. Commins 2006, pp. 200–201.

56. N. Delong-Bas 2004, pp. 224–25; D. Commins 2006, p. 172.

57. On this, see S. Schwartz 2002, pp. 70–71; N. Delong-Bas 2004, p. 229.

Chapter 5: Eastern Designs and Holy War

1. T. Hammes 2004, pp. 158ff.; F. Abdul Rauf 2004, pp. 240–41; G. Posner 2005, p. 97; S. Schwartz 2002, p. 152; A. Rashid 2002, p. 58; G. Michael 2006, p. 194; R. Dreyfuss 2005, pp. 260ff., 263.

2. A. Rashid 2002, pp. 315ff.; G. Kepel 2002, p. 315; who recognized that the most potent weapon in their armory was the ability to portray the Soviet invasion as a threat to Islam; see also A. Rasanayagam 2005, pp. 219–20; F. Gerges 2006, p. 109; D. Gold 2003, p. 129.

3. T. Hammes 2004, p. 131; C. Unger 2004, pp. 5, 21, 99; G. Kepel 2002, p. 314.

4. C. Unger 2004, pp. 102–3; M. Sageman 2004, p. 35; S. Schwartz 2002, pp. 160ff.; A. Rashid 2002, p. 319; O. Roy 1994, p. 11; S. Coll 2004, p. 204; D. Commins 2006, pp. 186ff.; L. Wright 2006, p. 103; R. Dreyfuss 2005, pp. 278–84. P. Bergen 2006, pp. xxxii, 24, 32–33,45–46, 92, 97; D. Gold 2003, pp. 97, 128. Operating on $600 million in charitable contributions from sundry Islamic countries, bin Laden likewise *personally* funded this operation at a cost of $25,000 a month. He would assume control of it on November 24, 1989, when, following a schism within the ranks of the insurgents, 'Azzam mysteriously fell victim to a car bomb.

5. P. Bergen 2001, p. 50; T. Hammes 2004, pp. 131–32; M. Sageman 2004, p. 34; A. Rasanayagam 2005, p. 221; R. Wright 1985, pp. 248–50.

6. M. Huband 1999, pp. 2–3, 8ff. The Soviet commitment to Afghanistan was substantial. By 1981, its troop presence had reached 105,000 soldiers and its annual war expenditure had risen to $5 billion. See also G. Kepel 2004, p. 84; T. Hammes 2004, loc. cit.; S. Coll 2004, pp. 162–63; A. Rasanayagam 2005, p. 220; L. Wright 2006, pp. 101, 111; P. Bergen 2006, pp. 49ff., 58.

7. O. Roy 1994, pp. 116ff.; S. Coll 2004, pp. 89–90; A. Rasanayagam 2005, pp. 218–19. Prince Turki subsequently left his U.S. ambassadorial posting in late 2006.

8. See R. Aslan 2005, p. 259; ICG 2004, pp. 3–4; J. Kelsay 1993, p. 61; A. Rashid 2002, pp. 318ff.; D. Gold 2003, p. 126ff.

9. C. Unger 2004, pp. 97–98; S. Coll 2004, pp. 46, 51; W. Phares 2005, pp. 111ff.; L. Wright 2006, pp. 99ff.; R. Gates 1996, pp. 132, 144; R. Dreyfuss 2005, pp. 256ff., 264ff.

10. M. Huband 1999, p. 9; R. Baer 2003, p. 100; Jamestown Foundation 2004, pp. 185–86; A. Rasanayagam 2005, p. 105; F. Gerges 2006, p. 172ff.; L. Wright 2006, pp. 102–4; R. Dreyfuss 2005, pp. 266ff., 271.

11. M. Huband 1999, pp. 9–10; S. Coll 2004, pp. 65–66, 81–82; D. Commins 2006, p. 172.

12. S. Huntington 1996, p. 247. Policy analyst Serge Trifkovic (2002, p. 211) places total U.S. financial commitments to Operation Cyclone at in excess of $4 billion; whereas A. Rashid (2002, p. 57) places the mujahidin's collective take from all sources at $10 billion. See S. Coll (2004, p. 134) who describes their motivations for jihad. Likewise see M. Yousef and M. Adkin 1992, pp. 95–96; A. Rasanayagam 2005, pp. 107ff. (p. 107 quoted), 112, 220; R. Dreyfuss 2005, pp. 274, 278; P. Bergen 2006, p. 49; M. Urban 1988, p. 244.

13. C. Unger 2005, p. 104; B. Rubin 1995, pp. 20–23; A. Rashid 2002, pp. 468–69; G. Michael 2006, p. 195; R. Dreyfuss 2005, pp. 245, 277.

14. B. Rubin 1995, loc. cit.; G. Posner 2005, p. 115; A. Rasanayagam 2005, p. 108; A. Rasanayagam 2005, p. 116; G. Michael 2006, p. 195.

15. M. Stremecki 1988, p. 227; C. Unger 2005, p. 104; S. Coll 2004, pp. 149ff.

16. G. Kepel 2004, p. 52; G. Posner 2005, p. 113; D. Commins 2006, p. 172.

17. M. Huband 1999, pp. 10–11; S. Huntington 1996, p. 247.

18. Interview with bin Laden cited in A. Rashid 2000, p. 132; idem. 2002, p. 321; L. Wright 2006, pp. 129ff.

19. M. Huband 1999, loc. cit.; G. Kepel 2004, p. 86; C. Unger 2004, p. 97; A. Rashid 2002, p. 313; S. Coll 2004, p. 89; D. Commins 2006, p. 186; A. Rasanayagam 2005, pp. 123, 125; L Wright 2006, pp. 99–100, 103–4, 130ff., 137; P. Bergen 2006, pp. 76, 87.

20. M. Fandy 1999, p. 179; G. Kepel 2004, p. 53; B. Lewis 2003, pp. 62–63, 161; A. Rashid 2002, pp. 317ff.; W. Phares 2005, pp. 122–24; A. Rasanayagam 2005, pp. 188ff.; F. Gerges 2006, pp. 113–14; P. Bergen 2006, p. 390; G. Fuller 2003, p. 10.

21. Azzam quoted in G. Kepel 2002, p. 147; M. Sageman 2004, p. 3; S. Schwartz 2002, p. 165; R. Dreyfuss 2005, pp. 288ff.

22. S. Schwartz 2002, p. 156; D. Commins 2006, pp. 175–76; F. Gerges 2006, pp. 114, 226; L. Wright 2006, pp. 105–6, 163.

23. M. Fandy 1999, p. 185; T. Lippman 2004, pp. 315–16; S. Schwartz 2002, p. 155.

24. F. Abdul Rauf 2004, p. 242; G. Kepel 2002, p. 10; S. Coll 2004, pp. 201ff.; D. Commins 2006, pp. 175–76; R. Peters 1976, pp. 174–75.

25. G. Kepel 2002, p. 219; R. Dreyfuss 2005, pp. 302, 312; P. Bergen 2006, pp. 108ff.

26. G. Kepel 2002, p. 317; A. Rasanayagam 2005, pp. 29ff., 230; P. Bergen 2006, pp. 98, 112–113.

27. A. Cordesman and N. Obaid 2005, p. 11; N. Delong-Bas 2004, pp. 267–68. T. Hammes 2004, p. 133; J. Bradley 2005, pp. 69ff.; G. Posner 2005, pp. 136ff.; J. Corbin 2002, p. 27; T. Lippman 2004, p. 316; C. Unger 2005, pp. 143–44; L. Wright 2006, pp. 194–96. Bin Laden's proposal to the Saudi Defense Minister Prince Sultan was accompanied by a ten-page detailed plan whereby the bin Laden family construction company would build the requisite fortifications needed for the country's defense. In April 1994, the Kingdom froze bin Laden's in-country assets and formally revoked his citizenship at the order of King Fahd, seizing his passport reportedly at the request of then Pakistani prime minister Benazir Bhutto who had accused him of meddling in Pakistani internal affairs. On this, see P. Bergen 2006, pp. 98ff., 151–53.

28. G. Kepel 2004, pp. 87–88; C. Unger 2005, pp. 149ff.; S. Schwartz 2002, p. 182; A. Rashid 2002, pp. 322–23. In a May 2003 document, al-Qaeda explains: "The ruler of a country is the one who has the authority in it. . . . The real ruler is the Crusader United States. The subservience of (Muslim) rulers is no different from the subservience of the amirs or governors of provinces to kings or presidents. The rule of an agent is the rule of the one who made him his agent." See R. Pape 2005, p. 118; W. Phares 2005, p. 203.

29. G. Kepel 2004, pp. 72, 88; idem. 2002, pp. 12, 317; T. Hammes 2004, p. 133; T. Lippman 2004, pp. 316ff.; M. Sageman 2004, p. 44; A. Rashid 2002, pp. 323ff.; D. Commins 2006, p. 187; A. Rasanayagam 2005, pp. 222–23; L. Wright 2006, pp. 130,

164ff.; P. Bergen 2006, pp. 149ff. Indeed, as noted, al-Qaeda literally means "the base."

30. G. Kepel 2004, p. 91; idem. 2002, p. 12; R. Baer 2003, pp. 20, 105; G. Posner 2005, p. 76; S. Coll 2004, p. 276; A. Rasanayagam 2005, p. 229; P. Bergen 2006, pp. 155–57; M. Huband 2004, p. 109.

31. R. Miniter 2004, p. 67; A. Rashid 2002, loc. cit.; G. Kepel 2002, pp. 13, 227; D. Commins 2006, p. 188; W. Phares 2005, p. 158.

32. On these developments, see T. Hammes 2004, pp. 138–39, 162ff.; A. Rasanayagam 2005, pp. 203–4; L. Wright 2006, p. 122. Beside Pakistan, Saudi Arabia and the United Arab Emirates would diplomatically recognize the Taliban regime.

33. On these developments, see T. Hammes 2004, p. 162; A. Rashid 2002, pp. 425ff., 444; P. Bergen 2006, pp. 161ff.

34. See statement of U.S. assistant secretary of state Robin Raphael at the United Nations on November 18, 1996, cited in P. Bergen 2006, pp. 176–77, 330–36; A. Rashid 2000, p. 178; M. Sageman 2004, pp. 45ff., 52; G. Michael 2006, p. 201. Though the United States did succeed in eliminating the Taliban regime in 2001, al-Qaeda's senior leadership as well as Mullah 'Umar managed to escape through allied Afghani lines during Operation Anaconda.

35. A prominent Middle East political observer speaking on a condition of anonymity.

36. G. Kepel 2004, pp. 71–72; A. Rasanayagam 2005, p. 237; R. Dreyfuss 2005, p. 302.

Chapter 6: How Western Jihad Created Al-Qaeda

1. J. Stern 2003, p. 29; A. Rasanayagam 2005, pp. 228ff.

2. M. Huband 1999, pp. 13–14; G. Posner 2005, p. 113; A. Rashid 2002, p. 118; P. Bergen 2006, pp. 144ff.

3. M. Sageman 2004, p. 38; M. Huband 1999, loc. cit.; G. Kepel 2002, pp. 217, 300.

4. A statement made on the Sunday talk show, *Meet the Press*, in late 1996.

5. Osama bin Laden, "Declaration of Holy War Against the American Occupiers of the Two Holy Mosques," August 23, 1996; see also N. Delong-Bas 2004, pp. 271–72; T. Hammes 2004, pp. 144ff. (to which America responded by freezing up to $300 million of bin Laden's international financial assets).

6. G. Kepel 2002, p. 13; P. Bergen 2006, pp. 161, 166.

7. G. Kepel 2004, p. 92; The strategy's implementation would begin six months later with twin attacks on the U.S. embassies in Kenya and Tanzania on August 7, 1998—the exact anniversary of the date when, eight years earlier, Saudi King Fahd invited American troops into the Kingdom to defend it against a possible invasion from Iraq. (Likewise see G. Kepel 2002, pp. 317–19; D. Commins 2006, pp. 188–89; R. Peters 1976, p. 175.)

8. Sources cited in preceding footnote; M. Sageman 2004, pp. 19–20; D. Commins 2006, p. 196; Q. Wiktorowicz 2006, pp. 29–30; P. Bergen 2006, p. 183.

9. Ibidem.

10. Ibidem.

11. Ibidem.

12. Bin Laden 1996 published interview with journalist Robert Fisk cited in N. Delong-Bas 2004, p. 277; see also B. Lewis 2003, loc. cit.; P. Bergen 2006, pp. 115, 374–75. Those who are wont to equate Saudi Arabia and al-Qaeda, therefore, should carefully reflect upon a Web site message (available online at www.gal3ah.net) attributed to bin Laden posted on December 16, 2004, which begins—

The government of Riyadh has entered into an international alliance with the infidel crusaders led by Bush against Islam and its peoples

—as well as the fact that al-Qaeda openly takes credit for bombing three residential compounds in Riyadh on May 12, 2003, killing thirty-five and wounding over two hundred, including Saudi Muslims.

13. Bin Laden remarks aired in Al-Jazirah TV Qatar, on October 7, 2001, and reprinted in the *Boston Globe* on October 8, 2001; see also B. Lewis 2003, pp. 147, 162–63.

14. Ibid.

15. On this, see B. Lewis 2003, pp. xxix, 160ff.; A. Rasanayagam 2005, p. 229; L. Wright 2006, p. 158; P. Bergen 2006, p. 183.

16. G. Kepel 2004, pp. 165ff. Indeed, this ruling attributed to Prophet Muhammad would become al-Qaeda's slogan.

17. Cited in B. Lewis 2003, pp. 157–58; G. Michael 2006, p. 260.

18. Al-Zawahiri 2001, passim.

19. On the evolution and rationalization of this exegetical extrapolation, see G. Kepel 2004, pp. 73–74.

20. G. Kepel 2004, pp. 1–2; al-Zawahiri cited in M. Sageman 2004, pp. 20, 22.

21. P. Bergen 2006, pp. 60–61, 177–78.

22. On this see H. Al-Banna n.d., pp. 75–108; R. Mitchell 1969, pp. 8ff. This Isma'iliyah complex would grow to consist of four mosques and a separate headquarters by the onset of 1932.

23. R. Mitchell 1969, pp. 28, 182. The Brotherhood was reportedly also concurrently in contact with, and courted by, the Nazis.

24. R. Mitchell 1969, pp. 9, 28–32, 39–40 (who cites Hassan al-Banna's autobiography as his source); R. Dreyfuss 2005, pp. 47ff., 82ff. MI6 was created when the British Secret Service Bureau was divided into MI5 (domestic) and MI6 (foreign) intelligence branches in 1909.

25. R. Mitchell 1969, pp. 12ff.; Z. Kaplinsky 1954, p. 378; R. Dreyfus 2006, pp. 57–58, 63–65, 126.

26. R. Mitchell 1969, pp. 5, 13–16, 32; E. Kedourie 1966, pp. 54–58; R. Dreyfuss 2005, pp. 48ff., 55ff., 106–7.

27. R. Dreyfuss 2005, pp. 58–59, 64–65.

28. M. Copeland 1969, pp. 48, 58, 184, 185–86; R. Dreyfuss 2005, pp. 86–87, 91–93, 102, 163, 204; R. Baer 2003, pp. 95–99.

29. B. Lewis 1953, pp. 311–24, passim; B. Dreyfuss 2005, pp. 83, 193; M. Boulby 1999, p. 43.

30. K. Cragg, 1954, pp. 127–38 passim.

31. Letter by W. Eddy, 1951, in U.S. National Security Archives, passim, as reported by R. Dreyfuss 2005, pp. 88–89.

32. R. Dreyfuss 2005, pp. 109–10, 114ff.

33. Ibid. pp. 155ff., 162ff., 190ff., 195ff., 211ff.

34. M. Yousef and Y. Adkin 1992, p. 16; R. Dreyfuss 2005, p. 218, 245.

35. A. Rashid 2000, p. 179; R. Dreyfuss 2005, p. 328.

36. R. Dreyfuss 2005, pp. 305ff. Indeed, Saddam was reportedly irrevocably opposed to al-Qaeda and the feelings were mutual, as bin Laden is said to have despised Saddam Hussein, deeming him to be an infidel. On this, see P. Bergen 2006, pp. 111–12, 170, 179, 350, 361. (And it comes with some irony that Hussein was the first of the two to be captured by U.S. military forces.)

37. Nasser quoted in R. Dreyfuss 2005, p. 120.

Chapter 7: Is Western Democracy the Answer?

1. National Intelligence Council, "National Security Estimate," January 2007, p. 1.

2. K. Abu al-Fadl 2004, p. 4; G. Fuller 2003, p. 121.

3. B. Lewis cited by C. Stevenson 2002, passim; Binder cited by G. Kramer 1997, p. 71; both cited by K. Abu al-Fadl 2004, p. 52; G. Fuller 2003, p. 25. The issue at stake is that while the corpus of Prophetic Tradition does serve as a moral exemplar, it does not directly translate into modern political institutions.

4. B. Lewis 2002, p. 159; A. Shadid 2002, p. 64.

5. A. al-Na'im 1996, passim; J. Esposito 2005, pp. 67ff.; R. Aslan 2005, p. 266; F. Gerges 2006, pp. 16ff.

6. B. Lewis 2002, pp. 100–101.

7. J. Kelsay 1933, p. 108.

8. Tribal law (a'raf), which is an early form of common law, of course, predated the rise of Islam.

9. Ibn Qutaybah 1963, vol. 1, p. 2.

10. F. Abdul Rauf 2004, pp. 88–90.

11. K. Abu al-Fadl 2004, p. 11; S. Bar 2006, p. 87.

12. M. 'Imarah 1979, pp. 431–32; though Mu'tazalite scholar Abu Bakr al-'Assam (d. 826) contended that this power reposes exclusively with the public at large.

13. R. Firestone 1999, pp. 117–124; K. Abu al-Fadl 2004, p. 66. In so doing, therefore, this so-called Constitution of al-Madinah marked a formal transition between the kinship system of rule that had long characterized pre-Islamic society and the formal system of governance prescribed by the new Muslim ummah.

14. K. Abu al-Fadl 2004, p. 65.

15. B. Lewis 2003, pp. 6–7.

16. B. Lewis 1988, passim; A. Rasanayagm 2005, p. 205.

17. F. Abdul Raof 2004, pp. 106–7; G. Fuller 2003, p. 25.

18. B. Lewis 2003, p. 44; F. Abdul Raof 2004, p. 107.

19. F. Abdul Raof 2004, pp. 148ff., 178; not to mention the striking parallels between the time-honored Supreme Court precept of *stare decisis* and closing of the Islamic *bab al-ijtihad*.

20. O. Roy 1994, pp. 44ff. In addition, Islamic law recognizes the principle of *al-siyasah al-shari'iyah* whereby rulers may issue decrees and regulations so long as they do not conflict with the *shari'ah*. On this, see D. Commins 2006, p. 117.

21. M. Rasheed 2002, pp. 67–69; D. Commins 2006, p. 90; G. Fuller 2003, p. 61.

22. Qur'an 3:159, 42–38; A. al-Na'im 1996, pp. 78–79; J. Esposito 2005, pp. 264ff.; M. Fandy 1999, pp. 39, 243.

23. M. Habeck 2006, p. 150.

24. B. Lewis 2003, pp. 111, 112, 118.

25. G. Fuller 2003, pp. 133ff.

26. Based on a transcript of meeting produced by author who personally attended the session.

27. T. Friedman, February 1, 2006, editorial page.

28. A. Cordesman 2006, p. 104.

29. Here, the "Alaskan General Stock Ownership Corporation," created to equitably distribute that state's oil wealth to its citizens, may serve as an appropriate model.

Chapter 8: Is Eastern Capitalism the Answer?

1. F. Abdul Rauf 2004, pp. 151–52.

2. S. Glain 2004, p. 15.

3. G. Kepel 2002, pp. 65–67.

4. Calculations performed on World Bank and United Nation economic databases.

5. S. Schwartz 2002, p. 155.

6. S. Glain 2004, pp. 19–20; G. Fuller 2003, pp. 27–28, 34, 78, 130.

7. B. Lewis 2003, pp 113–14, 118.

8. On these developments, see G. Kepel 2002, pp. 70ff.; indeed, more than 1,500 mosques financed with Saudi resources, as well as 210 Islamic centers, and more than 2,000 schools were built globally in this period.

9. G. Kepel 2002, p. 71.

10. Only now is the Kingdom belatedly effectively addressing that disequilibrium through its new privatization initiatives.

11. Though due to recent dramatic increases in oil revenues, Saudi year-end per capita GDP rose to $13,325 and was projected to reach $15,620 in 2006. On the serious socioeconomic consequences of this precipitous relative GDP decline, see S. Trifkovic 2002, pp. 246ff.; G. Kepel 2004, pp. 168ff.

12. Concurrently, its adult male unemployment rate is conservatively estimated at 12–15 percent and only about 5 percent of women participate in the labor force.

13. On these trends, see G. Heck 2005, pp. 23ff.

14. M al-Rasheed 2002, pp. 153–54, 169. Their demand for stricter application of *shari'ah* law was, in fact, formally petitioned to King Fahd by fifty-two Islamic activists in May 1991.

15. M al-Rasheed 2002, p. 155.
16. SAMBA, December 2006, passim.
17. Indeed, for the first half decade of the new millennium, Saudi GDP growth has recorded a laudatory average annual growth approaching 4 percent. Concurrently, inflation has held at an extremely low rate tracking in the 0.5 percent annual range.
18. On these significant reforms, see G. Heck 2005, chapter 5, passim.
19. G. Heck 2005, pp. 120–25.
20. S. Glain 2004, pp. 61, 305.
21. G. Fuller 2003, pp. 203–4.
22. Ibid., pp. 25, 141.
23. Ibid., p. 141.

Chapter 9: Epilogue: Reaping the Whirlwind

1. D. Long 1999, p. 121.
2. See B. Lewis 2003, pp. xx–xxi; A. Abu Khalil 2004, p. 42; K. Salibi 1980, p. 1.
3. L. DeLong-Bas 2004, pp. 7–8.
4. D. Long 1997, p. 110.
5. B. Lewis 2003, p. xxii.
6. D. Long 1997, p. 108.
7. B. Lewis 2003, pp. xxx, 37, 47–49. This is not surprising since, unlike jihad for Muslims, the Crusades were a late development and of relatively short duration.
8. B. Lewis 2003, pp. xxx, xxxi.
9. B. Lewis 2003, pp. 4–5, 25.
10. B. Lewis 2003, p. 137; S. Coll 2004, p. 138.
11. M. Juergensmeyer 2001, pp. 216–17; G. Fuller 2003, p. 186.
12. B. Lewis 2003, pp. 27–28; G. Fuller 2003, p. 197.
13. M. Juergensmeyer 2001, pp. 216–41.
14. B. Lewis 2002, p. 151; L. Wright 2006, pp. 38–39.
15. B. Lewis 2002, p. 152.
16. See B. Lewis 2003, p. 4; S. Huntington 1996, passim, and p. 218 in particular.
17. S. Huntington 1996, passim; G. Fuller 2003, p. 85.
18. R. Aslan 2005, p. 254; M. Huband 1999, pp. 89ff.
19. National Intelligence Council, "National Security Estimate," January 2007, p. 1.
20. L. Griffith 2002, pp. 213–14; P. Pillar 2001, p. 218. Or to invoke the emotive slogan of those eighteenth-century U.S. Founding Fathers who also were denounced as terrorists: "Live free or die!"
21. B. Lewis 2003, p. 108; R. Baer 2003, pp. 207–8; G. Kepel 2002, pp. 64ff.; R. Dreyfuss 2005, p. 205; G. Fuller 2003, p. 61. In the more modern context, Hamas may be perceived as an organization that employs political terror in support of a nationalistic cause.
22. N. Delong-Bas 2004, p. 290; R. Wright 1985, p. 288. Here, the distinction must be made between militant Islam, which is usually malignant, and activist Islam, which is generally benign and most often positive.

23. Perhaps modeled after the Georgetown University "Center for Muslim Christian Understanding" or the University of Birmingham's "Center for the Study of Islam and Christian-Muslim Relations."

24. J. Voll 1983, p. 33.

25. R. Bulliet 2004, p. 136; G. Fuller 2003, pp. 13, 16. This is a Middle East phenomenon famously described by Egyptian President Nasser in the 1950s as a "role in search of an actor."

26. See J. Esposito 2005, pp. 116–17.

27. A. al-Na'im 1996, passim; J. Esposito 2005, pp. 67ff.; R. Aslan 2005, p. 266; F. Gerges 2006, pp. 16ff.

28. Reza Aslan on *Meet the Press*, March 25, 2005.

29. To be credible, it likewise must be consistent. It cannot afford double standards. It cannot look the other way when terrorists with stashed munitions take refuge in mosques in direct contravention of the Qur'anic Surat al-Baqarah 1:191 admonition "fight them not at the Sacred Mosque unless they first fight you there," yet then castigate attacking peacemakers who seek to flush them out. It cannot randomly condemn other militaries for engaging in military action during the sacred month of Ramadan in the manner widespread when American marines attacked the insurgent stronghold of Fallujah in Iraq on *laylat al-qadr* (27 Ramadan = night of power = the night that the Qur'an was revealed to Prophet Muhammad by the Archangel Gabriel) on November 10, 2004—all the while cognizant that some of the most successful Muslim attacks in history have occurred in the month of Ramadan.

Indeed, this contention is itself predicated upon a misconception as the sacred months wherein cessation of war, as prescribed in the so-called sword verse Surat al-Tawbah 9: 5, do not refer to Ramadan at all, but instead to the ancient pilgrimage cum trading months of the last twenty days of Dhu al-Hijjah, the entire months of Muharram and Safar, and the first ten days of Rabi' al-Akhir. In short, it cannot be both ways. Militant Islamists cannot, on the one hand, extol militant jihadis yet, on the other, condemn countervailing "crusades" while expecting to retain a modicum of credibility within the civilized opinion of the outside world. On this see R. Firestone 1999, pp. 61–62, 74, 84–85; P. Bergen 2006, p. 57.

30. G. Fuller 2003, p. 161.

31. R. Miniter 2004, p. 60; C. Unger 2004, pp. 236–45, 250; G. Kepel 2002, p. 2.

32. Osama bin Laden media interview with ABC News correspondent John Miller, May 28, 1998, replicated in B. Lewis 2003, pp. 162–64. On this perceived American weakness, see also W. Phares 2005, pp. 217–18; T. Hammes 2004, pp. 151–52; F. Gerges 2006, pp. 204–5; L. Wright 2006, pp. 188–89; P. Bergen 2006, pp. 137–38. Bin Laden reportedly originally reached this assessment of a perceived weakness in America's character and will from the withdrawal of American marines from Beirut in mid-1983 and again in October 1993, when two American helicopters shot down in Mogadishu prompted President Clinton to withdraw U.S. troops from a humanitarian peace-keeping mission in Somalia.

33. MEMRI, no. 476 (Washington: March 5, 2003); Decision Support Systems 2001, passim; G. Michael 2006, p. 300; P. Bergen 2006, pp. 286–87, 311, 316.

34. See B. Lewis 1992, pp. 99ff. and sources cited in preceding footnote.

35. G. Fuller 2003, p. 87.

36. S. Huntington 1996, p. 311.

37. G. Kepel 2004, pp. 285–86; G. Fuller 2003, p. 15 Indeed, in the second half of the twentieth century, Arab socialism failed spectacularly in Algeria, Yemen, Egypt, Syria, Iraq, and elsewhere throughout the Middle East.

38. S. Schwartz 2002, p. 177; A. Shadid 2002, p, 291; G. Michael 2006, p. 112; P. Bergen 2006, p. 389.

39. B. Lindsey 2002, pp. 271–72; G. Michael 2006, pp. 112ff.

40. On this, see G. Kepel 2004, pp, 150–51; ibid. 2002, p. 7; W. Phares 2005, pp. 80–82.

41. G. Fuller 2003, p. 87.

42. M. Fandy 1999, p. 240; G. Kepel 2004, pp. 286–87; D. Commins 2006, pp 204, 209.

43. B. Lindsey 2002, p. 273; W. Mead 2004, p. 191.

Appendix A

1. On this, see al-Tabari 1879–1901, series II, vol. 1, pp. 85–115. This argument is made by Majid Khadduri 1955, passim; W. Phares 2005, pp. 26–27; and S. Bar 2006, p. 1.

2. See M. Khadduri 1955, pp. 4, 8, 14, 206–9.

3. See Qur'an 38:25.

4. See Thomas Arnold 1924, "Chapter 1," pp. 349–57.

5. H. Kelsen 1946; p. 8. As in the Qur'anic verse Surat al-Baqarah 276: "God hath allowed selling and forbidden usury."

6. See J. Schacht 1950, passim. In Arabia, the Hanbali School, as represented by renowned thirteenth-fourteenth–century Damascus lawgiver Ibn Taymiyah (d. 1327), was later adopted by the Wahhabi movement.

7. cf. M. Khadduri 1966, passim; H. Kelsen 1946, pp. 343, 363; H. Krabbe 1922, p. 236.

8. Al-Tabari 1937, pp. 60–64; M. Khadduri 1955, pp. 44–46.

9. M. Khadduri 1955, p. 48.

10. Ibid., pp. 55–57.

11. Ibid., pp. 69–70.

12. See J. Von Elbe 1939, pp. 665–88; C. Phillipson 1911, vol. 2, p. 180; A. D'Entreves 1948, pp. 59–61; J. Epstein 1935, passim; W. Ballus 1937, pp. 32–60.

13. M. Khadduri 1955, pp. 60–61, 94.

14. Other species of nonmilitant jihad specified by the sources included the struggle against the devil (*jihad al-shaytan*), a struggle against oneself (*jihad al-nafs*), and the campaign to spread Islamic values (*jihad al-tarbiyah = jihad al-da'wah = jihad al-lisan wa al-qalam*). It is in this context that the fifteenth-century Arab historian Ibn Khaldun (1965, vol. 2, p. 823) distinguishes between wars of jihad and justice (*hurub al-jihad wa al-'adl*) and wars of sedition and anarchy (*hurub al-baghi wa al-fitnah*). (See R. Peters 1996, pp. 116ff., 165).

15. Al-Mawardi 1853, p. 89; al-Bukhari 1864, vol. 2, p. 222; al-Shaybani 1917, vol. 1, pp. 6, 7, 9, 31; R. Peters 1996, p. 86.

16. Al-Mawardi 1853, pp. 58, 79.

17. Al-Tabari 1879–1901, ser. I, vol. 5, pp. 2273–76; Ibn 'Abd al-Hakam 1922, pp. 63–65; Ibn al-Qalanisi 1932, pp. 48, 68, 90, 269–72; W. Stevenson 1907, pp. 220–24, 269–84.

18. M. al-Shaybani 1917, vol. 1, p. 87; S. Bar 2006, pp. 30, 37. Typically, such circumstances arose if the Islamic force was outnumbered 2:1, although the Qur'an speaks of a requisite 10:1 disparity.

19. M. Shafi'i 1903–1908, vol. 4, pp. 103–4; M. Khadduri 1955, pp. 144–45; S. Bar 2006, p. 18.

20. M. Khadduri 1955, pp. 152–53.

21. On this, see al-Tabari 1937, pp. 66–67.

22. M. al-Zubaydi 1893, vol. 3, p. 229; E. Calverly 1925, p. 148.

23. Al-Mawardi 1853, p. 272; M. Khadduri 1955, pp. 158–59.

24. On this, see M. Khadduri 1955, pp. 162ff.

25. Ibidem; N. Aghnides 1916, p. 355.

26. M. Khadduri 1955, pp. 167–69.

27. Ibidem.

28. S. Bar 2006, pp. 21–22.

29. Al-Tabari 1937, p. 15; M. Khadduri 1955, pp. 202–3, 210ff.; R. Peters 1996, p. 157.

30. M. Khadduri 1955, pp. 251ff.; S. Bar 2006, pp. 18ff.

31. Al-Shafi'i 1903–1908, vol. 4, p. 110; al-Tabari 1937, pp. 19–20; ibid. 1879–1901, ser. 3, vol. 2, p. 696; Abu Yusuf 1933, pp. 19ff.; al-Shaybani 1917, vol. 3, pp. 119, 307–38; M. Khadduri 1955, pp. 251ff., 273.

32. See M. Khadduri 1955, pp. 239ff.

33. Al-Ya'qubi 1883, vol. 2, pp. 83–84.

34. See Abu Yusuf 1933, pp. 188–89; al-Shaybani 1917, vol. 4, pp. 66–67.

35. On these missions, see M. Khadduri 1939, pp. 15–16; H. al-Misri 1982, pp. 334–35.

36. On these various diplomatic embassies, see Einhardus 1840, years 787, 801, vol. 43, pp. 114, 123–24, 806, 831; al-Mas'udi 1861–1877, vol. 8, pp. 157–58; al-Rashid b. Zubayr 1959, pp. 48–49, 54, 57; M. Khadduri 1939, pp. 15–16; F. Buckler 1931, pp. 21ff., 40; B. Lewis 1982, pp. 92–93, 209; G. Levi della Vida 1954, pp. 21–38; W. Heyd 1885, vol. 1, pp. 90–91; M. Hamidullah 1953, pp. 272–300; M. Khadduri 1955, pp. 245–48.

37. M. Khadduri 1955, p. 248.

38. Again, on these various diplomatic embassies see Einhardus 1840, years 787, 801, vol. 43, pp. 114, 123–24, 806, 831.

39. Einhardus 1895, p. 831; F. Buckler 1931, p. 40.

40. See al-Mas'udi 1861–1877, vol. 8, pp. 157–58; al-Rashid b. Zubayr 1959, pp. 48–49, 54, 57; M. Khadduri 1939, pp. 15–16; F. Buckler 1931, pp. 21ff., 40; B. Lewis 1981, pp. 92–93, 209; W. Heyd 1885, vol. 1, pp. 90–91; S. Runciman 1935, p. 610; E. Johnson 1927, p. 245.

41. cf. Einhardus, *M.G.H.* 1923, p. 48, note 2.

42. Monk of St. Gaul, *M.G.H.* 1884, vol. 2, pp. 14, 27.

43. W. Heyd 1885, vol. 1, pp. 89–91; F. Buckler 1931, pp. 3ff.; E. Lévi Provençal 1937, pp. 1–24. Carolingian royal court documents similarly provide indications of

this sovereign interest in promoting commerce. Various *capitularia* (edicts) issued by Charlemagne, in particular, show his concern for preserving the operational integrity of the market-based economy that he was then seeking to establish. As such, the decrees contain explicit regulations for regulating and controlling market prices.

44. See S. Bolin 1953, pp. 24ff.; E. A. Ashtor 1970, pp. 175ff.

45. Abu Yusuf 1933, pp. 188, 190, 132–33; al-Ghazali 1899, vol. 2, p. 201.

Appendix B

1. On this see Aristotle 1946, bk. 1, ch. 8; M. Juergensmeyer 2001, pp. 25–26; L. Griffith 2002, pp. 27–29; M. Khadduri 1966, pp. 15ff.

2. M. Haleem 1999, p. 62; A. al-Na'im 1996, p. 144–47. Gods of terror, of course, were not the exclusive domain of the heavenly religions. Phobos was a Greek god of terror; a neo-Punic inscription refers to a contemporary god as: *b'il chrdt* = lord of terror. See L. Griffith 2002, p. 32; S. Bar 2006, p. 25.

3. R. Firestone 1999, p. 15; S. Bar 2006, pp. 25–26. Of the thirty-six references to jihad within the Qur'an, no more than fourteen have a direct military connotation.

4. Though frequently an intermediate status, abode of truce, *Dar al-Sulh*, was likewise recognized (as opposed to *salam*, a lasting peace). Concurrently, those entering the Dar al-Islam were often treated differently depending upon their mode of entry, with those entering peacefully (in a state of reconciliation = *sulhan*) afforded greater leniency than those annexed by conquest (*'anwatan*)—which was the Islamic juridical equivalent of the Roman *vi et armis*. On this see B. Lewis 2003, p. 37.

5. E. Lane 1865, book 1, part 2, p. 473; R. Firestone 1999, pp. 16–17; S. Bar 2006, pp. 25–29. *Jihad* is a third form verbal noun from *jaahada,* deriving from the triliteral root "*j*" "*h*" "*d*."

6. M 'Ali 1973, pp. 12–13; R. Firestone 1999, pp. 17–18.

7. cf. T. P. Schwartz-Barcott 2004, p. 305, note 83.

8. In this, one finds striking parallels to Pope Innocent III's (1198–1217) proclamation of Crusade asserting that a failure to participate in holy war was tantamount to "infidelity to Christ." On this see J. Kelsay and N. T. Johnson 1990, p. 37.

9. See al-Tirmidhi 1873, vol. 1, p. 145; Zayd b. 'Ali 1919, nos. 539, 544.

10. See al-Muttaqi al-Hindi 1894, vol. 2, pp. 193ff.

11. Ahmad Ibn Hanbal 18073; see also Ibn Majah 3002, and al-Nisa'i 4138.

12. Al-Kaya al-Harasiy 1983, 1:89; R. Peters 1996, p. 1; B. Lewis 2003, p. 30.

13. The al-Madinah edition does, though, translate *qital* as *jihad* in Surat al-Baqarah 2:216, "*kutiba alaykum al-qital wa huwa kurhun lakum*" (jihad is ordained for you though you dislike it); whereas 'Ali translates the term as "fighting" and Pickthall translates it as "warfare." An exception where they do appear in conjunction is Surat al-Nisa' 4:76: *Allidhina amanu yuqatilunafi sabil Allah.* (Those who believe fight to kill in the way of Allah.)

14. Islamic historian John Kelsay (1993:106–7) seeks to make a distinction between two separate forms of Islamic warfare: regular jihad and irregular jihad.

The rules of warfare delineated in this chapter define "regular jihad" as designed to capture and hold territory carried on between conflicting groups. "Irregular jihad," in turn, includes insurgencies and internal rebellions—precepts in direct contravention of classic Islamic concepts of combat governed by varying precepts; the so-called rules for insurgencies (*ahkam al-bughat*) governing (1) those who rebel (*khuruj*) (2) in the pursuit of good and the denial of evil while (3) possessing the power (*shawkah*) to prevail.

Pursuant to them, to be sanctioned, an insurgency must have political legitimacy and authority (*competence de guerre*). In its legitimate pursuit, would-be rebels must be pursuing the duties of (1) imposing order; (2) putting down wrongdoing; and (3) obeying God. The approach thus emphasizes the precept of *jus in bello* to the subordination of that of *jus ad bellam*. (On this see J. Kelsay 1993, pp. 82ff.; J. Kelsay and N. T. Johnson 1990, pp. 37, 150, 154–55, 158–60, 163–64; S. Bar 2006, p. 26.)

15. Y. Aboul-Enein and S. Zuhur 2004, p. 15. In his explanation of this verse, 'Abd Allah Yusuf 'Ali, in his translation of the Qur'an (1993, p. 257, note 737), interprets this verse as "one of the strongest possible condemnations of individual assassination and revenge."

16. On this, see A. L. Hussein 1979, pp. 45–50; S. Bar 2006, pp. 59ff., wherein the issue of whether one deliberately placing himself in harm's way in the course of conduct of war is martyrdom or suicide is addressed.

17. Al-Bukhari 1:223, 2:53, 1205.

18. J. Esposito 2005, p. 14; T. P. Schwartz-Barcott 2005, p. 93, note 15; Pickthall also observes the terms *martyr* and witness are synonymous in the Qur'an; as does Wehr, who deems *shahiid* to be a variant of *shaahid* (witness). This, then, is not unlike the English word *martyr*, which derives from the Greek *martys*—also meaning *witness*. Yet whereas in the Judeo-Christian context, it is used to denote someone willing to suffer death rather than renounce faith, in its Islamic counterpart, it is normally used to describe someone who dies pursuing jihad.

19. Al-Khatib al-Tabrizi, as related by W. Reich 1990, pp. 117–18.

20. W. Reich 1990, p. 197. In their approaches to martyrdom and suicide, Christian and Jewish doctrines, it should be noted, do not substantially differ from that of Islam in their view of the martyr (*shahiid*) as a military phenomenon and suicide as a deviant one.

21. See *Sahih al-Bukhari* in: *Recueil des Traditions Mahométanes*, vol. 1, p. 363; vol. 2, pp. 223–24, 273; vol. 4, pp. 71, 124, 243, 253–54, 320, 364; F. Rosenthal 1946, passim.

22. J. Kelsay and J. T. Johnson 1990, p. 64; G. Fuller 2003, pp. 89–90.

Appendix C: Islam's Code of Conduct for Pursuing "Just Peace"

1. On this, see M. Khadduri 1966, pp. 15ff.; R. Aslan 2005, pp. 99ff.

2. See G. Fuller 2003, pp. 246–47. While each religion views its creed as universal and God's final revelation, however, Christianity and Islam share a perhaps unique faith in a conviction that theirs is the exclusive reflection of God's full final message.

3. Al-Baladhuri 1978, pp. 241–42; idem. 1866, p. 336. Al-Bayhaqi (1961, p. 233–34) also relates a version of this story.

4. On this see G. Fuller 2003, pp. 146–47.

5. G. Fuller 2003, loc. cit.

6. K. Armstrong 1993, pp. 82, 108–11. This proclamation differed somewhat in its wording from what today is known as the Nicene Creed, which was actually composed at the Council of Constantinople in 381 A.D.

7. G. Fuller 2003, p. 147.

8. Cf. R. Spencer 2005, passim; B. Ye'or 2002, passim.

9. J. Esposito 2005, p. 15.

10. S. Runciman 1992, p. 1.

11. S. Runciman 1992, loc. cit.; K. Armstrong 2001, pp. 532–33. In commemoration, a small mosque, the Mosque of Omar, preserved intact today stands on the exact spot in tribute to the event.

12. The sixth Fatimid Caliph al-Hakim was an exception to this rule of tolerance.

13. On this, see F. Abdul Rauf 2004, pp. 2–3.

14. J. Esposito 2005, p. 59.

15. J. Esposito 2005, loc. cit.

16. Cf. I. Manji 2004, passim; F. Abdul Rauf 2004, passim.

Appendix D: The Use of Qur'anic Verses as Militant Propaganda

1. See B. Lewis 1981, pp. 12ff.

2. On this, see M. al-Husayni 1975, pp. 9–16, passim.

3. For examples of such coins, see W. Tiesenhausen 1873, specimen no. 2542; A. E. Vivas 1893, p. 374; S. Lane Poole 1875, specimen no. 153; H. Hazard 1952, p. 218. See also F. Yusuf 2003, pp. 23, 64, 111.

4. See F. Yusuf 2003, pp. 67–76.

5. W. Qazan 1983, no. 416; S. I. Kashif 1950, p. 98; F. Yusuf 2003, pp. 76–77.

6. N. Daftar n.d., pp. 85–86.

7. F. Yusuf 2003, pp. 86–87.

8. M. al-'Ushsh 1984, specimen no. 1775.

9. W. Tiesenhausen 1873, specimen no. 1560; C. M. Fraehn 1826, p. 4. See coin specimen no. MS 16209, Iraqi National Museum.

10. The reverse of this particular coin also bears the surname Jibril in a possible reference to Jibril b. Bakhtishu, court physician of Caliph Harun al-Rashid.

11. S. Shamma' 1995, specimen no. 631.

12. G. Miles 1938, specimen nos. 96G and 96H; M. al-'Ushsh 1984; see also specimen no. 1899. Indeed, when the sons of the rebel al-Surri b. al-Hakam were slain on the battlefield by al-Ma'mun's commander, 'Abd Allah b. Tahir, in Safar, May 626, al-Ma'mun ordered struck commemorative coins carrying that date and the name of his commander, together with the *laqab*, "the victorious" (*al-Mansur*).

13. See F. Yusuf 2003, pp. 91–97. This verse likewise would appear on coins issued by the Umayyads in al-Andalus as well as the Mongols in Iran.

14. See F. Yusuf 2003, pp. 23, 64.
15. Ibid., pp. 76–86.
16. Ibid., pp. 88–91.
17. Ibid., pp. 98ff.
18. Ibid., pp. 27, 103ff.

Bibliography

CLASSIC SOURCES

Abu Yusuf. *Kitab al-Kharaj*. Cairo: 1933.

'Ali, 'Abd Allah Yusuf. *The Meaning of the Holy Qur'an*. Brentwood: 1993.

Al-Ansari, 'Umar b. Ibrahim al-Awasi.' *Tafrij al-Qurub fi Tadbir al-Hurub*. George Scanlon, ed. Cairo: 1961.

Aristotle. *Politics*. E. Barker, trans. New York: 1946.

Al-Baladhuri. *Futuh al-Buldan*. M. de Goeje, ed. Leiden: 1866.

———. *Futuh al-Buldan*. R. Radwan, ed. Beirut: 1978.

Al-Banna, H. *Mudhakkarat al-Da 'wah wa al-Di'ayah*. Cairo: n.d.

Al-Basr. *Futuh al-Sham*. Calcutta: 1853–1854.

Al-Bukhari. *Sahih. I: Recueil des Traditions Mahométanes*. Leiden: 1862–1908

———. *Kitab al-Jami 'al-Sahih*. M. Krehl, ed. Leiden: 1864.

Al-Dabbi. *Bughyat al-Multamis fi Ta'rikh Rijal al-Andalus*. F. Codera and J. Ribera, eds. Madrid: 1884–1885.

Al-Darimi. *Musnad*. Delhi: 1919.

Einhardus. *Annales Francorum: Monumenta Germaniae Historica (M.G.H.)*. G. Teulet, ed. Paris: 1840.

———. *Annales Regni Francorum: (M.G.H.)*. G. H. Pertz and F. Kurze, eds. Hanover: 1895.

———. *Scriptores Einhardus Vita Karoli Magni Imperatoris: (M.G.H.)*. L. Halphen, ed. Paris: 1923.

Al-Ghazali. *Kitab al-Wajiz*. Cairo: 1899.

Al-Hilali, M. and Khan, M. *The Noble Qur'an*. Al-Madinah: 1996.

Ibn 'Abd al-Hakam. *Futuh Misr wa Akhbaruha*. C. C. Torrey, ed. New Haven: 1922.

Ibn 'Asakir. *Al-Ta'rikh al-Kabir*. 'A. Qadir Badran, ed. Damascus: 1914–1932.

Ibn al-Athir. *Al-Kamil fi al-Ta'rikh*. C. J. Tornberg, ed. Leiden: 1851–1867.

Ibn Khaldun. *Al-Muqaddimah: Kitab al-'Ibar wa Diwan al-Mubtada wa al-Khabar.* Cairo: 1867–1965.

———. *Muqaddimat Ibn Khaldun.* Beirut: 1978.

Ibn Majah. *Sunan.* Cairo: 1895.

Ibn al-Qalanisi. *The Damascus Chronicle of the Crusades.* H. A. R. Gibb, trans. London: 1932.

Ibn Qayyim. *I'lam al-Muwaqqi'in 'an Rabb al-'Alamin.* Cairo: n.d.

Ibn Qutaybah. *'Uyun al-Akhbar.* Cairo: 1963.

Ibn Taymiyah. *Al-Fatawa al-Kubra.* Cairo: 1961–1966.

———. *Al-Hisbah fi al-Islam.* Cairo: 1976.

Al-Idrisi. *Nuzhat al-Mushtaq fi Ikhtiraq al-Afaq.* Beirut: 1899.

Al-Kaya al-Harasiy. *Ahkam al-Qur'an.* Beirut: 1983.

Al-Maqqari. *Nafh al-Tib min Ghusn al-Andalus al-Ratib.* R. Dozy, ed. Leiden: 1885.

Al-Maqrizi. *Kitab Ighathat al-Ummah bi-Kashf al-Ghummah.* J. D. al-Shayyal and M. Ziyadah, eds. Cairo: 1957.

Al-Mas'udi. *Muruj al-Dhahab wa Ma'adin al-Jawhar.* A. C. de Meynard, ed. Paris: 1681–1877.

Al-Mawardi. *Kitab al-Ahkam al-Sultaniyah.* M. Enger, ed. Bonn: 1853.

Monk of St. Gaul ("Monachus Sangallensis"). *Gesta Karoli Magna: Scriptores Sacri II: Monumenta Germaniae Historica (M.G.H.).* Hanover: 1884.

Muhammad ibn 'Abd al-Wahhab. In *Mu'allafat al-Shaykh al-Imam Muhammad bin 'Abd al-Wahhab: al-Fiqh.* Riyadh: 1881.

———. "Kitab al-Tawhid." Vol. 1.

———. "Kitab al-Jihad." Vol. 2.

———. "Fatawa wa Masa'il al-Imam Muhammad ibn 'Abd al-Wahhab."1881, vol. 3.

Al-Muttaqi al-Hindi. *Kanz al-'Ummal fi Sunan al-Aqwal wa al-Af'al.* Hyderabad: 1894.

Pickthall, M. *The Qur'an Translated.* New York: 1955, Washington, D.C.: 2005.

Al-Rashid b. Zubayr. *Kitab al-Dhakha'ir wa al-Tuhuf.* M. Hamidullah, ed. Kuwait: 1959.

Al-Shafi'i, M. *Kitab al-Umm.* Cairo: 1903–1908.

Al-Shaybani, Muhammad b. Hassan. *Al-Sirar al-Kabir.* Hyderabad: 1917.

———. *Kitab al-Makharij fi al-Hiyal.* J. Schacht, ed. Leipzig: 1930.

———. *Kitab al-Iktisab fi al-Rizq al-Mustatab.* M. 'Arnus, ed. Cairo: 1938.

Al-Tabari. *Ta'rikh al-Rusul wa al-Muluk.* M. de Goeje, ed. Leiden: 1879–1901.

———. *Kitab al-Jihad.* J. Schacht, ed. Leiden: 1937.

Al-Tirmidhi. *Al-Sahih.* Cairo: 1866–1873.

Al-Waqidi. *Kitab Maghazi Rasul Allah.* A. Von Kremer, ed. Calcutta: 1855–1856.

Al-Ya'qubi. *Ta'rikh al-Ya'qubi.* M.-Th. Houtsma, ed. Leiden: 1883.

Al-Zubaydi, M. *Ithaf al-Sadah Sharh Ihya' 'Ulum al-Din.* Cairo: 1893.

Zayd b. 'Ali. *Majmu 'al-Fiqh.* E. Griffini, ed. Milano: 1919.

MODERN REFERENCES

Abdul Rauf, F. *What's Right with Islam.* San Francisco: 2004.

Abu al-Fadl, K. *Speaking in God's Name.* Oxford: 2003.

———. *Islam and the Challenge to Democracy*. Princeton: 2004.

Aboul-Enein, Y. and Zuhur, S. *Islamic Rulings on Warfare*. U.S. Army War College Foundation, Carlisle Barracks: 2004.

Abu Khalil, A. *The Battle for Saudi Arabia*. New York: 2004.

Abulafia, D. "Asia, Africa, and the Trade of Medieval Europe." *Cambridge Economic History of Europe*. Cambridge: 1987.

Aghnides, N. *Mohammedan Theories of Finance*. London: 1916.

'Ali, M. *Al-Jihad fi al-Shari 'ah al-Islamiyah*. Cairo: 1973.

Armstrong, K. *A History of God*. New York: 1993.

———. *The Battle for God*. New York: 2000.

———. *Holy War: The Crusades and their Impact on Today's World*. New York: 2001.

Arnold, T. *The Caliphate*. Oxford: 1924.

Ashtor, E. A. "Quelques Observations d'un Orientalist sur la Thèse de Pirenne." *JESHO*, 1970, vol. 13.

Aslan, R. *No God but God*. New York: 2005.

Baer, R. *Sleeping with the Devil*. New York: 2003.

Ballis, W. *The Legal Position of War: Changes in its Practice and Theory*. The Hague: 1937.

Bar, S. *Warrant for Terror*. Lanham, MD: 2006.

Bawer, B. *While Europe Slept: How Radical Islam Is Destroying the West from Within*. New York: 2006.

Bergen, P. *Holy War Inc.: Inside the Secret World of Osama bin Laden*. New York: 2001.

———. *The Osama bin Laden I Know*. New York: 2006.

Bieler, A. *La Pensée Éonomique et Sociale de Calvin*. Geneva: 1959.

Blankenhon, D. et al., eds. *The Islam-West Debate*. Lanham, MD: 2005.

Bolin, S. "Muhammad, Charlemagne, and Ruric." *Scandinavian Economic History Review*, 1943, vol. 1.

Boulby, M. *The Muslim Brotherhood and the Kings of Jordan*. Atlanta: 1999.

Bradley. J. *Saudi Arabia Exposed*. New York: 2005.

Brinton, C. et al. *A History of Civilization: 1715 to the Present*. Vol. 2. Englewood Cliffs, NJ: 1960.

Brydges, H. *An Account of the Transactions of His Majesty's Mission to the Court of Persia in the Years 1807–1811, to which is appended a Brief History of the Wahauby*. London: 1834.

Buckler, F. *Harunu'l-Rashid and Charles the Great*. Cambridge: 1931.

Bulliet, R. *The Case for Islamo-Christian Civilization*. New York: 2004.

Calverly, E. *Worship in Islam*. Madras: 1925.

Center for Law and Military Operations. "Basic Principles of the Law of War." *Marine Corps Gazette*, October 2002.

Clough, S. *The Rise and Fall of Civilization*. Westport, CT: 1951.

Cohen, J. *Protestantism and Capitalism: The Mechanisms of Influence*. New York: 2002.

Coll, S. *Ghost Wars*. London: 2004.

Commins, D. *The Wahhabi Mission and Saudi Arabia*. London: 2006.

Copeland, M. *The Game of Nations*. New York: 1969.

Corbin, J. *Al-Qaeda: The Terror Network that Threatens the World*. New York: 2002.

Cordesman, A. "Winning the War on Terrorism." *Middle East Policy*. Vol. 13, no. 3. Washington: 2006.

Cordesman, A. and Obaid, N. *Al-Qaeda in Saudi Arabia: Asymmetric Threats and Islamic Extremists*. CSIS. Washington: 2005.

Croce, B. *Uomini e Cose della Vecchia Italia*. Bari: 1927.

Crotty, R. *When Histories Collide: The Development and Impact of Individualistic Capitalism*. Walnut Creek, CA: 2001.

Daftar, N. *Al-Maskukat*. Baghdad: n.d.

Decision Support Systems. "Al-Qaeda's Endgame? A Strategic Scenario Analysis." November 2, 2001. available online at www.metatempo.com

Delong-Bas, N. J. *Wahhabi Islam: From Revival and Reform to Global Jihad*. Oxford: 2004.

Dodge, T. *Inventing Iraq*. New York: 2003.

Donner, F. *The Early Islamic Conquests*. Princeton: 1981.

Dreyfus, R. *Devil's Game: How the United States Helped Unleash Fundamentalist Islam*. New York: 2005.

Ehrenkreutz, A. S. "Another Orientalist's Remarks Concerning the Pirenne Thesis." *JESHO*, 1972, vol. 15, pt. 1.

Esposito, J. *Islam: The Straight Path*. New York: 2005.

d'Entreves, A. *Aquinas: Selected Political Writings*. Oxford: 1948.

Epstein, J. *The Catholic Tradition of the Law of Nations*. London: 1935.

Evans, M. *Beyond Iraq: The Next Move*. Lakeland: 2003.

Al Fahad, A. "From Exclusivism to Accommodation: Doctrinal and Legal Evolution of Wahhabism." *New York Law Review*, vol. 79, May 2004.

Fandy, M. *Saudi Arabia and the Politics of Dissent*. New York: 1999.

Fanfani, A. *Catholicism, Protestantism, and Capitalism*. Norfolk, VA: 2003.

Firestone, R. *Jihad: The Origin of Holy War in Islam*. New York: 1999.

Fouda, Y. and N. Fielding. *Masterminds of Terror: The Truth Behind the Most Devastating Attack the World Has Ever Seen*. New York: 2003.

Fraehn, C. M. *Recensio Numorum Muhammadanorum*. Petropoli: 1826.

Fregosi, P. *Jihad in the West: Muslim Conquests from the 7th to the 21st Centuries*. New York: 1998.

Friedman. T. "Addicted to Oil." *New York Times*, February 1, 2006.

Fuller, G. *The Future of Political Islam*. New York: 2003.

Gaffney, F. *War Footing*. Annapolis, MD: 2006.

Al-Gar, H. *Wahhabism: A Critical Essay*. New York: 2002.

Garfinle, A. *A Practical Guide to Winning the War on Terror*. Stanford: 2004.

Gates, R. *From the Shadows*. New York: 1996.

Gerges, F. *Journey of the Jihadist*. New York: 2006.

Glain, S. *Mullahs, Merchants, and Militants*. New York: 2004.

Gold, D. *Hatred's Kingdom: How Saudi Arabia Supports the New Global Terrorism*. Washington: 2003.

Griffith, L. *The War on Terrorism and the Terror of God*. Grand Rapids, MI: 2002.

Habeck, M. *Knowing the Enemy*. New Haven: 2006.

Haleem, M. *Understanding the Qur'an: Themes and Style*. London: 1999.

Al-Hamad, T. "Tawhid al-Jazirah al-'Arabiyah." *Al-Mustaqbal al-'Arabi*, 1986.

Hamidullah, M. "Embassy of Queen Bertha to Caliph al-Muktaf Bi'llah in Baghdad." *Journal of the Pakistan Historical Society*, 1953.

———. *Muslim Conduct of State*. Lahore: 1966.

Hammes, T. *The Sling and the Stone: On War in the 21st Century*. St. Paul, MN: 2004.

Haykal, M. H. *The Life of Muhammad*. Indianapolis: 1976.

Hazard, H. *The Numismatic History of Late Medieval North Africa*. New York: 1952.

Heck, G. *Saudi Arabia Transcendent: An Evolving Modern Economy*. Riyadh: 2005.

Helms, C. *The Cohesion of Saudi Arabia: Evolution of Political Identity*. Baltimore: 1981.

Heyd, W. C. *Histoire du Commerce du Levant au Moyen Âge*. Leipzig: 1885.

Hitti, P. *History of the Arabs*. London: 1970.

Hollenbach, D. *Nuclear Ethics: A Christian Moral Argument*. New York: 1983.

Hsu, T. *Target: Saudi Arabia: Essays on the Campaign Against the Kingdom*. Washington: 2005.

Huband, M. *Warriors of the Prophet: The Struggle for Islam*. Boulder: 1999.

———. *Brutal Truths: Fragile Myths*. Boulder: 2004.

Huntington, S. "The Clash of Civilizations." *Foreign Affairs*, vol. 72, no. 3, 1993.

———. *The Clash of Civilizations: Remaking the World Order*. New York: 1996.

Al-Husayn, M. B. "Dirasah Tahliliyah 'an Nuqud al-Di'ayah wa al-A'lam wa al-Munasabat." *Al-Maskukat*, no. 6, 1975.

Hussein, A. L. *Al-Islam wa al-Harb*. Riyadh: 1979.

'Imarah, M. *Al-Islam wa Falsafat al-Hukm*. Beirut: 1979.

ICG (International Crisis Group). *Saudi Arabia Backgrounder: Who are the Islamists*. Middle East Report 31. Riyadh: September 21, 2004.

Jamestown Foundation. *Unmasking Terror*. Washington: 2004.

Johnson, E. "The Alleged Frankish Protectorate in Palestine." *American Historical Review*, 1927.

Juergensmeyer, M. *Terror in the Mind of God: The Global Rise of Religious Violence*. Berkeley, CA: 2001.

Kaplinsky, Z. "The Muslim Brotherhood." *Middle Eastern Affairs*, December 1954.

Kashif, S. I. *Misr fi 'Asr al-Ikhshidiyin*. Cairo: 1950.

Kedourie, E. *Afghani and Abduh: An Essay on Religious Unbelief and Political Activism in Modern Islam*. New York: 1966.

Kechichian, J. *Succession in Saudi Arabia*. New York: 2001.

Kelsay, J. *Islam and War*. Louisville, KY: 1993.

Kelsay, J. and J. T. Johnson, eds. *Just War and Jihad: Historical and Theoretical Perspectives on War and Peace in Western and Islamic Traditions*. New York: 1991.

———. *Cross, Crescent, and Sword*. New York: 1990.

Kelsen, H. *General Theory of Law and State*. Cambridge: 1946.

Kepel, G. *Jihad: The Trail of Political Islam*. Cambridge: 2002.

———. *The War for Muslim Minds*. Cambridge: 2004.

Kennedy, P. M. *The Rise and Fall of the Great Powers*. New York: 1989.

Khadduri, M. *Al-Silat al-Dibulmasiyah bayna Harun al-Rashid wa Sharlaman*. Baghdad: 1939.

———. *War and Peace in the Law of Islam*. Baltimore: 1955.

———. *The Islamic Law of Nations: Shaybani's Kitab Siyar*. Baltimore: 1966.

Khalidi, R. *Resurrecting Empire: Western Footprints and America's Perilous Path in the Middle East*. Boston: 2004.

Krabbe, H. *The Modern Idea of the State*. New York: 1922.

Kramer, G. "Islamist Notions of Democracy." In *Political Islam: Essays from the Middle East Report*. J. Beinin and J. Stork, eds. Berkeley, CA: 1997.

Kushner, H. *Essential Readings on Political Terrorism: Analyses of Problems and Prospects for the 21st Century*. Lincoln, NE: 2003.

———. *Holy War on the Home Front*. New York: 2004.

Lackey, D. *The Ethics of War and Peace*. Englewood Cliffs, NJ: 1988.

Lane. E. *An Arabic English Lexicon*. London: 1865.

Lane Poole, S. *Catalogue of Oriental Coins in the British Museum*. London: 1875–1890, 10 vols.

Laoust, H. "Ibn 'Abd al-Wahhab, Muhammad." *Encyclopedia of Islam*, vol. 3, new ed. Leiden: 1971.

Laquer, W. *The Origins of Terrorism*. Baltimore: 1990.

———. *Terrorism: A Study of National and International Political Violence*.

Lawrence, B. *Shattering the Myth: Islam Beyond Violence*. Princeton: 1998.

Lévi Provençal, E. "Un Échange d'Ambassades entre Cordove et Byzance au Ix^e Siècle." *Byzantion*, 1937, vol. 12.

Lewis, B. "Islam and Communism." 1953; reprinted in *The Middle East in Transition*. Walter Laquer, ed. New York: 1958.

———. "The Return of Islam." In *Religion and Politics in the Middle East*. Michael Curtis, ed. Boulder, Colo.: 1981.

———. "Islamic Revolution." *The New York Review of Books*, vol. 34, nos. 21–22, January 1988.

———. *The Muslim Discovery of Europe*. London and New York: 1981.

———. "Rethinking the Middle East." *Foreign Affairs*, Fall 1992.

———. *What Went Wrong?* New York: 2002.

———. *The Crisis of Islam*. New York: 2003.

Lindsey, B. *Against the Dead Hand*. New York: 2002.

Lippman, T. *Inside the Mirage: America's Fragile Partnership with Saudi Arabia*. Boulder, CO: 2004.

Long, D. *The Kingdom of Saudi Arabia*. Gainesville, FL: 1997.

Lopez, R. S. *Settecento Anni Fa: il Ritorno all'Oro nell'Occidente Duecentesco*. Naples: 1955.

Mackey, S. *The Saudis: Inside the Desert Kingdom*. New York: 1987.

Manji, I. *The Trouble with Islam*. New York: 2004.

MacDonald, D. "The Caliphate," *Muslim World*, vol. 7, 1917.

Marsden, P. *The Taliban: War, Religion, and the New Order in Afghanistan*. London: 1998.

Marshall, P., ed. *Radical Islam's Rules*. Lanham, Md.: 2005.

Mead, W. *Power, Terror, Peace, and War*. New York: 2004.

MEMRI (Middle East Media Research Institute). "Bin Laden's Sermon for the Feast of the Sacrifice." *Special Dispatch Series No. 476*. Washington: March 5, 2003.

Michael G. *The Enemy of My Enemy: The Alarming Convergence of Militant Islam and the Extreme Right*. Kansas: 2004.

Miniter, R. *Shadow War: The Untold Story of How America is Winning the War on Terror*. Washington: 2004.

Al-Misri, H. *Tijarat al-'Iraq fi al-'Asr al-'Abbasi*. Alexandria, VA: 1982.

Mitchell, R. *The Society of the Muslim Brothers.* London: 1969.

Mowbray, J. *Dangerous Diplomacy.* Washington: 2003.

Murawiec, L. *Princes of Darkness.* Lanham, MD: 2005.

Al-Na'im, 'A. *Toward an Islamic Reformation.* Syracuse: 1996.

Naji, A. *The Management of Savagery.* West Point: 2006, available online at www.ctc .usma.edu/naji.asp

Nasr, S. N. *Islamic Science: an Illustrated Study.* Kent: 1976.

National Intelligence Estimate. *Prospects for Iraq's Stability.* January 2007.

Novak, M. *The Universal Hunger for Liberty.* New York: 2004.

Obaid, N. "The Power of Saudi Arabia's Islamic Leaders." *Middle East Quarterly.* Washington: September 1999.

Pakkiasamy, D. "Saudi Arabia's Plan for Its Changing Work Force." Migration Policy Institute. Washington: November 1, 2004.

Pape, R. *Dying to Win: the Strategic Logic of Suicide Terrorism.* New York: 2005.

Patai, R. *The Arab Mind.* New York: 2002.

Peters, R. *Jihad in Classical and Modern Islam.* Princeton: 1996, 2005.

———. *Islam and Colonialism: the Doctrine of Jihad in Modern History.* The Hague: 1979.

Phares, W. *Future Jihad.* New York: 2005.

Phillips, K. *Boiling Point.* New York: 1993.

Phillipson, C. *The International Law and Custom of Ancient Greece and Rome.* London: 1911.

Pillar, P. *Terrorism and U.S. Foreign Policy.* Washington: 2001.

Posner, G. *Secrets of the Kingdom.* New York: 2005.

Qazan, W. *Al-Maskukat al-Islamiyah.* Private Collection. Beirut: 1983.

Ramadan, T. *Western Muslims and the Future of Islam.* Oxford: 2004.

Rasanayagam, A. *Afghanistan: A Modern History.* London: 2005.

Al-Rasheed, M. *A History of Saudi Arabia.* Cambridge: 2002.

Rashid, A. *Taliban: Militant Islam, Oil, and Fundamentalism in Central Asia.* London: 2000; Waterville: 2002.

Read, P. *The Templars.* Cambridge: 1999.

Reich, W. *Origins of Terror: Psychologies, Ideologies, Theologies, State of Mind.* Washington: 1990.

Rentz, G. *Muhammad ibn 'Abd al-Wahhab (1703–4–1792 and the Beginnings of the Unitarian Empire in Arabia).* Doctoral dissertation. University of California, Berkeley: 1948.

Rodinson, M. "La Marchand Musulman." In *Islam and the Trade of Asia.* Oxford: 1970.

———. *Islam and Capitalism.* London: 1978.

———. *Mohammed.* Ann Carter, trans. New York: 1991.

Rosenthal, F. "On Suicide in Islam." *JAOS*, vol. 66, 1946.

Roy, O. *The Failure of Political Islam.* C. Volk, trans. Cambridge: 1994.

Rubin, B. *The Search for Peace in Afghanistan: from Buffer State to Failed State.* New Haven, CT: 1995.

Runciman, S. *A History of the Crusades.* Cambridge: 1966.

———. "Charlemagne and Palestine." In *English Historical Review*, 1939.

———. *The First Crusade.* Cambridge: 1992.

Sageman, M. *Understanding Terror Networks*. Philadelphia: 2004.

Salibi, K. *A History of Arabia*. New York: 1980.

SAMBA (Saudi American Bank). *Saudi Arabia's 2007 Budget, 2006 Performance*. Riyadh: December 2006.

Satloff, R., ed. *War on Terror: The Middle East Dimension*. Washington: 2002.

Sayyid Qutb. *This Religion of Islam (Hadha al-Din)*. Palo Alto, CA: 1967.

———. *Signposts (Milestones)*. Karachi: 1968.

Schacht, J. *The Legacy of Islam*. Oxford: 1931.

———. *The Origins of Mohammedan Jurisprudence*. Oxford: 1950.

———. "The Schools of Islamic Law and Later Development of Jurisprudence." *Law in the Middle East*. vol. 1, 1955.

Schwartz, S. *The Two Faces of Islam: The House of Saud from Tradition to Terror*. New York: 2002.

Schwartz-Barcott, T. P. *War, Terror, and Peace in the Qur'an and in Islam*. Carlisle Barracks: 2004.

Shadid, A. *Legacy of the Prophet*. Boulder, CO: 2002.

Shamma', S. *Ahdath Asr al-Ma'mun kama Tarwiyuhi al-Nuqud*. Irbid: 1995.

Sombart, W. *Der Moderne Kapitalismus*. Munich: 1916.

Soroush, Abdolkarim. *Reason, Freedom, and Democracy in Islam*. Oxford: 2000.

Spencer, R. *The Myth of Islamic Tolerance*. New York: 2005.

Stern, J. *Terror in the Name of God: Why Religious Militants Kill*. New York: 2003.

———. *The Ultimate Terrorists*. Cambridge: 1999.

Stevenson, C. "Lewis Tells Audience of Difficult Choices Facing the Islamic World." *Daily Princetonian*. Princeton: November 11, 2002.

Stevenson, W. *The Crusades in the East*. Cambridge: 1907.

Stremecki, M. "Among the Afghans." *Washington Quarterly*, vol. 11, no. 3, Summer 1988.

Sulayman, 'I. "Dinar Nadir li'l-Khilafah al-Mustadi bi-Amri Allah." *Al-Maskukat*. vol. 3, 1973.

Tawney, R. *Religion and the Rise of Capitalism*. New York: 1926 and 1960.

Tiesenhausen, W. *Monnaies des Khalifes Orientaux*. St. Petersburg: 1873.

Torrey, C. C. *The Commercial Theological Terms in the Koran*. Leiden: 1895.

Trifkovic, S. *The Sword of the Prophet*. Boston: 2002.

Udovitch, A. *Partnership and Profits in Medieval Islam*. Princeton: 1970.

Unger, C. *House of Bush: House of Saud*. New York: 2004.

Urban, M. *War in Afghanistan*. London: 1988.

U.S. Department of Justice. "Military Studies in the Jihad Against Tyrants." Captured al-Qaeda training manual. Federal Bureau of Investigation. Washington, DC. November 2001.

U.S. National Security Council. "National Intelligence Estimate." Washington: April 2006.

———. "National Intelligence Estimate: Prospects for Iraq's Stability: A Challenging Road Ahead." Washington, DC. January 2007.

Al-'Ushsh, M. "Misr: Al-Qahirah 'ala al-Nuqud al-'Arabiyah al-Islamiyah." *Abhath al-Nadwah al-Duwaliyah li-Ta'rikh al-Qahirah*. Cairo: 1971, no. 2.

———. *Al-Nuqud al-'Arabiyah al-Islamiyah al-Mahfuzah fi al-Mathaf al-Qatari*. Vol. 1. Al-Dawhah: 1984.

Vivas, A. E. *Monedas de las Dynastias Arabigo-Españolas*. Madrid: 1893.

Voll, J. "Renewal and Reform in Islamic History: Tajdid" and Islah. In *Voices of Resurgent Islam*, J. Esposito, ed. New York: 1983.

Von Elbe, J. "The Evolution and Concept of Just War in International Law." *American Journal of International Law*, vol. 33, 1939.

Wansbrough, J. *Qur'anic Studies*. Oxford: 1977.

Weber, M. *The Protestant Ethic and the Spirit of Capitalism*. New York: 1958.

Wiktorowicz, Q. "The New Global Threat: Transnational Salafis and Jihad." *Middle East Policy*, vol. 8, no. 4, 2001.

———. "A Genealogy of Radical Islam." *Studies in Conflict and Terrorism*. Vol. 28. 2005.

———. "Anatomy of the Salafi Movement." *Studies in Conflict and Terrorism*. Vol 29. 2006.

Wright, L. "The Man Behind bin Laden." *New Yorker*, September 16, 2002.

———. *The Looming Tower: Al-Qaeda and the Road to 9/11*. New York: 2006.

Wright, R. *Sacred Rage: The Wrath of Militant Islam*. New York: 1985.

Ye'or, B. *Eurabia: The Euro-Arab Axis*. Madison, Wis.: 2005.

———. *Islam and Dhimmitude: Where Civilizations Collide*. Lancaster, Pa.: 2002.

Yousef, M. and Adkin, M. *The Bear Trap*. Lahore: 1992.

Yusuf, F. *Nuqud al-Kharijin 'ala al-Khilafah al-Islamiyah fi Sharq al-'Alam al-Islami*. Cairo: 1991.

———. *Al-Ayat al-Qur'aniyah 'ala al-Maskukat al-Islamiyah: Dirasah Muqaranah*. Riyadh: 2003.

Al-Zawihiri, A. "*Knights Under the Prophet's Banner*." December 2, 2001, part 11, available online at www.fas.org

Zuckerman, M. "A Hang Tough Nation." *Newsweek*, October 24, 2005.

Index

Aaron of Alexandria, 28
'Abbasids, 28, 46
'Abduh, Muhammad, 51, 103
Abdullah (King), 138
acculturation, 112
Adelard of Bath, 29
al-Afghani, Jamal al-Din, 51, 103
Afghanistan, 76, 156; bin Laden in,
    93–94; CIA in, 12; jihad in, 57, 86,
    94; post Soviet invasion, 89–96;
    "reborn," 93; Soviet Union's
    invasion of, 12–13, 18, 83–89;
    Taliban in, 93–94; U.S. arms to,
    88–89
"age of Arab cold war," 54
Age of Engagement, 26
Age of Ignorance, 49
aggression: initiation of, 41;
    Muhammad Ibn al-Wahhab and,
    74–75. See also war
ahadith, 47, 49, 152
ahl al-hall wa al-'aqd, 115
Ahmadinijad, Mahmud, 121
algebra, 30
Al-Ittihad al-Islami, 87
Allah, 41–42, 76; as head of
    church/state, 113; as source of

authority, 162; U.S. at war against,
    98
Al-Majest (Ptolemy), 29
aman, 168–69, 174
America. *See* United States
Amin, Hafiz Allah, 83
amir al-jihad, 57
Amnesty International, 66, 150
analogy, 47, 163
al-Ansari, 'Umar, 36
Anas, Malik b., 114
al-Anfal, Surat, 4, 177
anti-Christ, 5
anticommunism, 104, 105
anti-Western sentiment, 67
Apostates from Hell, 63
Apostles of Heaven, 63
Arabian Peninsula, 25; as Islam in
    microcosm, 23; isolation of, 143–45;
    political events in, 54–63;
    unbelievers in, 77
Arab-Jewish War (1948), 103–4
Arabs, 23, 144
Arab socialism, 55
Arafat, Yasser, 14
Archimedes, 29
Aristotle, 29, 175

About the Author

Gene W. Heck is a senior business development economist operating in Saudi Arabia and throughout the Middle East. Prior to joining the private sector, he was a member of the United States Diplomatic Corps, with postings to the U.S. embassies in Saudi Arabia and Jordan.

Dr. Heck has served as U.S. commercial attaché to Saudi Arabia, as senior U.S. treasury economic advisor to the Saudi Arabian Ministry of Finance and National Economy, as well as a governmental relations officer with Arabian American Oil Company (ARAMCO).

Dr. Heck holds a doctorate and three master's degrees from the University of Michigan, Ann Arbor; a master's degree (MPA) in public administration from Golden Gate University, San Francisco, California; and has completed the requisite course work for a master's degree in Arab economic history from the University of Jordan. He also serves as an adjunct professor of government and history with the University of Maryland.